3 UA
   #23
   H783
   2009

Gender, Human Security and the United Nations

This book examines the relationship between women, gender and the international security agenda, exploring the meaning of security in terms of discourse and practice, as well as the larger goals and strategies of the global women's movement.

Today, many complex global problems are being located within the security logic. From environmental concerns to HIV/AIDS, state and non-state actors have made a practice out of securitizing issues that are not conventionally seen as such. As most prominently demonstrated by the UN Security Council Resolution 1325 (2001), activists for women's rights have increasingly framed women's rights and gender inequality as security issues in an attempt to gain access to the international security agenda, particularly in the context of the United Nations. This book explores the nature and implications of the use of security language as a political framework for women, tracing and analyzing the organizational dynamics of women's activism in the United Nations system and how women have come to embrace and been impacted by the security framework, globally and locally. The book argues that, from a feminist and human security perspective, efforts to engender the security discourse have had both a broadening and limiting effect, highlighting reasons to be skeptical of securitization as an inherently beneficial strategy.

Four cases studies are used to develop the core themes: (1) UN implemention of Security Council Resolution 1325; (2) the strategies utilized by those advocating women's issues in the security arena compared to those advocating for children; (3) the organizational development of the UN Development Fund for Women and how it has come to securitize women's rights; and (4) the activity of the UN Peacebuilding Commission and its challenges in gendering its security approach.

The work will be of interest to students of critical security studies, gender studies, international organizations, and international relations in general.

Natalie Florea Hudson received her PhD in Political Science from the University of Connecticut and is an Assistant Professor at the University of Dayton. She specializes in gender and international relations, human rights, international security studies, and international law and organization.

Routledge Critical Security Studies series

Titles in this series include:

Securing Outer Space
Edited by Natalie Bormann and Michael Sheehan

Critique, Security and Power
The political limits to emancipatory approaches
Tara McCormack

Gender, Human Security and the United Nations
Security language as a political framework for women
Natalie Florea Hudson

Gender, Human Security and the United Nations

Security language as a political framework for women

Natalie Florea Hudson

LONDON AND NEW YORK

First published 2010
by Routledge
2 Park Square, Milton Park, Abingdon, Oxon, OX14 4RN

Simultaneously published in the USA and Canada
by Routledge
270 Madison Avenue, New York, NY 10016

Routledge is an imprint of the Taylor & Francis Group, an informa business

© 2010 Natalie Florea Hudson

Typeset in Times New Roman by
GreenGate Publishing Services, Tonbridge, Kent
Printed and bound in Great Britain by
TJI Digital, Padstow, Cornwall

All rights reserved. No part of this book may be reprinted or reproduced
or utilised in any form or by any electronic, mechanical, or other means,
now known or hereafter invented, including photocopying and recording,
or in any information storage or retrieval system, without permission in
writing from the publishers.

British Library Cataloguing in Publication Data
A catalogue record for this book is available
from the British Library

Library of Congress Cataloging-in-Publication Data
Hudson, Natalie Florea.
Gender, human security and the United Nations : security language as a
political framework for women / Natalie Florea Hudson.
p. cm.
Includes bibliographical references.
1. National security--United States. 2. Women and peace--United States.
3. United Nations. I. Title.
UA23.H783 2009
355'.033082--dc22
2009011830

ISBN 10: 0-415-77782-8 (hbk)
ISBN 10: 0-203-86990-7 (ebk)

ISBN 13: 978-0-415-77782-7 (hbk)
ISBN 13: 978-0-203-86990-1 (ebk)

For my parents,
DeWayne and Bobbi Florea

Contents

Acknowledgments		viii
List of abbreviations		x

1 Women, peace, and security: an introduction   1

2 Women's activism in the context of the security debate: theoretical underpinnings   22

3 The security framework in practice: the case of Security Council Resolution 1325   44

4 Women and children: comparative frameworks and strategies within the Security Council   67

5 The United Nations Development Fund for Women: working its way into the security sector   95

6 The United Nations Peacebuilding Commission: a litmus test for assessing the status of women, peace, and security   119

7 Women, peace, and security: not the final analysis   143

Appendix A	155
Appendix B	159
References	164
Index	181

Acknowledgments

This book tells the story of the strength, intellect, and drive of the world's women. This is the story of what is possible when such dedicated women join forces and create networks among themselves in their efforts to establish human security and durable peace in their communities. Without these incredible women, this book would not be possible. I am grateful to these women for the work that they do, knowing that they often face insurmountable obstacles on a daily basis. Many of these women graciously took the time to sit with me and share their experiences. The many women (and some men) that I interviewed for this research are an inspiration to me, and I look forward to the day that I can share their stories of strength, faith, and love with my own two young daughters.

Throughout this journey, I have been blessed by a number of tremendous mentors. First and foremost, I am indebted to Mark A. Boyer for his support, encouragement, and most importantly, his friendship. My research also benefited from the guidance and insight of Shareen Hertel, whose intellect, UN-know-how, and energy continue to inspire me. Jennifer Sterling-Folker, Elizabeth Hanson, and Richard Hiskes also provided invaluable feedback throughout the process of this research, and I am grateful for their continual support. I am also indebted to Margaret Karns, who took me under her wing at a very young age and continues to be my mentor and friend today.

Beyond these immediate mentors, my intellectual horizons have been profoundly influenced by the pioneering and often path-breaking work of feminist scholars in the field of security studies, including Carol Cohn, Cynthia Enloe, Spike Peterson, Anne Sisson Runyan, J. Ann Tickner, and Sandra Whitworth. It is my hope that this book makes a small contribution to understanding just how gendered security is, how much women's voices matter, and how much work is left to do—another niche in the security studies armor, perhaps.

At the University of Dayton, the Political Science Department, Human Rights Studies Program, and Women's and Gender Studies Program have been extremely supportive in my research and a particularly congenial place to work. I owe a special debt of thanks to Chris Duncan who not only supported me throughout the entire book writing process, but also worked very hard to protect my time so that I could see this project through. I would also like to thank Ellen Fleischmann and Mark Ensalaco for their helpful comments on the manuscript in its earlier stages.

Acknowledgments   ix

Michael Butler and Christopher Paskewich also deserve special mention as they helped me sort through the many fuzzy beginnings of this research, convincing me to press on with my grand ideas. I also want to thank Anat Niv-Solomon, Joseph Young, and Karen Barnes for their moral support and constructive criticism at various points of this project.

At various stages, this research has received financial support from the Graduate School at the University of Connecticut as well as from the University of Dayton Research Institute. Some of the material included in Chapters 2 and 3 was drawn from two previously published articles, "Engendering UN Peacekeeping Operations," *International Journal* LX(3): 785–806 (2005) and "Securitizing Women's Rights and Gender Equality," *Journal of Human Rights* 8(1): 52–70 (2009). Some of the findings in Chapter 5 appeared in a short opinion piece in *WIIS Words, Women in International Security* (Summer 2007: 5–6), entitled, "A Development Fund Takes on Police Work." I am grateful to these publication outlets for allowing me to reprint this material in this book.

Finally, a special thanks to my sister and brother, Audra Disser and Patrick Florea, for their encouragement and friendship; to Sarah, for always listening when the work became overwhelming; to Pam, Andrea, Jamie, and the wonderful teachers at the Bombeck Family Learning Center, for providing loving care for our two precious girls; and to Phil and Joy Hudson, for their generosity, office space, and delicious meals.

I dedicate this book to my parents. I am so grateful to my mother, Bobbi Florea, for her unwavering support and unconditional love. My father, the late DeWayne D. Florea, dreamed bigger dreams for me than I did, and even though he did not get to see the completion of this project, he is very much a part of it as he continues to be a part of me in everything that I do and everything that I am. Lastly, I thank my husband, Peter, who is my rock, my confidant, and my partner in this life. Without his love, his humor, and his faith in me, this book would not have been possible. This is for him. Laney and Adelyn will have to wait for the next one.

List of abbreviations

AFWIC	African Women in Crisis
CC	Consultative Committee (UNIFEM)
CEDAW	Convention on the Elimination of all Forms of Discrimination against Women
CEDC	Children in Especially Difficult Circumstances
COPRI	Conflict and Peace Research Institute, Denmark
CPA	Child Protection Advisers
CRC	Convention on the Rights of the Child
CS	Copenhagen School
CSW	Commission on the Status of Women
DAW	Division on the Advancement of Women
DCAF	Geneva Centre for the Democratic Control of the Armed Forces
DDR	Disarmament, demobilization, and reintegration
DPKO	Department of Peacekeeping Operations
ECOSOC	United Nations Economic and Social Council
FAO	Food and Agriculture Organization
FST	Feminist Security Theory
GA	General Assembly
GAD	Gender and development
GAU	Gender Affairs Unit
GBV	Gender-based violence
IDSA	Institute for Defense Studies and Analysis
IGO	Intergovernmental organization
INSTRAW	United Nations International Research and Training Institute for the Advancement of Women
IR	International relations
KWAHO	Kenya Water for Health Organization
MARWOPNET	Mano River Union Women Peace Network
NAP	National action plans
NATO	North Atlantic Treaty Organization
NGO	Non-governmental organization
NGOWG	NGO Working Group on Women, Peace and Security

List of abbreviations xi

OC	Organizational Committee (Peacebuilding Commission)
OECD	Organization for Economic Cooperation and Development
OSAGI	Office of the Special Adviser on Gender Issues
PBC	Peacebuilding Commission
PBF	Peacebuilding Fund
PBSO	Peacebuilding Support Office
SC	Security Council
SCR	Security Council Resolution
SRSG	Special Representative to the Secretary-General
SSR	Security Sector Reform
UDHR	Universal Declaration of Human Rights
UN	United Nations
UNDP	United Nations Development Program
UNECA	United Nations Economic Commission for Africa
UNESCO	United Nations Educational, Scientific and Cultural Organization
UNFPA	United Nations Population Fund
UNICEF	United Nations Children's Fund
UNIFEM	United Nations Development Fund for Women
UNIHP	United Nations Intellectual History Project
VFDW	Voluntary Fund for the Development of Women
WGLL	Working Group on Lessons Learned (Peacebuilding Commission)
WID	Women in development
WILPF	Women's League for International Peace and Freedom
WPS	Women, Peace, and Security

1 Women, peace, and security

An introduction

> I am of two minds on this regarding human rights, meaning that I believe that in an ideal world we should be caring and paying attention to and promoting and protecting human rights because they are so fundamental to the dignity of human beings not because they can become threats to security. At the same time, I know that politicians, the political establishment in general, not just the establishment, but political people who are in politics in general—whether civil society or government—they respond, their lights go up when they hear security aspects, you know, conflict. It's sort of sexy and alive, you know buzzers. And so, then what is left to strategizers like me when I have to deal with sometimes, very often, marginalized issues and peoples. I have to remind them—those politicians, whether in the UN or government or whatever—on the threat of security. So, if you don't take care of these people they are going to revolt and have a revolution—you know, briefly speaking.
>
> Interview, UN official 2006

As the quotation above demonstrates, language is arguably one of the most powerful tools in world politics today. The words one chooses, the tone one takes, and the arena in which one speaks all constitute important decisions with often lasting political implications. Essentially, how one frames an issue matters greatly (Butler & Boyer 2003), and language must be seen as more than mere rhetoric (Cohn 1987). Framing not only determines whether and how issues get onto the political agenda, but also how issues are given meaning, operationalized, and adopted into the norm-building process even before becoming part of the official agenda (Keck & Sikkink 1998a; Joachim 2007). Framing governs the actors that are engaged and those that are excluded; frames control the issues that are on and off the agenda (Bob 2005; 2008). In this way, discursive positioning and conceptual frameworks are critical for those involved as well as those not involved in the process (Carpenter 2005; 2007). Nowhere is the power a particular discourse—the "framings of meaning and lens of interpretation" (Hansen 2006: 7)—more evident than the case of framing women's rights and gender equality as matters essential to the promotion and protection of international peace and security.

2 Women, peace, and security

In analyzing how a particular global network of women activists has used the language of security, this research sheds light on the nature and implications of the security framework as a political process. More specifically, activists for women's rights and gender equality concerns have recently framed their concerns as security issues attempting to make them integral to the international security agenda, particularly in the context of the United Nations (UN).[1] From gender-mainstreaming initiatives to the "Interagency Taskforce on Women, Peace, and Security," there has been a clear push from UN agencies, United Nations Development Fund for Women (UNIFEM) specifically, as well as from certain middle-power national governments, such as Canada and Norway, and various non-governmental organizations, chiefly the NGO Working Group on Women, Peace, and Security (NGOWG) to put women's rights on the security agenda.[2] This group of state and non-state actors constitutes a dynamic transnational network, known as the Women, Peace and Security (WPS). One of the most concrete and prominent policy outcomes from this network has been UN Security Council Resolution (SCR) 1325, the first Council decision recognizing the importance of women in international peace and security, making women and women's needs relevant to negotiating peace agreements, planning refugee camps and peace-keeping operations, reconstructing war-torn societies, and ultimately making gender equality relevant to every single Security Council action (Rehn & Sirleaf 2002).[3] Although this project is about much more than SCR 1325, this "living document" does inform and underscore every aspect of this research as it is a "productive force" in shaping ideas and actions on women and gender as well as the discursive construction and conduct of security by the UN and the relationship between the two regimes (Cohn et al. 2004).[4]

This strategy of securitizing women's rights within the UN system can also be understood in the context of the broader push by many global actors to humanize security. As my research demonstrates, however, humanizing security is not necessarily the same as securitizing "non-traditional" security concerns and this has significant implications for a range of actors and issues attempting to become part of the security mainstream. Today, many complex global problems are being located within the security logic. Issues, such as the environment (Deudney 1990; Kakonen 1994; Litfin 1999) and HIV/AIDS (Price-Smith 2001; Chen 2003; Prins 2004; Elbe 2006), are just a couple of examples that demonstrate how both state and non-state actors use the security framework to draw attention to their particular concerns, challenging the conventional and narrow definitional boundaries associated with international security. This framework relies upon the utilitarian assumption that these issues need to be addressed because they are essential elements to establishing international peace and security. This justification has led to a debate on what should be considered in the realm of international security, as many scholars have made a practice out of securitizing issues that are not conventionally seen as such. And for better or for worse, this strategy of securitizing non-military matters is not limited to the academic community.[5] International organizations, particularly the UN, also employ this security discourse attempting to raise international awareness and policy-oriented attention toward various issues. In light of the human security rhetoric (recognizing the individual as the referent of security), it is not surprising that the concerns of women are increasingly framed within the security discourse.

Although the purpose of this book is not necessarily to demonstrate the many ways in which the lack of women's rights and gender inequality present valid security concerns, the critical role that women and gender issues play in constructing enduring international peace and security, particularly as far as the UN is concerned, will become manifest throughout my case studies.[6] The aim of this book is to explore the process of securitization: whether or not it leads to audience acceptance, the ability of the securitizing actor to "break free of procedures and rules he or she would otherwise be bound by" (Buzan et al. 1998: 25), and what this process means for both the international security agenda as well as the world's women.[7] Clearly, invoking specific gendered understandings of security not only affects the nature of security, but such frames can impact the women's movement at various levels. Working from the assumption that the UN is a norm-influencing global governance institution, and what happens in the Security Council has real implication for the meaning and practice of security as we move into the twenty-first century, three basic questions emerge and guide the rest of the book:

1   How is security defined *and* practiced within the context of international organization?
2   In what ways, if any, has women's activism been able to challenge traditional conceptions of security?
3   What are the implications of the "security framework" for the broader goals of the women's movement?

Overall, these questions interrogate the meaning of security, in terms of discourse and practice, particularly from a feminist perspective. But it is not just a matter of what women or a gender perspective does for the security agenda, but understanding the implications of the security framework for the global women's movement as well.

In short, this project goes beyond a debate of security at the conceptual level to examine how the application of this security framework affects policy and practice for these non-traditional security issues and actors. In other words, does the security framework really help bring global attention to issues and groups of people that are normally marginalized? Has it meant more resources and more involvement by state and non-state actors? These questions not only have important policy implications, but normative ones as well. Should these issues be framed as security issues? Can we really assume that the security language is inherently beneficial for those concerned with empowering women around the world?

As these more normative questions suggest, there is reason to be skeptical of the security discourse as a necessarily "good" framework when it comes to women's emancipation (Whitworth 2004). How movements frame their causes

4   *Women, peace, and security*

matters, in terms of outcomes, strategy, actors involved, opportunity structures, and in this case, future gender roles and relationships in societies transitioning from conflict and war. Thus, it is important to ask not only what women's activism brings to the security arena, but what the arena does for women—what does it mean to securitize women's rights and gender equality. This latter point reflects a gap in the existing research on gender mainstreaming in all arenas, as it "tends to ignore the challenge faced by feminist activists in remaining true to their political goals when they are caught up in a mainstreaming policy 'victory' that may be very real, but also very compromised" (Cohn 2003–04: 11). This project addresses this gap in terms of theoretical, practical, and normative consequences.

Research design

This research is both theoretically driven and policy-oriented. With regard to the former, this project offers the building blocks necessary to advance theory making in three respects (Van Evera 1997). First, it addresses a real need to expand the scope of security studies beyond military–strategic research to something more reflective of the range of security threats that the world currently faces (Klare 1998). Even in the last decade, scholars where critiquing security scholarship; for example, Baldwin (1997: 9) argues, "Paradoxical as it may seem, security has not been an important analytical concept for most security studies scholars."[8] This is particularly true from the perspective of feminist security theory (Blanchard 2003) and those advocating for human security (Axworthy 2001). Second, this research traces and analyzes the organizational dynamics of women's activism in the UN system and how women have come to embrace and have been impacted by the security framework, globally and locally. Lastly, this project provides insight into practical strategies utilized by transnational advocacy networks in the development and implementation of international human rights norms. From a policy perspective, this research explores the utility of mechanisms, such as the security discourse, in empowering groups advocating for women's rights and gender equality. As important, this research examines how such language may also be limiting for the world's most marginalized sect of society.[9]

Scope and limitations

It is necessary to explain a number of caveats before proceeding in order to guide the reader's expectations in terms of the scope and limitations of this project.

Theory

With regard to theory, this project utilizes three theoretical paradigms that taken together help to answer the research questions. While it is ambitious to take up three bodies of literature—critical security studies, feminist international relations theory, and women's activism as a transnational network and social movement—each provides the insights and context necessary to develop a comprehensive and

Women, peace, and security 5

intelligent analysis. By beginning with security studies, one can easily see how traditional approaches to security have been inadequate, substantively and methodologically. Concepts, such as human security and securitization, help to demonstrate security as a process to be widened and deepened and as an analysis that serves a political and normative role. Feminist international relations theorists have long been critical of such traditional approaches to security and can help explain the conceptual, cultural, and linguistic barriers and practices that have segregated women's rights and gender equality norms from security discourse in both theory and practice. Feminist theory also provides useful warnings regarding the adoption of gender language for politically expedient ends. Lastly, by placing women's activism in the context of theory on transnational advocacy and social movement strategy, the research is able to situate the security framework within the broader goals of the global women's movement, contributing to our understanding of strategies utilized by contemporary social movements. These theoretical perspectives are explored in more detail in Chapter 2.

Why the UN?

Although there are many locales to explore security discourse or women's activism, the UN is the most logical starting point for studying the two together at the global level.[10] The mere fact that the UN Security Council—the center of UN power and primary decision-making body in the area of international peace and security—recognized with SCR 1325 the need to adopt a gender perspective and to make women central to all aspects of the peace process, as both victims and agents of conflict and conflict resolution, is momentous. The world's largest international organization has now publicly declared that attention to women and gender is integral to "doing security." As Carol Cohn rightly argues, "even if at this point the Security Council's re-visioning of security is more rhetorical than practical, it still puts the UN far ahead of any academic security studies or international relations programme" (Cohn et al. 2004: 139).

Furthermore, despite American feminists' general disregard for the UN, this global body remains a significant organization for many, particularly those in the developing world. It became evident in the research for this project, that for many women in many war-torn regions and the many local, national, and international non-governmental organizations (NGOs) that those women form, what happens at the UN matters a great deal. UN activity has long had real implications for women on the ground, and women from the developing world follow the UN's work very closely (Jain 2005). As Berg (2006: 333) maintains, "work on gender could be one of the UN's most fundamental contributions to human betterment."[11]

In terms of both gender equality and international security, the UN greatly contributed to the development of ideas and norm diffusion. As the United Nations Intellectual History Project (UNIHP) demonstrates, the UN is a laboratory for growing ideas that drive human progress.[12] Through an extensive historical analysis of both written and oral accounts, the UNIHP series illustrates how ideas formed within and among UN officials change discourse, shape institutional

6   Women, peace, and security

development, and even influence state interests.[13] Given that from its inception maintaining peace and security has been and continues to be the most important function of the organization, notions of humanizing security and securitizing women's rights within the UN is significant. Shifting from approaches such as comprehensive or collective security to the latest buzzword—human security— has particular relevance for the UN and its work on women's rights and gender equality issues.

As early as 1980 with the UN-sponsored Brandt Commission, the organization was pushing an expanded understanding of security. The first of two reports, *North-South: A Programme for Survival*, calls "for a new concept of security that would transcend the narrow notions of military defense and look more towards the logic of a broader interdependence" (124).[14] More recently, the 2004 High-Level Panel on Threats, Challenges and Change appointed by the former Secretary-General Kofi Annan concluded:

> the biggest security threats we face now, and in the decades ahead, go far beyond States waging aggressive war. They extend to poverty, infectious disease and environmental degradation; war and violence within States; the spread and possible use of nuclear, radiological, chemical and biological weapons; terrorism; and transnational organized crime. The threats are from non-State actors as well as States, and to human security as well as State security.
>
> (UN 2004: 1)

As an organization committed to international peace and security, but with member states keeping national security interests of sovereign states at the top of the agenda, the UN is a prime institutional focus for studying the nature and tension of international security, its existence as a substantive policy framework, its relation to national security approaches, and the impact of such an approach on different issue areas that clearly fall under the rubric of human security. Sadako Ogata, Co-Chair of the UN Commission on Human Security argues:

> The United Nations stands as the best and only option available to preserve international peace and stability as well as protect people ... The issue is how to make the United Nations and other regional security organizations more effective in preventing and controlling threats and protecting people, and how to complement state security with human security at the community, national, and international levels.
>
> (2003: 5)

Despite its many weaknesses, the UN does play a significant role in promoting and creating certain norms, including norms and values surrounding the meaning and approaches to international security.[15] Given the UN's role in norm creation and its mission of promoting and protecting international peace and security, the organization is a good starting point for understanding the process of securitization and its impact on non-traditional security concerns, such as women's rights and gender equality. This book is in part a response to Inis L. Claude Jr.'s commitment and call for serious study of the UN and the development of realistic and sophisticated understanding of the nature of the organization, its possibilities and limitations, and its merits and defects.

> Above all, we need to examine the United Nations in its political context, regarding it as essentially an institutional framework within which states make decisions and allocate resources, arranging to do a variety of things with, to, for, and against each other.
>
> (Claude Jr. 2004: xiii)

This theoretical tension surrounding the meaning of security as well as the existence of human security—at least in rhetorical form—within the United Nations is the foundation for this project.

Definitions and terminology

There are several important clarifications to make regarding the concepts used throughout this project.

Gender is usually misunderstood and misused as the term is so often equated with "women." This is in part because women are usually the ones to bring attention to gender issues. This can be explained by the unequal ordering of gender power that systemically and routinely disadvantages women.[16] Thus, the incentives for women to take up gender issues are obvious, which only further substantiates the perception that gender issues refer to women's issues only.

Rather than an oversimplified simile for women, questions about gender relate to the assumptions made about people with male or female bodies and the roles attached to those bodies that prescribe what people are like and should be like in a particular culture. Moreover, there are values placed on these roles constructing gendered hierarchies where masculinity and femininity become dependent on each other for meaning (Peterson & Runyan 1998). Former UN Secretary-General Kofi Annan in his report on "Women, Peace, and Security" defines gender as:

> the socially constructed roles ascribed to women and men, as opposed to biological and physical characteristics. Gender roles vary according to socio-economic, political, and cultural contexts and are affected by other factors, including age, race, class and ethnicity. Gender roles are learned and changeable. Gender equality is a goal to ensure equal rights, responsibilities and opportunities for women and men, and girls and boys, which has been accepted by Governments.
>
> (2002: 4)

Women as a group is also an oversimplified term. Thanks to the challenges posed by women of color and women of the Global South, however, feminists have

8   *Women, peace, and security*

ceased to claim a common identity (Mohanty et al. 1991). Understanding that gender identities cannot be separated from race and class, it is important to ask "Which women are you talking about?" In the field of security and conflict, researchers and policy-makers have been slow to identify the diverse role that women play as community leaders, combatants, enablers, peace activists, and of course, as victims.[17] Problems arise when scholars and policy-makers addressing post-conflict reconstruction assume that women "naturally" fall into the latter two categories or when intersections with race, ethnicity, and socio-economic status are simply overlooked.

With the 1995 Beijing Platform for Action, 183 UN Member States established *gender-mainstreaming* as a global strategy for achieving gender equality. In July 1997, the UN Economic and Social Council (ECOSOC) defined gender-mainstreaming as follows:

> Mainstreaming a gender perspective is the process of assessing the implications for women and men of any planned action, including legislation, policies or programmes, in any area and at all levels. It is a strategy for making the concerns and experiences of women as well as of men an integral part of the design, implementation, monitoring and evaluation of policies and programmes in all political, economic and societal spheres, so that women and men benefit equally, and inequality is not perpetuated. The ultimate goal of mainstreaming is to achieve gender equality.[18]

As this definition indicates, gender mainstreaming is more than just a Western, liberal project aimed at inserting more women in decision-making bodies and existing political structures. It goes beyond an additive approach to something with far more transformative potential because it is a "strategy to re-invent the processes of policy design, implementation, and evaluation" (True 2003: 371). From this perspective, gender mainstreaming is quite radical in that it recognizes both men and women's role in making processes, programs, and practices more gender sensitive from the very beginning.

The transformative agenda of gender-mainstreaming is best articulated in the language of SCR 1325 through which the *"Women, Peace, and Security" network* has been instrumental in drafting, proposing, and implementing. This network refers to a community of advocates in and around the UN that have been a part of getting women on the international security agenda.[19] The NGO Working Group on Women, Peace, and Security is the driving force in this network.[20] The original Working Group members include Amnesty International, Women's Commission for Refugee Women and Children, International Alert, Women's Caucus for Gender Justice, the Hague Appeal for Peace, and Women's International League for Peace and Freedom (WILPF).[21] Among UN agencies, UNIFEM—the UN Development Fund for Women—continues to be a central actor in this network.[22] As for UN Member States, a coalition of 23 countries led by Canada supports this network through the establishment of "Friends of 1325."[23] Academics from all parts of the world have also been a large part of this network, as individuals and as

Women, peace, and security 9

organized groups.[24] An example of the latter is the Boston Consortium on Gender, Security and Human Rights.[25] As this list demonstrates, this network includes state and non-state actors, activists and academics, and rights-based groups and peace-based groups.

This network has come to be the driving force for defining and applying the *Security Framework* for women's rights and gender issues. The security framework refers to the type arguments made and the justifications set forth to draw attention to and prioritize women's rights and a gender-sensitive perspective. The framework operates from the premise that women's rights and gender equality situated in a human rights frame or even a moral frame are not enough and simply not as effective in generating awareness, response, and commitment. Therefore, the framework highlights how protecting and promoting the rights of women is a fundamental component of establishing international peace and security—the driving mission of the UN.[26] The idea is that security needs women, as much as women need security. The security language serves as a framework for action through discursive positioning that situates women as central, or at least part of, the security agenda. This frame highlights how women's rights and gender equality can contribute to international peace and security, and therefore constitute vested interest for many national and international leaders. As Sanam Anderlini (2000: 3) argues, it is not a matter of what women stand to gain from inclusion into the peace process, but rather "what peace processes stand to lose when women's wealth of experiences, creativity, and knowledge are excluded."

With this framework, targeting the UN Security Council became critical. As Carol Cohn argues, "The ideas of mobilizing to influence the Security Council, and to get a Security Council Resolution on women and armed conflict, represents a new and important strategy" (Cohn 2004: 8). Although this strategy is new in terms of its target, as the Security Council in a very non-conventional arena for those advocating gender equality and women's rights, it does, however, rely upon very traditional stereotypes of women as peacemakers and nurturers of society.[27] Nonetheless, the notion of women as more peaceful or collaborative serves a political function in terms of narrow national interest, rather than any sort of moral or altruistic obligation.[28] In this sense, the security framework presents the integration of women and a gender perspective as an untapped resource that can greatly improve the UN's ability to establish and maintain international peace and security.[29]

Methodology

Data collection for this study relied on several sources. Most importantly, the analysis relies on interviews with scholars and policy-makers that have been a part of the UN system and/or the WPS network since its inception.[30] Most interviews were conducted in New York during numerous interview trips.[31] Interviewees included current and former UN personnel, staff from relevant NGOs, and scholars professionally affiliated with the UN. Phone and email interviews have been conducted in cases where interviewees were outside the United

10 Women, peace, and security

States. Interviewees represented a diverse group, ranging in nationality, gender, and status/experience within the UN. Using the "snowball sampling method," the number of interviews exceeded thirty-five (Ackerly et al. 2006: 11).

This project also relies heavily on textual analysis and archival research of UN documents, both public and internal.[32] These include but are not limited to annual reports, committee reports, convention and conference reports, independent assessments, relevant Security Council and General Assembly resolutions and declarations, and Secretary-General statements. These primary sources as well as select secondary sources also help form a robust structural analysis of relevant UN agencies and funds in terms of administrative changes, budgetary allocations, leadership shifts, and the often complex relationship that exists between these groups. Thus, the strategy of this project was to "incorporate material and ideational factors rather than privilege one over the other" (Hansen 2006: 23) in order to "illustrate how ... textual and social processes are intrinsically connected and to describe, in specific contexts, the implications of this connection for the way we think and act in the contemporary world" (George 1994: 191).

With regard to methods used in the project, I also acted as a participant-observer as both a member of a UN-accredited NGO and as a researcher. For the former, I attended the Sixth Anniversary events of SCR 1325 in New York City from October 23 to 26, 2006. Through the Huairou Commission, a transnational network committed to supporting women's grassroots movements, I was able to attend both public and closed meetings at UN headquarters and parallel NGO meetings also taking place in New York. Of particular interest, I observed an Arria formula meeting,[33] where women's civil society groups were able to address and debate with Security Council Members as well as the Security Council open debate on SCR 1325. As an academic researcher, I also observed and participated in two virtual community discussions on gender and security sector reform in April and May of 2007. These online communities, facilitated by the United Nations International Research and Training Institute for the Advancement of Women (INSTRAW), brought together over thirty practitioners currently working in the field to share their experiences making security sector reform gender-sensitive and gender-inclusive. The participants were an equal mix of UN personnel and non-state actors from all over the world.[34] Both experiences as a participant-observer provided great insights and many first-hand accounts that informed this research.

Overall, the methodological approach operates from the premise that "the way to study securitization is to study discourse" (Buzan et al. 1998: 25). In other words, in order to understand how international security is constructed and conducted, one must not only talk to the people involved, but pour over official and unofficial documents as well to really deconstruct the significance of the language—that which is articulated and is left out. Establishing a standard of rhetoric, a commonly understood language, is not only a tool with which to hold governments accountable, it is also constitutive for what is brought into being. My methodology is distinct in its reflexivity, and derives its strength from the "juxtaposition and layering of many different windows" through which to look at the nature of security discourses in relation to women and gender (Cohn 2006: 93).[35]

Women, peace, and security   11

While some of these windows were part of my original research design others were opportunistic and emerged as I collected the data. Chapters 4 and 5 are particularly reflective of the latter approach. Similar to the work of Carol Cohn, the persuasiveness of my case studies taken together relies upon the "multiplicity of spaces within which I trace metaphoric gendered themes and their variations" in the production of international peace and security (2006: 107).

Genesis of 1325

Before moving on, it is important to briefly discuss some of the background on how SCR 1325 and the WPS network came to be. Although the emergence and development of this activism has been well documented, it has been done so in a fragmented way.[36] No one piece offers a comprehensive narrative, and thus, it is important to synthesize this information for a solid knowledge-base. In order to understand where we are going, we must understand where we have come from— the root values and objectives that motivated this particular initiative to engage and attempt to influence the UN Security Council, *the* global governance institution in matters of peace and security.

The 1995 Beijing Platform for Action laid the conceptual foundation in its articulation of women and armed conflict as one of the twelve strategic objectives.[37] In 1998, the Commission on the Status of Women (CSW) took up this theme and discussed the obstacles to implementing the Beijing chapter on women and armed conflict. According to two UN officials who were part of the process, "the NGO network began to appear informally at the 1998 meeting" of the CSW. They go on to say, "With many women from a number of different conflict zones attending, it was here that the idea to advocate for a Security Council resolution was first raised" (Cohn et al. 2004: 131). As one NGO activist at the time points outs, "Frankly, at the time, I had no idea what it really meant to get a Security Council resolution. But I knew it would create a mandate for our work" (interview, March 2007). After the CSW, the NGO Working Group on Women, Peace, and Security officially formed and agreed to pursue two specific recommendations: to encourage women's participation in peace agreements and to push for the convening of a special session of the Security Council on women, peace, and security (Hill et al. 2003: 1258).[38]

Although UNIFEM did informally support some of the Working Group's members in 1998–1999, it did not get directly involved with the working group until 2000.[39] This more formal partnership really started to take shape with a conference organized by International Alert, one of the NGOs party to the WPS network. The conference was focused on a global campaign to bring women to the negotiation table, and International Alert brought UNIFEM on as an integral partner in supporting local women's peacebuilding work.[40] Thus, through this partnership with International Alert, UNIFEM became initially involved in the WPS network (former UNIFEM official, interview 2007).

Although the NGO Working Group initiated this notion of working for a Security Council Resolution on women, UNIFEM played a major role in circulating

12   Women, peace, and security

it among members of the Security Council and proved to be a critical access point for such non-state actors to influence state actors. One NGO official that was involved during that time recounted:

> Noeleen Heyzer [the executive director of UNIFEM] hosted a cocktail party in March of 2000 and invited the Security Council President at the time, Ambassador Anwarul Chowdhury of Bangladesh. At the party she gave him copies of the draft [for a potential resolution] to give to the rest of the Council. Then, he came out with his speech on International Women's Day, and it was so important in drawing attention to the campaign.
>
> (Interview, 2007)

Numerous studies on SCR 1325 find this speech given by the Council President at the time to be a major turning point.[41] Not only was it the first time that the President of the Security Council addressed the International Women's Day proceedings, but it was also significant in what he said. He recognized that:

> peace is inextricably linked with equality between women and men. They affirm that the equal access and full participation of women in power structures and their full involvement in all efforts for the prevention and resolution of conflicts are essential for the maintenance and promotion of peace and security.
>
> (SC/6816 2000)[42]

Thus, he squarely placed the women's rights (minimally understood) and gender equality in the security framework. As one UNIFEM official remembers:

> I think the main turning point was when Bangladesh passed the presidential statement. I think that is when people at the SC recognized that WPS was not an issue for the GA only and that the SC could not just talk about civilian protection and children in armed conflict, but that there really was this debate that had to be had on WPS. So it really was Bangladesh that turned the corner and then Namibia during their presidency. You know the country has been very progressive. Women have been active in the liberation struggle and afterward in their post-conflict reconstruction. So Namibia also took this forward and really encouraged UNIFEM to formulate some solid thinking around this.
>
> (Interview, August 2006)

Others have described Chowdhury's speech as a "crucial rhetorical act" (Cohn 2003–04: 4) that provided a "shot of enthusiasm and encouragement for the women gathered at the CSW by linking equality, development, and peace, and the need for women's urgent involvement in these matters" (Hill et al. 2003: 1257). Another former UNIFEM official described this security framework as a "lens for all three things, opening up women's situation vis-à-vis equality, development and peace" (interview, December 2007).[43] These speech acts not only served to further mobilize the women's organizations into an effective and heterogeneous transnational advocacy network, but they also helped further by opening political space for this network to operate.

As previously noted, the government of Namibia was also critical in this process. In May 2000, the Government of Namibia and the Lessons Learned Unit of the UN Department of Peacekeeping Operations (DPKO) organized a seminar on mainstreaming gender in peace operations, which resulted in the Windhoek Declaration and the Namibia Plan of Action.[44] Because Namibia hosted this meeting, the NGO Working Group saw Namibia as a logical entry point for discussing the possibility of holding an open session on women during Namibia's October presidency of the Security Council (Hill et al. 2003: 1259). Beginning with Namibia, NGO Working Group began forming alliances with sympathetic states on the Council at the time, which included Canada, Bangladesh, and Jamaica. But during this time NGOs intentionally downplayed their role in pushing this issue onto the security agenda, as they understood it was vital that Namibia did not appear to be NGO-led. Felicity Hill, a founding member of the Working Group, describes the process:

> Through a series of meetings and papers, NGOs supplied this core group of states with arguments about the *utility and advantages* of a Council debate on this subject, with talking points and recommendations to use in their discussion with other delegates. Only after they knew that states had begun the discussion between them, the NGO Working Group on Women, Peace and Security undertook a number of initiatives such as meeting with each remaining member of the Security Council, utilizing different arguments with each to advocate for a thematic debate and resolution on Women, Peace and Security.
> (2004–2005: 29–30, emphasis added)

Throughout the process, the NGOs worked tirelessly to educate the Council, "finding as much high quality relevant literature as they could ... comb[ing] through every UN document from the institution's inception, finding every reference any way relevant to the Women, Peace, and Security agenda" (Cohn 2003–04: 4). In this way, NGOs supplied UN officials with a "a compendium of 'agreed language' which showed the basis for committing themselves" to the resolution (Cohn 2003–04: 4). All the while they worked to create a resolution that appeared state-driven, not NGO-driven. All the while they worked to create a resolution that appeared state-driven, not NGO-driven.

As soon as Namibia agreed to host an open session on Women, Peace, and Security, the Working Group drafted the resolution. UNIFEM and the NGO Working Group arranged for women from conflict zones from around the world to address the Council in an Arria formula meeting, "bringing to men who rarely left NY a concrete, personal awareness of both women's victimization in war and their agency" (Cohn 2003–04: 5). The resolution was passed the day after the Arria formula meeting, and although there were a number of issues left off the

14   *Women, peace, and security*

final document, its preambular language was identical to the draft the NGO Working Group had submitted (Hill 2004–05: 30).[45]

Overall, the progressive leadership of Bangladesh and Namibia was very important. So too was the technical, financial, and institutional support of UNIFEM once they fully signed onto the Women, Peace, and Security campaign in early 2000. But in the end, it was the NGO Working Group that laid the "entire groundwork for this resolution, including the initial drafting, and the political work of preparing the Security Council members to accept that a resolution was relevant and had precedents in the Security Council's work" (Cohn 2003–04: 4).

A UN official, who was not directly part of the process, described WPS as a group that took advantage of "interagency networking" and the "growing concern within the UN system to mainstream human rights" (interview, October 2006). This focus on human rights had already emerged in the Security Council with its thematic focus on civilians and children in armed conflict in 1998–99.[46] Thus, the WPS network utilized a sort of "bandwagoning mechanism to see gender from a security perspective" (interview, October 2006). Another interviewee who was with UNIFEM at the time and directly involved in the WPS network related this bandwagoning strategy to:

> The human security agenda and the ways in which the Council started think-ing thematically about security: first with the protection of civilians during armed conflict and then children. It created this opportunity to look at gen-der issues. It had to do with a much broader securitization of politics in general, a question of framing and expediency. All of those factors brought it together.
>
> (Interview, December 2006)

But the concept of human security was consciously evoked for only a few actors in this process. One of the founding members of the NGO Working Group argues that although human security as a "fairly obvious concept was invoked, it was not the sustaining or enabling discourse that facilitated the NGO work on 1325" (Cohn et al. 2004: 135). Nonetheless, human security, and the Human Security Network more specifically, provided the legitimization that the Security Council needed to include issues, such as women, into its work in the late 1990s.[47] This network and the language it utilized created an entry point for issues that had long been seen as organizationally and substantively separate from the Council's man-date to be included as part of their agenda. According to Carol Cohn, without the Human Security Network, "the thematic resolutions (children and armed conflict; civilians and armed conflict; and 1325) could not have happened" (Cohn et al. 2004: 135). It was all part of a political space that was opened with the discourse surrounding human security.[48] In further support of this claim, a recent study of South African women involved in various peace-building projects concludes that "… from a gender perspective, the most significant document in human security" is SCR 1325 (Hamber et al. 2006: 490).[49]

Women, peace, and security 15

Within this context of human security and an organized and sophisticated women's network, SCR 1325 was unanimously adopted by the Security Council in October 2000. Scholars and practitioners, men and women have referred to SCR 1325 as a landmark document:

> It is not only a landmark document, it is potentially a revolutionary one. Its broadening of the gaze from the traditional political and military aspects of peace and security can and should do several different things at once: It affirms women's rights to protection and participation; and should it be widely implemented, women's experience of conflict and their ability to prevent or end it could be substantially transformed. What could also be transformed by this 'broadening of the gaze' is the mainstream belief in the adequacy of restricting one's vision to the traditional political and military aspects of peace and security. Resolution 1325, as it moves from rhetoric to reality, could potentially transform our ideas about the prevention of war, the bases for sustainable peace, and the pathways to achieve them.
>
> (Cohn 2004: 9)

This transformative potential is a result of the way gender and war are historically, inextricably linked.[50] As Joshua Goldstein (2001: 10–11) concludes, "Gender roles adapt individuals for war roles, and war roles provide the context within which individuals are socialized into gender roles." In this way, the transformation of gender relations may often demand significant changes in the war system first; at the same time, if the war system is to change or if war is to end altogether gendered identities and expectations may have to be reconstructed. The intricate interdependencies between gender and international security are significant, and any genuine shift in how gender roles are perceived by the Security Council has potentially profound consequences for the very nature of war itself.

To understand how the security framework and the WPS network have affected the war system in terms of socialized gender roles, I have developed four distinct, yet interrelated case studies. Each one provides a unique look into the ways in which the security discourse and SCR 1325 have been implemented and not implemented, used by other UN agencies outside the Council, and informed the development of emerging UN institutions and norms related to gender and security. These cases studies are not an exhaustive look at the security framework or at SCR 1325, but rather reflect multiple ways of examining international security discourses as they relate to women's rights and gender equality. These cases constitute Chapters 3 through 6 and are described briefly in the next section.[51]

Project roadmap

Understanding the origins of the WPS network and SCR 1325, raises further questions about how this security framework has been operationalized and implemented throughout the UN system. First, how have women's rights been

16   Women, peace, and security

securitized within by the Security Council in the last eight years? How has SCR 1325 been integrated into Council activity on the ground? Chapter 3, in addressing these questions, finds that despite the many institutional and attitudinal barriers, the adoption of SCR 1325 and the diffusion of norms from the WPS network is proof that ideas originating in women's movements and feminist theory are gradually becoming part of the practices and institutions of global governance, rhetorically, legally, and procedurally. Nonetheless, the chapter concludes that much of the progress associated with SCR 1325 reflects additive shifts rather than a transformative change to the way the UN does security, leaving much of the traditional security agenda very much intact. The tensions that emerge with this case study begin to point to some of the important differences between securitizing women's rights and humanizing security.

Given the many obstacles that the WPS network still faces, the second case study turns to a comparison of women's activism in conflict and post-conflict situations with those advocating for children in armed conflict. Chapter 4 contrasts these two vulnerable groups as a way of highlighting the unique (and not so unique) obstacles that women face in the Security Council. In analyzing the now six SC resolutions on children in armed conflict with SCR 1325 and the more recent SCR 1820,[52] I find that as much as women have gained in the UN system, they do face some unique structural, institutional, and attitudinal barriers that children do not particularly in the context of the security framework. This is partly explained by the transformative nature of the WPS agenda and the demand that the Security Council go beyond seeing women as victims. Simply stated, demanding women's inclusion into the decision-making process, poses a greater challenge to the existing power structure than demanding the protection of children during and after conflict. While children certainly have agency and fundamental human rights, they do not challenge existing power relations and embedded structures in the same way that women do.

Although Chapter 4 highlights the shortcomings and setbacks of the security discourse and SCR 1325 for the WPS network, it raises questions about what sorts of advantages or opportunities, if any, the movement has gained in utilizing this framework. Chapter 5 explores one way that the security discourse has benefited women beyond the scope of the Security Council through an organizational examination of UNIFEM, an institution created to deal with women's roles and concerns in economic development. As indicated in an earlier section of this chapter, UNIFEM has been an important actor in the WPS network, and therefore, it is important to understand how a *development* fund got in the business of international peace and security, a policy arena they had long been excluded from. Through an analysis of security sector reform in post-conflict situations, I find that the security discourse provides a new strategic entry point in terms of a basis for developing new partnerships and new resources that had not been available to UNIFEM before.

Lastly, Chapter 6 addresses questions about the future of the WPS network and SCR 1325 in guiding the work of the UN more broadly. The establishment of the

Women, peace, and security 17

UN Peacebuilding Commission (PBC) in 2005 presents an opportunity for the UN to fulfill and implement the principles set forth by SCR 1325, and therefore it serves as an ideal case study for evaluating how a gendered approach to security is being articulated and operationalized in its design, mandate, and activities. Given that the PBC is part of the larger efforts to reform the UN, this case also provides insight into the major tensions that women still face in challenging how the UN defines and pursues international peace and security in relation to broader socio-economic development goals. In addition, analyzing the progress and the many setbacks of the PBC, I find SCR 1325 coming full circle in this case study: a campaign that was initiated by NGOs continues to be driven by NGOs in its implementation.

Taken together, these chapters weave an intricate and complex story about the way in which this network of activists, and the policy commitments they were able to push through, have and have not fostered discursive change at the level of foundational concepts and subsequent practices with the UN system. This means acknowledging that as many doors as this framework may have opened, the security language has also posed significant limitations in just how far the WPS network can go in criticizing the fundamental assumptions of peace and security practice in a state-based system. In other words, many of the opportunities created by this discursive positioning rely upon state institutions for the realization and implementation. The shortcomings of the security language, particularly the essentialist assumptions of women as peacemakers that framework relies upon, cannot be ignored.

In the end, however, my research works from the premise that feminist scholars and activists need to be engaged with formal institutions of global governance, like the UN, but always analyzing the complexity of the impacts of that engagement along many different dimensions. Reaffirming Jacqui True's argument, it is "not how feminist scholars and activists can avoid cooptation by powerful institutions, but whether we can afford not to engage with such institutions, when the application of gender analysis in their policy-making is clearly having political effects beyond academic and feminist communities" (2003: 368). When one interviewee was asked about where her motivation to use the security discourse came from, she responded:

> Well, it came from my working at the UN for 27 years. It's something that you breathe working for the UN. I have to be strategic in my work. I have a very difficult and complex issue with a very small office. I had better be strategic in terms of how I create high profile. Of course, human rights create a high profile. But security takes it to a different level.
>
> (Interview, UN official, September 2006)

It is to that level that we now turn.

18 *Women, peace, and security*

Notes

1 From this perspective, "'security' is the move that takes politics beyond the established rules of the game and frames the issue either as a special kind of politics or as above politics" (Buzan et al. 1998: 23). Framing, therefore, is a strategy being employed by multiple actors at multiple levels.

2 It is important to note here that no organization, governmental or non-governmental, discussed in this research is necessarily uniform in its beliefs and strategies. Inter-agency tensions exist and not all are in support of the security framework for women's rights. Many still prioritize a rights-based approach over a security-based approach. This tension and its impact on policy are addressed in later chapters.

3 For the full text of this resolution, see http://www.un.org/events/res_1325e.pdf. For a summary, see Appendix A.

4 For more on women and security as "regimes" see Hill 2004–05.

5 Chapter 2 explores in more detail the positive and negative impacts of securitizing non-military or nonconventional security issues (and threats).

6 For a comprehensive and timely analysis of the importance of ensuring women's rights and gender equality in post-conflict situations, see Anderlini 2007.

7 Even those most engaged in studying securitization, namely scholars at the Copenhagen School, refrain from judging a particular security framework as accurate or not. The approach of the Copenhagen School is discussed in greater detail in Chapter 2.

8 In this sense, the meaning of security is assumed and agreed upon. It is a given not to be questioned. It is simply an end goal to be achieved. For more on this distinction of security as a means versus an end, see edited volume by Lipschutz (1995).

9 Other marginalized groups, such as refugees and internally displaced persons, have also been located within the security framework by activists in and around the UN. Although this group is beyond the scope of this book, it is certainly an area that merits further research.

10 The European Union, for example, has been engaged in this discourse and adopted several initiatives to better implement SCR 1325. For example, see http://ec. europa.eu/employment_social/gender_equality/index_en.html or http://ec.europa.eu/ employment_social/speeches/2003/ad290503_en.pdf.

11 Margaret Snyder, the first Executive Director of UNIFEM, has been quoted as saying, "I think the global women's movement would be lost or at least much weaker without the UN ... I think women captured the UN and made it their own vehicle for their movement to make sure that their movement was going to go ahead" (Weiss et al. 2005: 255).

12 For more information, see http://www.unhistory.org/.

13 See for example, Weiss et al. (2005).

14 Although the Brandt Reports focused on the global economy, they are significant here in that they link issues that historically have not been linked, such as the environment with trade with dependence with population and so forth. More broadly, they begin to construct the interdependencies between development with security.

15 Karns and Mingst (2004) confirm this normative role of the UN in terms of the human rights regime and the evolution of the idea of sustainable development. They also discuss the emerging norms surrounding human security and humanitarian intervention, particularly as they relate to the UN, although they are less certain that these norms have been confirmed by the international community.

16 As of December 2008, the Gender Development Index of the UN Human Development Reports illustrates that no country on earth accords women the same status and rights as men.

17 Enloe's work, particularly *Bananas, Beaches, and Bases: Making Feminists Sense of International Politics* (1989), was pioneering in this area.

Women, peace, and security 19

18 For more on this concept, see http://www.un.org/womenwatch/osagi/pdf/e65237.pdf.
19 For an idea of the range of members and scope of issues of this network, see www.peacewomen.org.
20 The role the NGO Working Group in the Genesis of 1325 is explained in further detail below.
21 Interestingly, as Carol Cohn points out, these Working Group members while all concerned with what was happening to women in wars, the majority do not define themselves as "anti-war," per se, nor as feminist. Only The Hague Appeal for Peace and WILPF are explicitly anti-war, anti-militaristic, and pro-disarmament, and of those two, only WILPF defines themselves as feminists. "What these differences meant concretely was that although all group members agreed that something had to be done to increase women's protection and participation, their own conceptual framings for how to do that were quite divergent" (Cohn 2003–2004: 12).
22 See for example, UNIFEM's web portal on "Women, Peace, and Security" at www.womenwarpeace.org.
23 For more on this network and other initiatives by the Canadian government to support SCR 1325, see http://www.dfait-maeci.gc.ca/foreign_policy/human-rights/women_peace-en.asp.
24 It is also worth noting here that SCR 1325 and WPS as a movement, campaign, and network have been part of International Studies Association (ISA) panels for at least the last seven years that this author has been in attendance.
25 For more information, go to www.genderandsecurity.org.
26 For more speeches using this framework, see the collection at http://www.peacewomen.org/un/6thAnniversary/Open_Debate/index.html.
27 In recent years there has been a substantial amount of anecdotal research asserting that women have a different understanding of peace, security, conflict resolution, and the use of force, given their socially constructed identities and experiences. Many make the case that the different identities, experiences and perspectives that women bring to peace missions allows them to be more constructive, inclusive, and sustainable. These assumptions are in part based on the male-dominated nature of the military system and warfare as explained by the intense socialization arguments set forth by Joshua S. Goldstein (2001) in his book, War and Gender: How *Gender Shapes the War System and Vice Versa*. Goldstein finds gender to be ontologically enmeshed in war, concluding that culturally constructed gender identities enable war.
28 Many have referred to this framework as the "practical 'use value' argument" (Isha Dyfan, as cited by Cohn et al. 2004: 137).
29 Such specific value-added, gendered arguments include notions that women are more likely to foster reconciliation (Hamilton 2000); women raise different issues than men, making the peace process more comprehensive and increasing national ownership (Anderlini 2000; Conaway & Martinez 2004); women control aggression better than men (DeGroot 2001); women are more collaborative and innovative negotiators (Olsson 2001: Florea et al. 2003); and women's organizations in general persistently advocate for peace (UNIFEM 2005).
30 In compliance with the Institutional Review Board at Office of Research Compliance at the University of Connecticut (Approval Protocol H06-061), and at the Research Institute at the University of Dayton all interviewees gave written and/or oral consent signaling their willingness to participate in the research project. They were given copies of a consent form along with a summary of the project and his/her rights as participants in the study. Given that many interviewees are still part of this ongoing political process and employed by the UN, national governments or non-governmental organizations, most interview attributions in this book are kept anonymous.
31 The interviews took place between March 2006 and November 2008.
32 Several interviewees shared internal documents with me during the interview process.

20 Women, peace, and security

33 Arria Formula meetings, named after their originator Ambassador Diego Arria (Venezuela), are informal gatherings that allow the Security Council greater flexibility to be briefed about international peace and security issues by actors with a given expertise that aren't necessarily government officials or UN delegations. This practice has been used frequently and has grown in importance since 1992 when it was first implemented. Most significantly, these meetings allow non-state actors, especially civil society organizations to address the Council directly. For more on this practice see http://www.globalpolicy.org/security/mtgsetc/arria.htm.

34 For more information on these two virtual discussions, see http://www.un-instraw. org/en/index.php?option=content&task=view&id=1048&Itemid=244.

35 This methodological approach is largely informed by feminist research in international relations, most especially Ackerly et al. (2006).

36 One possible exception here is the 2003 article by Felicity Hill, Mikele Aboitiz, and Sara Poehlman-Doumbouya, although this article focuses specifically on the role of NGOs. See also True-Frost (2007).

37 For the specific references to women and armed conflict in this document, go to http://www.peacewomen.org/un/ women/unwomenpeacedocs.html#16.

38 There were six original NGOs that formed the Working Group. Now there are twelve. For more information, see http://www.womenpeacesecurity.org/about/.

39 Carol Cohn maintains that although UNIFEM becomes very important to SCR 1325, from 1998 to early 2000 "the Working Group initiated and carried out this project for months despite what they felt was a clear message from women's advocates within the UN that the 'time isn't right, it couldn't happen, it isn't worth the effort" (2003–04: 5).

40 That conference led to the global campaign Women Building Peace: From the Village Council to the Negotiating Table. It was launched by International Alert in May 1999, with the support of 100 organizations worldwide, to respond to women's concerns about their exclusion from decision-making levels of peace, security, reconstruction and development processes. For more information, go to http://www.international-alert.org/.

41 Beyond issues of women and gender, international lawyers are beginning to study more closely the legal status of presidential statements. Dr. Jose Alvarez, Director of the Center on Legal Problems at Columbia Law School, recently spoke about presidential statements as intentionally weak, nonbinding documents that are beginning to develop into something that they were never intended to be, something closer to soft law. Speech given at the 2007 Academic Council on the United Nations System, New York, June 7, 2007.

42 For more, see http://www.peacewomen.org/un/UN1325/1325index.html. It is also worth noting that this language is very similar to that in the 1995 Beijing Platform for Action.

43 Equality, development, and peace was the theme of the Decade for Women (1975–1985). The Decade for Women is often seen as a vehicle that mobilized the world's women into the beginnings of the global women's movement. For more, see Antrobus 2004. The security language seems to shed new light on this old theme.

44 For the full text of this declaration, see http://www.peacewomen.org/un/ pkwatch/WindhoekDeclaration.html.

45 Although SCR 1325 represents the broadest political interpretation of gender issues ever articulated by the UN peace and security agenda, it does not, by any means, reflect the entire agenda of issues related to women, peace, and security. It does not for example address overall disarmament and the militarized approach of the UN system to establishing peace and security.

46 These resolutions are examined in great detail in Chapter 4.

47 The Human Security Network was formed in 1999 by several UN Member States. The Network includes Austria, Canada, Chile, Costa Rica, Greece, Ireland, Jordan, Mali, the Netherlands, Norway, Switzerland, Slovenia, Thailand, and South Africa as an

observer. The Network has a unique interregional and multiple agenda perspective with strong links to civil society and academia. The Network emerged from the land-mines campaign and was formally launched at a Ministerial meeting in Norway in 1999. For more, see http://www.humansecuritynetwork.org/network-e.php.

48 Also related here was Canada's role on the Security Council at the time. During its two-year term (1999–2000), the Canadian government in particular was part of "humanizing the Security Council" prior to SCR 1325. See Pearson (2001).

49 At the same time, however, it is important to understand that human security has not always been interpreted in such comprehensive terms or through such progressive leg-islation as SCR 1325. As Mary Caprioli (2004) convincingly demonstrates, the universal nature of human security can obscure the fact that key ideas promoted by that discourse—democracy and human rights—tend to have differential impacts on men and women and can be subsumed into traditional statist frameworks.

50 "Potential" is a key qualification here, as SCR 1325 seriously lacks enforcement mechanisms. The sources and implications for this lack of mechanisms are discussed more fully in Chapter 3.

51 Case selection for this project follows the criteria outlined by Van Evera (1997), par-ticularly in terms of maximizing the empirical scope, data richness, the resemblance of case background conditions to the conditions of current policy problems, appropriate-ness for controlled comparison with other cases (mainly using Mill's method of difference, and intrinsic importance.

52 The full text of SCR 1820 can be found in Appendix B.

2 Women's activism in the context of the security debate
Theoretical underpinnings

> The achievement of peace, economic justice, and ecological sustainability is inseparable from overcoming social relations of domination and subordination; genuine security requires not only the absence of war but also the elimination of unjust social relations, including unequal gender relations.
>
> J. Ann Tickner (1992: 128)

Given that "no other concept in international relations packs the metaphysical punch, or commands the disciplinary power, of 'security'" (Der Derian 1995: 24–25), it is not surprising that the meaning of security and how it is practiced and studied in international relations has long been a point of contention and debate. Although scholars began questioning conventional conceptualizations of security prior to the end of the Cold War (Ullman 1983), this debate has gained significant momentum in both academic and policy circles in recent years (Brown 2003). As notions of collective security, cooperative security, and human security have emerged, many are asking important questions regarding what should be considered in the realm of international security and what or who should be the primary referent of security be. In this way, security is often understood as an "essentially contested concept" characterized by "unsolvable debates about [its] meaning and application" (Buzan 1991: 7).[1]

While there is little agreement on how the nature of security is changing and to what extent such shifts in approach are occurring, most agree that the "classical approach to security is inadequate and that a broader, multisectoral approach to security is preferable to the traditional understanding of seeing security concerns as relating only to issues of militarized relations between competing states" (Sheehan 2005: 2–3).[2] Along these lines, scholars and policy-makers alike have made a practice out of securitizing global problems that are not traditionally seen as matters of security. In other words, the use of security language—security talk—as a political framework has increasingly been utilized for prioritizing unconventional security issues; because, as one study put it, "everyone agrees that "security issues" are important and deserving of national prominence and financial support" (Shultz, et al. 1993: 1). From concepts such as economic security (Dombrowski 2005) to food security (Cavalcanti 2005) and issues from the

Women's activism 23

environment (Deudney 1990; Kakonen 1994; Litfin 1999) to HIV/AIDS (Chen 2003; Elbe 2006; Price-Smith 2001; Prins 2004), a wide variety of non-military issues have been framed as security concerns.[3] These academic debates are reflective of the push in national and international policy arenas to expand the security agenda to better respond to the complex nature of human suffering and shifting threats to the dignity of the human race. Contrary to the optimistic projections of some analysts (Fukuyama 1992; Mueller 1989), the end of the Cold War has not resulted in diminished threats to world peace and security, but rather new and more complex ones.

This chapter will examine what meanings have traditionally been attached to security and how recent critics of the traditional approach seek to change it substantively and methodologically. In outlining the security debate, it will be important to examine theories of human security and the implications of this alternative approach. The notion of human security serves to open up the concept of security as a process to be widened and deepened. The widening aspect of the process is best understood in terms of securitization theory as pioneered by Barry Buzan, Ole Wæver, and the Copenhagen School (CS). On the other hand, deepening the meaning of security relies upon critical theory and its emphasis on emancipation to ask questions about the objectives and referents of security (Booth 1991; 1997). The CS and critical theory perspectives will be explored as they illustrate the political and normative role of security analysis. Turning then to feminists' insights on the study of security and its meaning for marginalized groups, one can see how feminist international relations (IR) theorists have long raised similar questions and critiques of security studies, traditionally defined. This review of the literature ends with contextualizing women's activism within this debate on the meaning and practice of security. This involves understanding the security framework as a particular strategy—a campaign—of the broader global women's movement to promote and protect women's human rights.

Conceptualizing security: its realist roots

Security comes from the Latin word *securitas* meaning freedom from care. It is not surprising then that from Roman times until the French Revolution, security was, as Emma Rothschild (1995) argues, a condition universally understood as pertaining to individuals. But as the Westphalian system consolidated in the eighteenth and nineteenth centuries, so too did the state's ethical claim to the primacy in security. Individuals entered into a bargain with states where "the individual accepted an obligation to contribute to the state's security and not to challenge the state in its quest to maximize a value that served individual and collective interest" (MacFarlane & Khong 2006: 6). In the twentieth century, security became increasingly synonymous with military preparedness as the preservation of state independence and autonomy became paramount in the pursuit of "national security" (Sheehan 2005). Although such an approach is certainly limited, it is straightforward in its focus on the state, as that which needs to be secured, and on the role of the military as the institution best positioned to provide security

24   Women's activism

against external threat (actual or potential) and establish conditions for economic growth (Bull 1977). As MacFarlane and Khong (2006: 1) best articulate:

> Security policy focused on the effort to sustain and promote the core values of states in their relations one with another. These core values were taken to be sovereignty and territoriality. The principle instrument of states in their quest for security was considered to be the military.

This perspective renders the term national security as the *raison d'être* of the state; this state-based conception of security is what came to dominate security studies and international relations during the twentieth century.[4]

Indeed, the field of security studies is often seen as "a child of Machiavellian and Hobbesian realism" where might makes right (Crawford 1991: 292). This association with the intellectual hegemony of realism can be characterized by the emphasis on military threats, states as actors, and orientation toward the status quo.[5] In other words, this "traditional" view of security centers on war and the military capacity to respond to external threats to the state (Wolfers 1962: 18), or as Walt (1991: 212) more recently maintains "the study of the threat, use, and control of military force." Thus, security studies and security-based organizations have long focused on foreign and defense policy mechanisms to avoid, prevent, and if need be win interstate military disputes (Baldwin 1995). And while realism was the dominant paradigm for understanding security throughout most of the Cold War, it was a perspective that did not go entirely unchallenged during this period.

As early as 1952, Arnold Wolfers argued that different states value security on varying levels and that the nature of security must be subjectively understood.[6] Although he was very much arguing from a realist perspective, speaking in terms of states in anarchy, military power, and armaments, he did open the door for a discussion of security that was both process-oriented and value-laden. He distinguished between the nature of security as an object (as a real threat) and as a subject (as a perceived threat), and recognized that both may be true at the same time. He made the point that the realist conception of security was not less idealistic than conceptions proposed by its critics, since "the demand for a policy of national security is primarily normative in character" (1952: 483). This means that even the traditional concept of security constitutes a series of value judgments and an ordered set of priorities in terms of public attention and governmental resources. Such recognition lays the groundwork for a discussion of security that is political and relative in conceptual and practical terms. From this perspective, the national security process demands more discussion and greater specification, "with respect to the actor whose values are to be secured, the values concerned, the degree of security, the kinds of threats, the means for coping with such threats, the costs of doing so, and the relevant time period" (Baldwin 1997: 17).

Despite this early and progressive conceptual analysis, it was not until the 1980s that more fundamental challenges to the meaning of security began to

Women's activism 25

emerge. Ken Booth describes the 1980s as a period that has seen a "growing unease with the traditional concept of security, which privileges the state and emphasized military power" together with a "frequent call for the broadening or updating of the concept of security" (Booth 1991: 317). Here is where Ullman's article that appeared in *the* flagship journal of realist security studies, *International Security*, is significant. While his article did call attention to environmental security issues, thus, challenging the dominant militaristic paradigm, in many ways the article was as important for when and where it appeared as it was for what it actually said (Sheehan 2005). Ullman argued that traditional military approaches to security lead to the underestimation of other security threats and contributed to the militarization of IR, yet he had difficultly defining an alternative security agenda that was not linked to the military agenda and that was not reliant upon the state for promotion and protection. In this way, it was not a particularly radical departure from the logic of realism in a substantive sense. In terms of its timing and location, however, it was important for the political space that it opened for more critical conversations to begin.

Another important critical theory perspective that emerged from the 1980s was Barry Buzan's *People, States, and Fear* (1983). Buzan effectively demonstrated how a "national security" approach automatically identified military issues with security, rendering other sorts of real world security threats invisible. From this perspective, he argued that the national security problem needed to be seen in terms of a general systemic security problem in which individuals, states, and the system all play a part, and in which economic, societal, and environmental factors can be as important as political and military ones (1991: 15, 368). Here, he maintained that the literature on security was "unbalanced"—with the conceptual literature largely lacking. Similarly, in 1989 Jessica Tuchman Mathews also argued that the concept of security needed to be rethought as "global developments now suggest the need for ... national security to include resource, environmental, and demographic issues," thereby challenging the use of national borders as the determinant of national security threats (1989: 162). All-in-all throughout the 1980s and particularly with the end of the Cold War, traditional realist conceptualizations of security were seen as increasingly unsatisfactory for failing to take into account important aspects of an emerging international policy agenda. In other words, security equals the absence of insecurity and the latter can be defined in many different ways.[7] Insecurity could be focused on military matters, but can also be expanded to include all aspects of human agency and natural phenomena that may have any impact on the security of people. In this sense, history, culture, and identity all interact to determine the discourse on security that will be most consistent with security conceptions, objectives, and policy.

Emergence of a human security agenda

The fall of the Berlin Wall only served to bolster critiques of realist notions of security and the narrow, militaristic policies that followed from such theory.

26   Women's activism

While attempts to redefine security in the post-Cold War era continued to be controversial and constantly shifting focus, consensus did emerge on two fronts.[8] First, it was impossible to ignore how globalization in all its speed, enormity, and complexity was impacting the security agenda at the local, national, and international level (Held & McGrew 2001). Along these lines, one could not refute Rosenau's argument that "more than ever, security is elusive, more than ever, it is embedded in the interaction of localizing and globalizing forces" (1994: 255). The increasing relevance and intensity of these local–global processes and interactions raised critical questions regarding the rationale for exclusive focus on the state and suggested that security might have other referent subjects and might be extended to issues beyond military capacity.[9]

On a second and related front, consensus emerged on the need to focus on the individual as the subject of security. This focus on the individual must be understood in the context of the 1990s where armed conflict was increasingly defined by intra-state violence, civilian targets, and gross and systematic human rights violations that impinged upon the credibility of the state's claim to primacy in security.[10] As Kal Holsti (1999: 302) argues, "most of the mass killings of [the twentieth] century have been organised by states against their own citizens," and nowhere was the line between protector and perpetrator more blurry than after the Cold War. It was at this time when human security became a buzzword in academic and policy circles.[11]

The term "human security" developed as a concept that can be compared and contrasted to the more traditional term of "national security," thereby directing attention to a wider spectrum of security threats, both within and outside of the state.[12] Problems lie in the fact that people can be insecure in a secure state and threats increasingly exist that lack identifiable enemies (Hamill 1998). This is where realist notions of security fall short. Kanti Bajpai observed that "realism's appropriation of the term security rests on the assumption that interstate war is the greatest threat to personal safety and freedom. This may or may not be the case, at any given time" (2000: 51). Human security, which is "not merely the absence of military conflict between states," is a direct response to this critique (Axworthy 2004: 348). As Lloyd Axworthy (2001: 19) explains, human security "puts people first and recognizes that their safety is integral to the promotion and maintenance of international peace and security."

One of the earliest statements concerning human security appeared in the 1994 *Human Development Report*. "The concept of security," the report argues, "has for too long been interpreted narrowly: as security of territory from external aggression, or as protection of national interests, or as global security from the threat of nuclear holocaust" (UNDP 1994: 22). The politics of security, the report made clear, must widen its focus and include not only "the security of borders [but] also ... the security of people's lives" (23).[13] The final report from UN Commission on Human Security further defined human security to mean "protecting fundamental freedoms ... protecting people from critical (severe) and pervasive (widespread) threats and situations." (*Human Security Now*, 2003: 4). The report connects different types of freedoms—freedom from want, freedom from fear, and freedom to take action on one's own behalf and offers two general strategies to address these fears: protection and empowerment.[14]

At its core, human security has come to have meaning in terms of the individual, moving beyond purely state-based notions of military and territorial security. Newman (2001: 239) asserts that human security in its broadest sense "seeks to place the individual—or people collectively—as the referent of security rather than, although not necessarily in opposition to, institutions such as territory and state sovereignty." This concept "reflects the impact of values and norms in international relations" and "embraces a range of alliances, actors and agendas that have taken us beyond the traditional scope of international politics and diplomacy" (Newman 2001: 240).[15] In its most basic form, security implies the absence of, or freedom from, threats to core values, such as survival, welfare or identity for individual human beings.

Many proponents of human security, however, do not see it as opposing or replacing traditional notions of security, but rather supplementing and complementing national security. According to the UN Human Commission on Human Security in its report, *Human Security Now* (2003: 4), human security complements state security in four respects:

1   Its concern is the individual and the community rather than the state.
2   Menaces to people's security include threats to the state and conditions that have not always been classified as threats to state security.
3   The range of actors is expanded beyond the state alone.
4   Achieving human security includes not just protecting people but empowering people to fend for themselves.

The report goes on to argue that human security and state security are "mutually reinforcing and dependent on each other" (6). While these tenets are certainly true, the report largely fails to address situations where human security and state security might be contradictory, and more importantly how the international community ought to handle such contradictions and trade-offs when it comes to prioritizing resources.[16] The four case studies that follow in this book problematize this assumed complementarity and shed light on the practical implications of these sorts of conceptual ambiguities.

The report, *Human Security Now*, also makes the case that human security is complementary to both human development and human rights. Human development has an optimistic quality that focuses on expanding opportunities for people so that progress is fair—"growth with equity" (10). Human security complements this approach by focusing on "downside risks"—protecting people "unforeseen downfalls, or reversals of development" (Ogata & Cels 2003: 275). For example, the Asian economic crisis of 1997–1999 made it painfully clear that even a very successful history of "growth with equity" can provide very little protection to those who are thrown to the wall when sharp economic downturn suddenly occurs. In terms of human rights, human security provides a "cognitive and practical framework for identifying the rights and obligations at stake in particular

28   Women's activism

insecure situations" (Ogata & Cels 2003: 275). In this way, human security provides a framework for action and a sense of urgency for protecting against certain human rights violations.[17]

Despite these loose conceptual boundaries, human security remains a highly contested and criticized concept, and "even some of the strongest proponents of human security recognize that it is at best poorly defined and unmeasured, and at worse a vague and logically inconsistent slogan" (King & Murray 2001: 591).[18] Even for those who find validity in the concept, human security is still an "underdeveloped approach to understanding contemporary security politics" (Thomas & Tow 2002: 177).[19] The major tensions and debates center on the following issues:

- Does the concept of human security make security so broad and all-encompassing that it renders the term meaningless? (Paris 2004)[20]
- Human security seems to have both universal application and particularistic (or individualistic) tendencies. How are these two seemingly oppositional characteristics reconcilable? (Hudson H. 2005)
- Does human security challenge or complement the role of the state? Does it reinforce the same structuring logic of national security, thus reinvesting the state with the responsibility of providing security (Berman 2007)? Or does it fundamentally change the way the international community approaches security (Hubert 2004)?

Furthermore, there is a tension within the human security approach between those who advocate "freedom from fear" and those who advocate "freedom from want"—physical safety and freedom concerns as compared to development and meeting basic needs.[21] These two approaches can be seen by contrasting UNDP documents with Canada's foreign policy on human security and is similar and even related to the strain within the human rights regime in terms of the division between civil and political rights and social, economic, and cultural rights.[22] Fen Hampson et al. (2001) further articulates the divisions within human security approaches by outlining three distinct but related strands of thought:

1   Rights Based Approach—focus on legal rights, rule of law, and treaty-based solutions to human security. Seeks to strengthen normative legal frameworks, internationally, regionally, and even nationally. IGOs and NGOs play a role here. Most pro-statist approach.
2   Humanitarian Approach—focus on the safety of peoples (freedom from fear). Seeks to protect individuals who are victims of war and allows for a large role for NGOs. Also, includes conflict prevention and post-conflict reconstruction efforts by looking at the underlying causes of conflict and violence. Often focuses on military threats.
3   Sustainable Development Approach—focus on equity and social justice (freedom from want). Includes mostly non-military threats (AIDs, environment,

Women's activism 29

poverty, drug trafficking). Began with FAOs use of the term 'food security' and articulated further by the 1994 *Human Development Report.*

What is important here is how different approaches identify different threats, different responses and mechanisms for dealing with these threats, and different actors, institutions and governance structures required to address these threats. But all focus on the basic security needs and minimal protection of individual human beings. Thus, while the focus on the individual has remained central, it is clear that human security has been legitimated and appropriated differently depending on its policy usage. The concept highlights the ways in which the international community still fragments and separates the development world from the human rights community from the security sector, oftentimes in problematic ways. Thus, as a holistic concept human security has the potential to serve as a bridging concept between development, human rights, and security, bringing the actors from these areas together to recognize the complex, interdependent, and even contradictory agendas and goals that exist between them.

Furthermore, human security has certainly served its purpose in problematizing mainstream approaches to security. It is analytically advantageous in the way that it switches "the referent from the state to individuals and shifting the focus from military threats to the state to political, economic, environmental, and gender-based threats to individuals" (MacFarlane and Khong 2006: 237). This switch is particularly "beneficial" when it is used as a vehicle to help garner resources and attention from policy-makers. Such a manipulation takes human security beyond a slogan or rallying cry to something with analytical traction. It is in this sense that human security becomes both a *conceptualization* that has allowed issues such as women and gender equality to be included in the security discourse and a *framework for action* that has the potential to change the way in which the international community approaches and addresses security problems and issues.

The wideners: Copenhagen and securitization theory

If human security is largely seen as a vertical shift in security studies, a horizontal shift is best understood in terms of securitization theory. Similar to human security, securitization theory does not seek to overturn traditional assumptions of security but rather works to coexist. In some ways, securitization theory can actually be understood as an attempt to bring the staunch realists and human security idealists together using the inner logic of traditional security studies. This means that in order to add something new to the ongoing debates on security, "we must begin with those debates, taking on the problematique, so that we can get at the specific dynamics of that field, and show how these old elements operate in new ways and new places" (Wæver 1995: 51). Ole Wæver goes on to argue:

By working from the inside of the classical discussion, we can take the concepts of national security, threat, and sovereignty, and show how, on the collective level, they take on new forms under new conditions. We can then

30   Women's activism

strip the classical discussion of its preoccupation with military matters by applying the *same* logic to other sectors, and we can de-link the discussion form the state by applying similar moves to *society*.

(1995: 51)

This suggests that the best way to broaden the concept of security is not through external criticism, but rather by challenging it from the inside and engaging with the concept's core assumptions. And the core is about survival—existential threats that create priorities for action and the use of exceptional measures.

This is the logic underpinning the theory of securitization as articulated by the "Copenhagen School." The Copenhagen School (CS) refers to a number of scholars who have produced a rich body of work with a significant degree of coherence and continuity coming from a project at the Conflict and Peace Research Institute (COPRI) in Denmark.[23] Barry Buzan, Ole Wæver, and Jaap de Wilde are among the usual suspects associated with this broadly social constructivist theory of security. From this perspective, security does not refer to an objective reality as a perception of threat, but rather to a speech act—"the *word* 'security' is the act; the utterance is the primary reality" (Wæver 1995: 55). Thus, securitization is the positioning through language of a particular issue as an existential threat to security. This approach allows for an engaging debate on widening the approach to security, and the CS does indeed identify five sectors where security threats to human collectivities could emerge: military, political, economic, societal, and environmental.[24] The CS is careful not to privilege one sector over another, but rather understand what differentiates security and the process of securitization from that which is merely a political process. In other words, "security" is "the move that takes politics beyond the established rules of the game and frames the issue either as a special kind of politics or as above politics" (Buzan et al. 1998: 23).

While there are several aspects and strands of speech act theory, this project privileges Austin's and Searle's treatment of the speech act, as they are the authors from whom the CS examination of speech act originally draws.[25] According to Austin, certain statements do more than merely describe a given reality and, as such, cannot be determined as true or false. Rather, these utterances bring to fruition a specific action; they "do" things. "They are 'performatives' as opposed to 'constatives' that simply report states of affairs and are thus subject to truth and falsity tests" (Balzacq 2005: 175). Thus, the meaning of the word lies in its usage and not in some analytical or philosophical definition.

For the CS, securitization goes beyond politicization. Thus, any given issue can be placed on a larger spectrum ranging from an issue not of public debate or government decision (the non-politicized) to an issue part of public policy and government dealings and resources (the politicized) to an issue "presented as an existential threat, requiring emergency measures and justifying actions outside the normal bounds of political procedure" or the securitized (Buzan et al. 1998: 25).[26] This theory raises the questions of whether women's rights and gender equality in armed conflict have really moved beyond the politicized to the securitized and if so, what the value is in making this shift along the spectrum. This move—this intersubjective process—can either be ad hoc or institutionalized given the varying nature of existential threats and the actors involved across time and space.

Securitization is not merely a symbolic or linguistic act, but a political one with real world implications. Not only can securitization legitimize the use of force and the ability of the state to take special measures, but it could also mean the allocation of a substantial proportion of the state's resources to address the problem. As Sheehan states, "To securitize an issue not previously deemed to be a security issue is to challenge society to promote it higher in its scales of values and to commit greater resources to solving the related problems" (2005: 52). Using security talk as a political framework for action elevates a particular issue or a vulnerable population, demanding that the issue or group be prioritized and be on the agenda. The human security discourse, for example, has been one way to securitize groups such as women and issues such as gender equality. Securitization is ultimately a strategy—a purposeful series of maneuvers for obtaining a specific goal—one that certainly merits analysis and evaluation.

Thus, while in theory securitization allows for a remarkable broadening of analysis well beyond the military security of the state, one of the stated goals of the CS,[27] it is at the same time structurally constrained

> by the differential capacity of actors to make socially effective claims about threats, by the forms in which these claims can be made in order to be recognized and accepted as convincing by the relevant audience, and by the empirical factors or situations to which these actors can make reference.
>
> (Williams 2003: 514)

This means that speech acts do not occur in a vacuum, but rather are embedded rhetorically, culturally and institutionally in ways that make them somewhat predictable and not wholly open or expandable. Further, because securitization relies upon "existential threats, emergency action, and effects on inter-unit relations by breaking free of the rules" it continues to be structurally based in existing authoritative structures (Buzan et al. 1998:26).[28] Along these lines, Wæver (1995) maintains that even a widened conceptualization of security cannot be understood outside of the context of authoritative structures, most especially those of national security, such as the police or military.[29] Thus, security as a speech act occurs in structured institutions where some actors are in positions of power by being generally accepted voices of security, by having the power to define it.

The relative success of securitization as a speech act points to important tensions regarding both ethical and practical dilemmas associated with the theory. As Balzacq (2005: 227) contends, securitization is not a conventional procedure but rather a "strategic (pragmatic) practice that occurs within, and as part of, a configuration of circumstances, including the context, the psycho-cultural disposition of the audience, and the power that both speaker and listener." In other words, securitization is a power-laden, historically informed process that carries with it certain entrenched connotations related to notions of defense, and institutions, like the military and the state. As numerous scholars have demonstrated, addressing an

32   Women's activism

issue in security terms can still evoke a "threat-defense" logic that is not inherently beneficial (Wæver 1995: 47).[30]

From this line of thinking, securitization is not always the preferred strategy in dealing with political problems because this strategy suspends the normal, deliberative processes of politics. For many, "desecuritization" is the preferred strategy as it results in keeping more issues within the deliberative process. This reasoning is rooted in the logic that security and insecurity do not constitute a binary opposition (Wæver 1995: 54–57).[31] As such security and insecurity both indicate the presence of a security problem, and the difference between the two is a matter of whether or not a measure was taken in response. When there is no security problem, one can cease to use the word security. This problematizes the notion that the goal should be to seek "security" for women, and suggests that the aim should be to transcend that terminology to a place where there is no security problem for these groups as a normal part of the political environment. "Consequently, transcending a security problem by politicizing it cannot happen through thematization in security terms (securitization), only away from such terms (desecuritization)" (Wæver 1995: 56). Ultimately, this challenges the assumption that security is inherently a positive value to be maximized, challenging the tendency "to elevate 'security' into a kind of universal good thing—the desired condition toward which all relations should move" (Buzan et al. 1998: 4).

Similarly, on a study of securitization of the HIV/AIDS epidemic, Elbe (2006) argues that security language often pushes national and international responses to particular social problems away from civil society into the hands of state institutions, which are limited by bureaucratic politics and which have the ability to override human rights and civil liberties and often the root of the problem for many of these newly securitized issues. Furthermore, the security language serves a political function by justifying any and all efforts in terms of narrow national interest, rather than altruistic or moral obligations. This normative dilemma begs the question—is it really better to make these issues "threats" as opposed to a normal (or natural) concern for society, particularly when those being threatened constitute approximately 50 percent of society?

While numerous critiques of this push for desecuritization exist, the most relevant for this research are the issues raised by Lene Hansen and her observation that securitization theory is lacking a gender perspective in at least two ways. The first, and more obvious critique, questions the presupposition of the securitization process that a speech act is in fact possible. This is problematic given that many women do not have a voice in international politics, and much of gender-based insecurity occurs in the private realm disconnected from (or ignored by) public discourse.[32] Lene Hansen (2000) characterizes this first barrier to gendering securitization as "security as silence," in which insecurity simply cannot be voiced because "raising something as a security problem is impossible or might even aggravate the threat being faced" (287). Furthermore, securitization limits the speech act to verbal communication, and as feminists have been arguing for years, communication is much more than verbal; it is often bodily and visual (Butler 1997). These important forms of communication are not accounted for by the theory.

Women's activism 33

The second area of exclusion is somewhat less obvious and more complex. Because gendered identities are intrinsically linked to other aspects of the subject's identity, specifically nationality, religion and economic status, gender does not establish a cohesive neat group of individuals to serve as a collective referent object of security. Hansen refers to this "intimate inter-linkage between the subject's gender identity and other aspects of the subject's identity" as the "subsuming security" problem (2000: 287). This multidimensionality of identities makes gender a tough fit the CS's qualification of referent object. In this sense, gendered identities are often characterized by their inseparability from other identities, creating great ambiguity of the gender security problem.

Thus, for women to become a referent object for security they need to find a way into international discourse as a mobilized collective to make their voices heard. Obviously, this is less ideal than a strategy securitizing discourse within national governments. But going through the international community to influence national policy seems one of few options available to women in setting the agenda and shaping international norms (Keck and Sikkink 1998a). To this end and as the proceeding chapters demonstrate, securitization theory is still a compelling way to understand women's activism at the international level, even in light of Hansen's important critiques. Securitization allows for the exploration of how security discourses are produced and what constraints or obstacles emerge for those involved. In the larger security studies debate, "...what is at stake is not simply the question of whether the concept of security should be expanded or not, but how certain threats achieve such a political saliency that they become the subject of security policies" (Hansen 2000: 306). From this perspective, the CS begins the dialogue for scholars and practitioners to explore the practical implications of the language they speak and the strategy behind frameworks they employ.

The deepeners: critical theory and emancipation

Nevertheless, Lene Hansen's critique of the CS points to certain assumptions about voice and referent objects embedded in securitization theory that actually play a role in reifying traditional practices and axes of power.[33] While the CS's approach to security studies can be broadly understood as critical, some maintain that it is "only marginally 'critical' in theoretical orientation" (Booth 2005: 271).[34] This means that the CS does not go far enough in articulating the political and normative role of security analysts and security studies. Critical theory more narrowly defined emphasizes the role of the analysts by drawing upon Antonio Gramsci and his discussion of the potential role of intellectuals in elaborating and setting forth an agenda of change. This strand of critical security studies, often referred to as the "Welsh School" approach, is openly committed to human emancipation, asking questions about who benefits and who loses because of particular political structures and ideological systems.[35] This is where critical theory parts ways with postmodernism, where simply "the unpacking of the meta-narrative *is* the point of analysis" (Sterling-Folker 2006: 162, emphasis in original). In general, critical theory not only seeks to deconstruct and problematize the liberal

34 Women's activism

meta-narrative, but does so with the practical and political intent to replace it with a narrative informed by the Enlightenment in order to achieve emancipation. In this sense, critical security studies are unashamedly normative, recognizing that, "theory is always for someone and some purpose" (Cox 1986: 207).

Although critical theory has its roots in Marxist-inspired dependency theory of the 1960s, critical security studies in international relations has its origins in Ken Booth's 1991 article, "Security and Emancipation." For Booth, the central question to ask was not "what counts as a security issue" but "whose security are we talking about?" Thus, security is about vulnerabilities and insecurities of individuals and emancipation is a "strategic process" and a "guide for tactical goal setting" (Booth 2005: 182). Specifically, he defines emancipation as:

> the theory and practice of inventing humanity, with a view to freeing people as individuals and collectivities, from contingent and structural oppression. It is a discourse of human self-creation and the politics of trying to bring it about. Security and community are guiding principles, and at this stage of history the growth of a universal human rights culture is central to emancipatory politics. The concept of emancipation shapes strategies and tactics of resistance, offers a theory of progress for society, and gives a politics of hope for common humanity.
>
> (Booth 2005: 181)

In other words, emancipation is a discursive and very political process that relies upon certain ideas about security, community, and human rights. Andrew Linklater (2005: 116) further defines emancipation in terms of "communicative action" with "dialogue and deliberation" constituting "the crucial link between political community and human security." Here, emancipation seeks to recover a voice for those without voice, representation or power (Wyn Jones 1999). This empowering theoretical approach is where the Welsh School enhances the Copenhagen School and its critique of mainstream realist security studies, and where the two bodies of literature bring critical security studies in line with feminist security studies. Both theories working together have particular relevance for the place of women's voices in security discourses, an issue that has long been problematized by feminist theorists.

Feminist weigh in: feminist security studies

While there is no one feminism, in most forms feminism resemble critical theory (Ackerly et al. 2006). As Leonard (1990: xxii) rightly points out, it is not just critical in terms of problematizing traditional security thinking (or other IR concepts for that matter) but also because it is a theory characterized by an "ongoing critical self-examination and consciousness-raising project" that seeks to practice emancipation rather than define it. Feminist security theory scholarship (FST) is very much part of this emancipatory project in challenging traditional security studies, and further enriching the human security approach, securitization theory,

Women's activism 35

and critical security theories more broadly. Eric Blanchard (2003: 1290) in a review of FST outlined this range of contributions in terms of "four theoretical moves." These moves are significant both in terms of theory and for those on the ground doing feminist security-based work; after discussing each of these moves in turn, I will then add a fifth theoretical move essential to the case studies that follow. FST is central to understanding how women's rights and gender equality issues have historically been related to international security, theoretically and practically speaking, and what this means for the future, particularly in terms of SCR 1325 and the WPS network.

Feminist IR theory begins with a criticism of realism and thus traditional approaches to security, in terms of both ontology and epistemology. Specifically, realism is exposed as an approach dominated by elite, white males where a patriarchal discourse renders its masculinist underpinnings as well as women invisible (Tickner 1992: 130).[36] For feminists, the key concepts of security and sovereignty and units of analysis like "state" and "international system" are indistinguishable from the patriarchal divisions of public/private (True 1996: 225); further, these concepts are gendered in their dependence upon women's subordination as a "domesticated figure whose 'feminine' sensibilities are both at odds with and inconsequential to the harsh realities of the public world of men and states" (Peterson & Runyan 1998: 68–69).[37] Cynthia Enloe's (1989) work is particularly insightful here. She demonstrates how gender roles and women contribute to and are impacted by traditional security issues (military bases and diplomacy) as well as security issues outside of the mainstream (sex tourism and peace movements). Her work not only establishes the feminist curiosity of asking "where are the women," but she also contests the restriction of security to simply "high politics." This critique not only highlights how women have been excluded from international security politics and decision-making roles, but how they have been seen as invisible and irrelevant from security studies and international relations theory more broadly.

As numerous feminists have argued, this exclusion and irrelevancy is a product of what Elshtain ([1987] 1995: 245) calls the "strategic voice," an authoritative discourse that is "cool, objective, scientific, and overwhelming male." The significant and exclusionary power of gendered language is further supported by the work of Carol Cohn (1987; 1993), and exemplifies the second theoretical push from FST: security for whom and by what means? J. Ann Tickner was a pioneer on these sorts of questions particularly in laying the groundwork for "a definition of security that is people-centered and transcends state and regional boundaries" (Tickner 1995: 192). This means recasting the state as the referent of security, understanding that the state is often part of the problem, thus, altering the means by which security is achieved. Moreover, Tickner recast the meaning of violence at the international, national, and family levels as interrelated, occurring in domestic and global spaces often beyond the reach of law.

Along these lines, constructions of security not only mask the security threats that women face during war, but also in the domestic sphere where masculinist social control is so often hidden. Thus, the women's security must be understood

36 Women's activism

as a continuum of violence ranging from direct physical attacks (murder and rape) to structural violence embedded in the ideological assumptions about "women's work" and peaceful, dutiful mothers (True 1996: 232). This focus on the interrelatedness yet individualized notions of violence fundamentally challenges the location of security within state boundaries and highlights women's everyday [in]security experiences. Security for women struggling everyday with patriarchy, as Christine Sylvester (1994: 183) observes, "is always partial ... elusive and mundane." From a feminist perspective, prioritizing order and the survival of the state has served to hide and maintain various forms of domination between women and men (and between men and men, and women and women). Thus, hierarchical social relations at all levels must be recognized and seemingly natural social dichotomies problematized before society can address the multilevel insecurities that exist. "In the final analysis, therefore, genuine security means the eradication of unjust social relations and divisive boundary distinctions" (Sheehan 2005: 126).

The third theoretical move by FST can be largely understood as those contesting and countering essentialist arguments that unreflectively link women to peace and what that link means for the conceptualization and operationalization of security.[38] If women have had any access to the securitization process it has been through reliance upon the stereotypical pacifist nature assigned to femininity and motherhood.[39] For example, Reardon (1993: 21) argues, "Women's traditional roles in engaging in multiple activities ... have given them this broad, integrated view of peace and security that provides a hopeful alternative to the more narrow and fragmented views ... of security policy formation." In other words, given women's socially constructed gender roles within society, many believe that women are more likely to approach security in a more holistic and constructive manner, emphasizing the individual as well as society needs in terms of equality, rights, dignity, and development. FST, however, is quick to point out how this essentialist view often obscures the diversity of women's different relationships with war and peace and as a result quickly devalues (once again) the range of women's contributions (Tickner 1999).[40]

The fourth area that Blanchard articulates for FST is the study of the role and meaning of masculinity as it "offers insight into the practices that sustain security" (Blanchard 2003: 1304). Women's inequality not only reflects disempowering ideas about vulnerable and dependent women, but also reproduces in contradistinction, ideas about men that normalize militarism as an expression of protective masculinity. As Otto (2004: 8) adds, "this conservative discourse of gender weights the credibility of approaches to peace and security according to their association with masculinity and femininity; put simply, (manly) militarism is valorized while (feminine) pacifists ways of thinking are considered cowardly." Sandra Whitworth's (2004) study on the entrenched relationship that exists between masculinity and militarism (also referred to as "realist hypermasculinity," see Zalewski & Parpart 1998) as demonstrated in UN peacekeeping operations further highlights the complex and problematic way that security is gendered. In short, an intricate web of gender roles and identities—including

Women's activism 37

masculinity—have always been present in understandings of international [in]security, its causes and its effects.[41]

In addition to Blanchard's four broad theoretical advances for FST, I add one more with regard to FST and the role of human security. While feminists have rightly been skeptical of human security as a potentially dangerous concept for collapsing masculinity and femininity into the term "human," ultimately concealing the gendered underpinnings of security practices, I argue that human security remains a bridging concept that brings feminists, critical theorists, and the CS together in new and potentially transformative ways.[42] It is important to recognize the common normative underpinnings of their scholarship as a way to bridge the gap between IR theories as well as the gap between security theory and practice. As Heidi Hudson (2005: 172) argues:

> After all, the goal of inter-paradigm dialogue is not greater synergy between alternative and mainstream discourse, but rather to create a fractured whole that—when synthesized—is richer and more authentic than the sum of its constituent parts. Now that is theoretical progress.

In sum, FST illustrates the many ways that security is gendered and how that social construct is created, learned, and sustained as collective projects.[43] It is not neutral, but rather a process constituted by value judgments and hierarchies of power. Thus, to insist that security is an objective reality to be defined, inevitably leads to "a coercive strategy to relegate the interests of the less powerful to the margins" (Zalewski 1996: 350). The goal continues to be to render the familiar strange—going below the surface and problematizing the naturalness of security (Harding 1991). As argued by Ken Booth, "To talk about security without thinking about gender is simply to account for surface reflections without examining deep down below the surface" (1997: 101). In building upon the work of critical security studies and expanding upon conceptual insights from the human security literature, FST serves as a theoretical gateway for understanding and analyzing the security discourse as a political framework for the world's women in the context of the United Nations, SCR 1325 and the 'Women, Peace, and Security' network. Before turning to the case studies, it is important to situate the security-based discursive strategy within the context of the broader global women's movement.

Discursive strategies of transitional women's activism

The critical feminist approach to security is reflected to a significant extent in the practice of many contemporary women movements. As J. Ann Tickner (1995: 190) maintains, women's movements are fluid and transitional, and a large number have emerged in recent decades that are committed to pursuing *human security* in the economic, ecological, and political domains. Thus, women's activism surrounding WPS is the promotion of an idea of security that is people-centered and process-oriented, and therefore, very much rooted in human security

38 Women's activism

and critical security studies (see, for example, Petchesky 2002). This activism demonstrates how women have been doing the crucial, but basic work of redefining the world from the point of view of women's lives, putting problems and issues on the agenda, and actually changing how people understand what the world is about (Bunch 2002; 2004). WPS, as a campaign within the broader women's movement must be understood then as a very intentional, strategic "discursive politics," a tactic described by Katzenstein (1996: 17) as "the effort to reinterpret, reformulate, rethink, and rewrite the norms and practices of society and state."[44] This campaign and its base in transnational women's networks illustrate how women have transformed the "terms and nature of the debate" (Keck & Sikkink 1998a: 3) in the context of international peace and security.

Similar to the economic development frames used by women in the 1970s and the "women's rights as human rights" frame in the 1990s, WPS is a framework used to make relevant and implement gender mainstreaming strategies within the international security arena.[45] And while gender mainstreaming strategies are a common theme now in peace and security policy circles, the strategy did not originate here. Emerging in international development circles, gender mainstreaming refers to the "places where choices are considered and decisions made that affect the economic, social and political options of large numbers of people. It is where the action is. It is where things happen" (Anderson 1993: 10). Because these places have traditionally been occupied by men, gender mainstreaming as a concept reflects a desire for women to be included at center-stage—to be part of the mainstream.[46]

In the development field, gender mainstreaming evolved from an earlier approach known as "women in development" (WID), which called for the "integration" of women into the current system (Baden & Goetz 1998). Dating back to the 1970s, this feminist approach to development saw the absence of women in development plans and policies as the central problem. Therefore, all efforts were focused on women with the goal of inserting women into the existing development paradigms in order to receive development assistance. Pearson & Jackson (1998: 4) articulated the movement as follows:

> WID movement had been premised on a notion that women were excluded from development and that there was a growing feminist analysis of the patriarchal nature of the state and the ways in which it ignored the interests of women ... this new scenario ... was able to insist that women were targeted as beneficiaries ...

WID focused primarily or exclusively on women—not on the relationships between women and men as the way to make development more effective (Abirafeh 2005). In doing so, development organizations policies rarely encourage interventions and "interact[ions] with male beneficiaries ... and therefore [are] afforded few opportunities to make men rethink and change unequal gender hierarchies" (Hyndman & de Alwis 2003: 216) that contribute to inequality and underdevelopment. Such one-sided "gender policies" are not transformative,

Women's activism 39

however, because they isolate women, portraying them primarily as victims and "the most vulnerable" (Carpenter 2003).

Despite efforts spanning two decades, the WID approach saw minimal progress in achieving real change for women. Any change that did occur was at the margins. Schalkwyk (1998: 3) argued that WID was ineffective because "significant change cannot be achieved by adding marginal programmes for women." The "add women and stir" approach of WID failed to take into account power relations and women as they relate to men, institutions, and the system itself.

Given such shortcomings, by the late 1980s the dominant approach shifted its emphasis from integration to what has been called "agenda-setting," implying that the goal is to transform the existing development agenda in order to empower women. The gender and development movement (GAD) sees the participation of women as decision-makers in determining development priorities and policies. In this sense, "Women not only become part of the mainstream, they also reorient the nature of the mainstream" (Jahan 1995: 13). From this perspective, the targets for change are the social structures and processes that have allowed gender inequalities to persist. The problem lies in unequal power relations that subsequently prevent equitable development and women's full participation (Connelly et al. 2000). Therefore, the aim cannot be just additive, it must be transformative as well.

Mainstreaming strategies emphasize "systematic procedures and mechanisms within organizations—particularly government and public institutions—for explicitly taking into account gender issues at all stages of policy making and programme design and implementation" (Baden and Goetz 1998: 20). This comprehensive strategy involves both integration and agenda-setting. It requires the analysis of the concerns and experiences of both men and women "as agents, not simply as recipients" (Connelly et al. 2000: 63). As understood by the international community, particularly the UN, the GAD approach underscores the notion that gender equality and inclusion are intrinsic to sustainable peace and security.[47] As Olsson and Tryggestad (2001: 1) argue, gender mainstreaming in the UN is about "equal access to and full participation of women in power structures and their full involvement in all efforts for the prevention and resolution of conflicts" and, therefore, is "essential for the maintenance and promotion of peace and security."

From this literature, we can understand WPS as a campaign engaged in framing women's rights as a matter of international peace and security within the context of the broader women's movement. It is part of a process of norm diffusion that builds upon the recognition of the centrality of women's rights and gender equality to the international development agenda and the human rights regime. In this sense, women and gender have already become part of the development and human rights discourse. To be sure, these discourses inform and are related to the security discourse, particularly through the concept of human security.

Conceptualizing human security from a critical, feminist perspective is essential to understanding how SCR 1325 and the WPS network have affected the international security agenda as well as what the security discourse and the subsequent

40 Women's activism

interaction with the international arena has meant for women's activism on the ground. As the proceeding case studies demonstrate, this is an ongoing, intersubjective, constitutive process; one that is political and dynamic. "Security is not a final moment, but a final moment that never comes, a modern technology of political practice" (Berman 2007: 35).

Notes

1 The notion of an "essentially contested concept" comes from W.B. Gallie, "Essentially contested concepts," in Max Black, ed., *The Importance of Language*, Englewood Cliffs, N.J.: Prentice-Hall, 1962: 121–146. Essentially contested concepts are said to be so value-laden that no amount of argument or evidence can ever lead to agreement on a single version as the correct or standard use. Baldwin (1997: 10–11) takes issue with this classification because a strict reading of an essentially contested concept would make any sort of conceptual analysis futile. Thus, I agree with Baldwin that "Since the analysis undertaken here purports only to improve current usage, and not to identify the single best usage, it is compatible with the weaker variant of the essential contestedness hypothesis" (10).
2 Notable exceptions certainly exist. Stephen Walt, for example, staunchly argues that "defining the field this way would destroy its intellectual coherence and make it more difficult to devise solutions to any of these important problems" (1991: 212–213). See Kolodziej 1992 for a critique of Walt's argument.
3 In surveying contemporary international relations literature, for example, it is now fairly common, for books on the environment or gender to include a chapter on security, and for books on security to include "at least a genuflection in the direction of gender analysis, environmental security, and other features of a wider approach" (Sheehan 2005: 3).
4 Some realists go as far to say that "realism was the dominant discourse from about the start of the late medieval period in 1300 to at least 1989" (Mearsheimer 1994/1995: 44).
5 Also important here is realist reliance on rationalists canons of science. Walt (1991: 222) argues, "Security studies seeks cumulative knowledge about the role of military force," as does Helga Haftendorn (1991: 12), who stresses the need "to construct an empirically testable paradigm" involving "a set of observational hypotheses."
6 More recently, Baldwin (1997: 14) clearly identifies an objective and a subjective interpretation for security when discussing the goals of security. He argues, "The value of an increment of national security to a country will vary from one country to another and from one historical context to another, depending not only on how much security is needed but also on how much security a country already has" (Baldwin 1997: 19).
7 For more analysis of this notion of "insecurity" see Bobrow (1996).
8 To a lesser extent, the end of the Cold War brought into focus concerns about excesses in defense spending giving impetus to rethinking approaches to security and restructuring resource allocation.
9 Emma Rothschild (1995) draws this distinction between vertical and horizontal expansion of security in "What is Security?" *Daedalus: Journal of the American Academy of Arts and Sciences* 124.
10 For an influential discussion of the changing character of war in the post-Cold War era, see Mary Kaldor, *New and Old Wars: Organized Violence in a Global Era* (Cambridge, UK: Polity Press, 1999). For a critique of Kaldor's argument, see Mats Berdal, "How 'New' Are 'New Wars'? Reflections on Global Economic Change and War in the Early twenty-first Century," *Global Governance* 9 (Oct–Dec 2003): 477–502.
11 MacFarlane and Khong (2006) point to numerous historical processes of the late nineteenth and early twentieth centuries that drew into question the state's capacity to

Women's activism 41

provide individuals protection from domestic and international anarchy. These processes including, but not limited to, decolonialization, industrialization, and globalization all served as important contextual factors for the movement towards focusing on individual security needs.

12 For more on the blurring of the line between internal and external security threat dimensions, see Neack 2007.

13 Expanding this notion, the report identified seven specific elements that comprise human security: economic security, food security, health security, environmental security, personal security, community security, and political security. Indeed, the drafters of the report did not want to establish any definitional boundaries, but rather promote the "all-encompassing and integrative qualities of the human security concept, which they apparently viewed as among the concept's major strengths" (Paris 2003: 255).

14 It is worth noting here that this two-part strategy is reflected in the baseline goals of SCR 1325 and the WPS network in its focus on protection and participation, as will be discussed in greater detail in Chapter 3 and 4.

15 Newman, like other proponents of human security, claims that traditional security—the military defense of territory—is necessary but it is not a sufficient condition for human welfare.

16 For more on the incompatibility of human and state security, see Abad, Jr. 2000.

17 The relationship between a rights-based approach and security-based approach will be explored further in the subsequent case studies.

18 A special issue of *Security Dialogue*, 2004 35(3), illustrates the controversial aspects of this concept theoretically, analytically, and practically speaking.

19 One exception here is the work led by Taylor Owen that has attempted to operationalize human security through the use of thresholds. See for example Owen and Liotta (2007).

20 See also MacFarlane and Khong's notion of conceptual overstretch (2006: 236–243).

21 This is often articulated as the narrow versus wide approach to human security. Narrow being freedom from violence and attack. Wide goes beyond that to include economic, social, and cultural threats to personal security. For more on this, see the debate in *Security Dialogue* 2004, 35(3).

22 See also Caroline Thomas (2001) for a developed argument that places human security squarely within the development paradigm. Simply states, she argues that human security can exist without "material sufficiency" as a precondition for other forms of security of the individual.

23 Jef Huysmans (1998b: 481) contends that it is best to understand this School as a "creative development" allowing its "ideas to grow and change ... for shifting and shuffling in the way they are developed." Such a sympathetic interpretation of a work is countered by McSweeney's 1996 critique of the School inconsistencies since its beginnings in 1985. See also Huysmans (1998a).

24 In the eyes of one supportive observer, the CS's approach to security is "possibly the most thorough and continuous exploration of the significance and implications of a widening security agenda for security studies" (Huysmans 1998b: 480).

25 See, for example, Austin (1962; 1970: 233–252; 1971: 13–22) and Searle (1969; 1977: 59–82; 1991: 254–264).

26 The image of a spectrum is a bit misleading. The image would have one believe that securitization is an intensification of politicization, but its process and outcomes can be quite incongruous. According to the CS, "Politicization means to make an issue appear to be open, a matter of choice, something that is decided upon and that therefore entails responsibility ... By contrast, securitization ... means to present an issue as urgent and existential, as so important that it should not be exposed to the normal haggling of politics but should be dealt with decisively by top leaders prior to other issues" (Buzan et al. 1998: 29).

42 Women's activism

27 The CS's 1998 collaboration began with the statement, "our approach is based on the work of those who for over a decade have sought to question the primacy of the military element and the state in the conceptualization of security" (Buzan et al. 1998: 1).

28 This is where Williams (2003) argues that securitization theory begins to resemble the concept of "the political" defined by Carl Schmitt and seemingly overlapping with post-war realism.

29 He maintains that security "has to be read through the lens of *national* security" (1995: 49).

30 See also Deudney 1990 and Elbe 2006.

31 It is important to note here that Wæver is accepting a logic of security that is negative and exclusionary, which leads him to argue for desecuritization.

32 Gender-based violence also occurs publicly in many situations. Honor killings in Pakistan are a vivid example of this. But even public gender-violence often silences its victims.

33 Buzan et al. (1998: 41) do acknowledge that "one danger of the phrases *securitization* and *speech act* is that too much focus can be placed on the acting side, thus privileging the powerful while marginalizing those who are the audience and judge of the act" (emphasis in the original).

34 For an insightful discussion on the ways in which the Copenhagen School and the Welsh School overlap and complement each other, see Browning and McDonald 2007.

35 It is important to note here that critical theorists' focus on deepening security is fundamentally and theoretically different than the vertical move by those advocating human security to include the individual as the referent of security. The goals of each approach are quite different. Critical security studies theory does seek to replace traditional, state-based approaches to security where order is prioritized over justice. The human security approach is far less radical and more complementary as previously discussed.

36 Not all feminist IR theory is critical and/or post-positivists. For brief, but thorough discussion of the ways in which "feminism is a multifaceted theoretical enterprise involving numerous variants that grapple with ontological, epistemological, and methodological issues as they relate to women and gender," see Sterling-Folker (2006: 243–251).

37 Runyan and Peterson further argue that characteristics of politics, such as order, power, autonomy, rationalism, states and security all reflect male domination and andocentric biases that in turn define the international system. Thus, feminine traits, such as dependency, emotion, people, justice, and subjectivity have no place for the way we study and the way we do politics, particularly security.

38 As Dan Smith (2001) describes, gender essentialisms both exaggerate alleged differences between men and women and obscure variation within these groups.

39 Framing women as peacebuilding resources uses what Helms (2003) calls "affirmative essentialism."

40 This essentialist argument not only idealizes women as peacemakers, but idealizes women who deviate (violent women) from this stereotypical gender role as either mothers, monsters, or whores (Sjoberg & Gentry 2007).

41 Many feminists see the study of masculinity as still in its infancy and an area deserving of further research.

42 This is similar to Whitworth's (2004) critique of gender mainstreaming as a concept that depoliticized women's issues and that has become confiscated by the masculine project.

43 That an issue such as rape was left out of constructions of "security" until the mid-1990s when governments at Beijing declared rape in armed conflict a war crime (and in some cases a crime against humanity and an act of genocide) demonstrates how important it is to include a gender focus in this realm.

Women's activism 43

44 Keck and Sikkink (1998b: 228) define campaigns "as sets of strategically linked activities in which members of diffuse principle networks develop explicit, visible ties and mutually recognized roles toward a common goal."

45 Zald (1996: 262) defines framing as the use of "specific metaphors, symbolic representations, and cognitive cues to name wrongs and propose or demand remedies." Political actors use frames to promote a coherent interpretation so as to shape the course of events in ways that they hope will produce a preferred policy outcome (Butler & Boyer 2003: 394).

46 This emphasis on women has been criticized by both scholars and practitioners. My argument, however, is premised on the assumption that if one is going to "gender mainstream," the majority of strategies must begin with women, given that they are the group of individuals that are almost always systematically excluded from decision-making bodies. Further, it is important to note that while most strategies of gender mainstreaming do aim for the inclusion of women and issues pertaining to women, there are some that are focusing on gender issues more broadly. One example was the 2004 CSW 48th annual session that focused on the thematic issue of "the role of men and boys in gender equality" in the process of conflict resolution. Thus, there is recognition within the UN for the need to apply gender more broadly by addressing the socialization process, which produces actions and attitudes for both men and women. Ideally, as more women are included, the focus of the gender-mainstreaming discourse will be increasingly able to focus its efforts on the actions and attitudes of men and women more equally.

47 The UN Economic and Social Council also gives a useful definition for gender mainstreaming, defined as the process of assessing the implications for women and men of any planned action, including legislation, policies, and programmes, in all areas and at all levels and as a strategy for making women's as well as men's concerns and experiences an integral dimension of the design, implementation, monitoring, and evaluation of policies and programmes in all political, economic, and societal spheres so that women and men benefit equally and inequality is not perpetrated. See United Nations, 1996. *Implementation of the Outcome of the Fourth World Conference on Women.* Report of the Secretary-General, A/51/322. New York: United Nations.

3 The security framework in practice

The case of Security Council Resolution 1325

> Expressing concern that civilians, particularly women and children, account for the vast majority of those adversely affected by armed conflict, including as refugees and internally displaced persons, and increasingly are target by combatants and armed elements, and recognizing the consequent impacts this has on durable peace and reconciliation.
>
> S/1325/2000

> Reaffirming the important role of women in the prevention and resolution of conflicts and in peace-building, and stressing the importance of their equal participation and full involvement in all efforts for the maintenance and promotion of peace and security, and the need to increase their role in decision-making with regard to conflict prevention and resolution.
>
> S/1325/2000

In October 2000 the Security Council unanimously adopted Resolution 1325 (SCR 1325), a landmark step in raising awareness of the impact of armed conflict on women and girls and in acknowledging the vital role of women's agency in conflict resolution and peacebuilding.[1] For the first time in the history of the UN, the Security Council formally decided on a gender issue, setting a new threshold of action for the Security Council, the UN system, and for all member states (Olsson & Tryggestad 2001). This watershed political framework demands that the Council engage in gender mainstreaming in all its work. This requires all actors involved in peacekeeping, peacebuilding, and post-conflict reconstruction to: 1) adopt gender perspectives in all levels of decision-making and to establish the equal participation of men and women in the maintenance and promotion of peace and security and; 2) take into account the special needs of women and girls during repatriation and resettlement, rehabilitation, reintegration, and post-conflict reconstruction.

As the above quotes from the resolution suggest, SCR 1325 outlines several explicit ways that the participation and protection of women further the goal of international peace and security. In other words, the resolution prioritizes

The security framework in practice 45

women's rights by highlighting their (assumed positive) impact on durable peace and security, which is the fundamental mission of the Council, and the UN more broadly. SCR 1325 is about promoting and protecting women *in order to create or preserve peace*. Thus, the aim of SCR 1325 is to develop "effective institutional arrangements to guarantee their protection and full participation in the peace process" so that they "can significantly contribute to the maintenance and promotion of international peace and security" (S/1325/2000).

Without a doubt, SCR 1325 has set a new threshold of action for the international community. As of January 2009, the resolution has been translated into ninety-five different languages providing important new leverage for local women's groups to claim a role in peace negotiations and post-conflict decision-making.[2] As one official from the UN Department of Peacekeeping Operations said, 1325 is:

> *a rallying point* for people concerned with gender issues as it provides a place to channel information and concerns before the SC. And it is a *framing resolution* for all peacekeeping operations. Every peacekeeping operation has a mandate with regard to ensuring gender issues. Even if we look at it as the progress not being as great as we would want it, the reality is—it has become part of the standard framework of peacekeeping missions and that is absolutely important. That is a major breakthrough.
>
> (DPKO official, 2006, emphasis added)

In this sense, 1325 is an ideal case study of the security framework as it presents women, a non-traditional security concern, as relevant to a traditional security body on the world stage, the Security Council. The resolution makes an intentional and instrumental argument for women's rights by emphasizing women's unique contribution to conflict resolution and the Council's mandate in peacekeeping. The preamble of the resolution notes "the important role of women in the prevention and resolution of conflicts and in peace-building, and stressing the importance of their equal participation and full involvement in all efforts for the maintenance and promotion of peace and security" and recognizes that "an understanding of the impact of armed conflict on women and girls, effective institutional arrangements to guarantee their protection and full participation in the peace process can significantly contribute to the maintenance and promotion of international peace and security" (S/RES/1325).

Securitization: making the instrumental argument

Advocates of 1325 noted that at that time (2000) "it was difficult to talk about rights at the Security Council because there was a position held by many that human rights was a prerogative of the General Assembly, not the Security Council" (UNIFEM official, 2006). So women's rights were presented not only in terms of the security needs of women during conflict, but what women—and gender equality—could contribute to lasting peace and security. In other words,

46   *The security framework in practice*

women need security and security needs women. And as many voices of UN officials who work with member states reiterated:

> Instrumental arguments are the only arguments that work with policy-makers. Nobody is interested in women because it is the right thing to do or because it's about human rights—nobody. And that's the best reason for working on gender in any area—just because it is right. We shouldn't have to make everything contingent upon positive social development or democratic or peace consequences. It's just right, but that just so doesn't wash. So, yes, instrumental arguments are very important.
>
> (UNIFEM official, 2006)

SCR 1325 is a clear case of the security framework and allows one to examine the impact of this discourse on the security agenda of the UN as well as on the work of the global women's movement. In other words, does SCR 1325 help bring global attention to issues and groups of people that are normally marginalized? Has it meant more resources and more involvement by state and non-state actors? Or has it resulted in narrow, limiting, or even militaristic responses to the complex social problems surrounding women and gender? These questions not only have important policy implications, but normative ones as well. Should these issues be framed as security issues? Can we really assume that the security language is inherently good for those concerned with empowering women around the world? And in the case of 1325, has the language really allowed for transformative change for women's rights in conflict and post-conflicts situations around the world.[3]

To answer these questions, this chapter employs several levels of analysis that identify categories of change in the context of the security agenda and Security Council activity. These analytical levels include shifts in rhetoric, legal mechanisms, and operational procedures within the UN system, as well as the existence of new actors, partnerships, and of course, resources that can be linked to the use of this framework. While these levels are not comprehensive in measuring the many impacts of SCR 1325, they should be understood as overlapping and interconnected.[4] The chapter concludes by exploring the implications of these shifts for the WPS network and what these shifts mean for the nature and future direction of the global women's movement.

Plenty of rhetoric to go around

At the rhetorical level, one does not have to go far to find countless statements and speeches from heads of state to UN leaders and agencies to other governmental and non-governmental organizations voicing commitment to the principles within the resolution. Every October for the past eight years governments have expressed support for 1325 in open debates within the SC, at Arria Formula meetings with civil society organizations, and at roundtables and panel discussions sponsored by both governmental and non-governmental actors. Similar to

The security framework in practice 47

previous anniversaries, speeches in October 2008 were made by all fifteen members of the SC as well as by another thirty-six Member States in support of 1325. In addition, leaders of various UN agencies including the UN Department of Peacekeeping Operations and the UN Development Fund for Women delivered speeches that focused on how 1325 was being implemented (and not implemented), and thus how the resolution was "working" on the ground. In these public statements of commitment, all were willing to put the concerns and rights of women within the framework and language of international peace and security, and to justify women's rights and gender equality as effective means to the promotion of international peace and security. This approach was articulated by Ms. Rachel Mayanja, Assistant Secretary-General, Special Adviser on Gender Issues and Advancement of Women, at the Security Council open date in 2008:

> Drawing on shared values of security, women come together around shared concerns—getting wells and schools, community health, nutrition and care for children and the elderly—engage in confidence-building programmes across communities and play a key role in fostering reconciliation both during conflict and after. Women's networks mobilize women across party lines and are sometimes able to build consensus around peace proposals. They are amongst the strongest advocates of transparent and accountable governance. In addition, they increasingly create national coalitions and international networks for peace and democracy, building blocks for future sustainable peace and gender equality … It is our duty and, indeed, our obligation to millions of women in conflict areas to use the opportunity offered by Security Council resolution 1325 (2000) to set in motion perhaps one of the most promising approaches to conflict resolution of this new century—a comprehensive approach based on inclusive values and gender equality.
>
> (Mayanja 2008: 4)

There are a number of points to make here. First, this framework is not just concerned with securing the rights of women, but also about highlighting how protecting and promoting the rights of women is a fundamental component to establishing international peace and security—the driving mission of the UN.[5] This framework and security language is important, particularly when talking about those at the margins trying to gain access to circles of power. As one UN program specialist stated, "Most men will listen if you frame the issue in their terms, which means reinforcing their cultural values" (UN official, 2006). Framing issues as vested interest for security seems to be somewhat of a universal value for many national leaders, particularly within the context of Security Council debates.[6]

For women on the ground, however, it is not simply rhetoric. The issues outlined in SCR 1325 are essential to their survival, to their security, and in this way, women make significant contributions to peace and security processes (Anderlini 2007). Irrespective of the framework used, establishing the language on this is a critical first step, and progress has been made on this front. From October 2000 to

48   *The security framework in practice*

August 2008, 102 out of 309, or 33 percent, of country-specific Security Council resolutions include language on women and gender.[7] The number of resolutions even mentioning women prior to 2000 is negligible. One interviewee summarized the significance of the discourse:

> you engage, you discuss, you argue, you advocate, whatever. Then you have a product that allows, that gives the policy weight, that raises the concerns and issues and then you have the potential to move the system ... You have to start by getting the language. You get the mandate and that leads to policy—crystallizes in a document ... Acceptance of the language is key. That's where you begin to change perceptions and understandings.
>
> (DPKO official, 2006)

As an observer—participant at the sixth anniversary 1325 events at UN Headquarters, I had the opportunity to speak with a number of women from grassroots organizations in various conflict zones in Africa, including Liberia, Burundi, and Sierra Leone. In their work to influence the peace process in their respective countries, they all spoke confidently about the way 1325 empowered them and other women in the region because they used the actual document to educate the men in power about their rights, as women.

But as feminists have long warned us, language is extremely powerful, entrenched, and never gender-neutral (Cohn 1987; Peterson & Runyan 1998). This has important implications for interpretations of security, and Security Council Resolutions specifically. With its emphasis on war and the use of force, the international security arena has been one of the most thoroughly gender-biased fields of international politics. It has been particularly difficult for women and feminists to break into this masculine and militarized discourse because the voices of women, particularly noncombatants, are perceived as unnatural, even "inauthentic" in this deeply entrenched system surrounding international security (Tickner 1998: 4). Given this conventional discourse, it is not surprising then that SCR 1325 lacks any critique of the continued militarized approach of the SC in its mission or any challenge toward total disarmament—two strongholds of the women's peace activism dating back to the emergence of the Women's League on International Peace and Freedom in 1915. This is particularly problematic as the world's military expenditures continue to rise, with a 34 percent increase from 1996 to 2005 (SIPRI Annual Yearbook 2006) and as WILPF was one of the founding organizations of the WPS network (as noted in Chapter 1). For many, this omission despite WILPF's involvement in the NGO drafting of SCR 1325 reflects a strategic move—and a trade-off—to create an entry point for WPS into the activities of a SC. Such a move is potentially problematic as it signals prioritizing security over peace and reinforcing the powers of the state to protect the most vulnerable and marginalized. SCR 1325 specifically implicates states in the provision of security of women in terms of protection, prosecution of war crimes, and in disarmament, demobilization, and reintegration programs (DDR). Security then largely goes unchallenged at the most basic level—as a masculinized project

The security framework in practice　49

reliant upon the state for implementation. And if SCR 1325 is not challenging some of the fundamentals of the international security apparatus, then is it not reinforcing it?[8] The research has shown that the state is often part of the problem when it comes to women's security, rather than part of the solution.[9] In short, what the language says and does not say has long-term implications for the UN Security Council's work in post-conflict societies and the potential to limit the more radical goals of the WPS movement in redefining the meaning of security at the turn of the century.[10]

Along similar lines, the language also has potentially negative implications for the way in which collectives of women are perceived. First, the security language still provokes threat-defense logic and thus has the ability to create public fear of people or groups of people that are placed within this logic. This means that security:

> carries with it a history and a set of connotations that it cannot escape. At the heart of the concept we still find something to do with defense and the state. As a result, addressing an issue in security terms still evokes an image of threat-defense, allocating to the state an important role in addressing it. This is not always an improvement.
>
> (Wæver 1995: 47)

Professor Alice Miller who has long worked on the trafficking of women notes how the security framework is detrimental in this way:

> What it sets up is a primary response of border control and prosecution. The focus is on the bodies crossing. Why they cross, and what they encounter all drops out of the picture. So even though the rhetoric is a high rhetoric from the Bush Administration—and they switch between women's rights and women's honor. They very quickly go from a discussion on women's rights and sexual labor to a very conservative discourse of saving women, not interested in the exploitation at the more general level. And the actual money that goes to direct services is very low, even though the rhetoric is high.
>
> (Interview, 2006)

One can see how this threat-defense logic would easily apply to women in conflict, particularly women refugees, and women with HIV/AIDs.[11] In a post 9/11 security environment, constructions of the feared "other" are easily identified and have real policy implications.

Second, and somewhat at the opposite end of the spectrum, the security language and SCR 1325 specifically tends to promote an essentialist view of women and the role that they play in post-conflict reconstruction, as mothers, nurturers, and peacemakers. This essentialist assumption that underlies the discursive position of SCR 1325, at least in part, has the potential to push post-conflict societies back to the status quo in terms of traditional gender roles.[12] Sjoberg (2006) articulates these roles in the narrative of just warriors and

50   *The security framework in practice*

innocent women, where women are the pacifist force in society in need of protection. Women are assumed to be above going to war, both in their passiveness and peacefulness. This implicit assumption follows in much of the language of SCR 1325 in that women's participation in the resolution of wars will make the peace more likely and more durable. Here, SCR 125 does not include all women. Instead, its focus is on *feminine* women whose passivity and pacifism are now valued, which further entrenches important ideas about how and why wars are fought.

Furthermore, even though the resolution uses the term gender eleven different times and women twenty-nine times, men are completely absent from the document. This follows what Connell (2005: 1806) suggests about "discussions of women's exclusions from power and decision-making [where] men are *implicitly* present as the power holders." Men are very much the absent presence. This is problematic at two levels. First, SCR 1325 associates gender with women further entrenching a concept of gender as a synonym for women.[13] This means that men and masculinity are taken for granted and rendered invisible in terms of understanding shifting political, social, economic, and cultural power-relationships that take place both during and post conflict. Second, the term "he" is used in the document embodying the subject of the Secretary-General, articulating a narrative of masculinity in which the Secretary-General is "urge[d] ... encourage[d] ... invite[d] ... request[ed]" to provide the women with whom the document is concerned with protection (S/1325/2000).

Following such essentialist language, SCR 1325 repeatedly associates women with children or girls as though the groups have indistinguishable traits. Conceptually bracketing these two collective nouns together is what Cynthia Enloe refers to as "womenandchildren"—the West's evocation of innocent, helpless, voiceless victims (as cited in Peters 2001).[14] This association has very serious implications for the so-called "agency" that SCR 1325 supposedly recognizes for women in conflict resolution and post-conflict reconstruction. Given that children are as a collective perceived as not fully mature and lacking the ability to think and act rationally, this stereotype denies women full personhood, limiting them as victims.[15]

In many ways, the security framework is not necessarily in line with the emancipatory vision of social change so central to the women's movement. In the end, the security language must be seen as a tool with great potential but by no means an inherent good. Furthermore, having the language is clearly not enough and potentially counterproductive or at least limiting in terms of how deeply the system is actually challenged. Nonetheless, that language must still be translated into policy, and then policy must be implemented. The residual theme at the UN when discussing SCR 1325, usually only in the month of October, is that national governments have fallen short of what is *required*. Rhetoric too often is not reality, particularly in the case of women's rights. This is where the next level of securitization comes into play: how can international and national law further securitize the rights of women, by translating the rhetoric into achievable policy standards?

International legal mechanisms

The WPS movement has been successful not only in raising awareness and pushing for a shift in language at the rhetorical level, but also as a driving force in establishing legal requirements. The process leading up to SCR 1325 in itself is an example of this, as discussed in Chapter 1. Security Council resolutions are legally binding to member states, and thus, at minimum set certain international standards of behavior and institutional process.[16] Implementing these standards at the national level, however, is essential. The United Kingdom, Norway, Sweden, Canada, Finland, Netherlands, and Denmark have all developed national action plans (NAP) on gender mainstreaming as a direct response to SCR 1325, and these national policies have helped to improve their donor relationships with the UN in terms of programming for women's rights (UNIFEM official, 2006).[17] In this sense, SCR 1325 has proven the potential to build upon existing international legal structures and subsequently integrated into governmental institutions at the national level. These national action plans are therefore a critical first step.

Any discussion of legal mechanisms protecting women's rights, however, must also account for the activity and presence of the Convention on the Elimination of All Forms of Discrimination Against Women (CEDAW)—*the* human rights treaty on women. In terms of legal mechanisms, SCR 1325 and CEDAW are logically interconnected, and therefore ought to be mutually reinforcing. As one of the eight major human rights conventions, CEDAW represents binding international legal obligations for those states that have signed and ratified the treaty.[18] The international law is monitored by CEDAW's committee, an expert body established to interact with state parties through periodic meeting and reporting. This procedure of actual dialogue where states submit reports regularly and the committee comments on the report provides an opportunity for the international community to analyze national anti-discrimination policies and push national governments to move closer toward the full implementation of CEDAW. While there are certainly states and non-state actors, particularly in conflict situations where 1325 is most relevant, that are not members and thus not bound by the treaty (for example, Somalia and Sudan), there are states emerging from conflict that are signing and ratifying human rights treaties for the first time, presenting a tremendous opportunity to incorporate both CEDAW and SCR 1325 standards into their post-conflict reconstruction and peace-building efforts. For example, Afghanistan and Timor-Leste became party to CEDAW in 2003, and according to the terms of the treaty, those states have one year to submit their first report. Not uncommon to reporting practices, however, these two member states have yet to submit their reports.[19] Still, given the emerging governing structures being rebuilt in these war-torn regions, CEDAW's monitoring and reporting structure can lay a solid foundation for the country in terms of their responsiveness and capacity in implementing these international legal standards, including SCR 1325.

Further, SCR 1325 has the potential to expand CEDAW's application in post-conflict societies that may not be party to the convention. Although SCR 1325 does not specifically refer to CEDAW, it does demand that all actors engaged in

52   The security framework in practice

every stage of conflict, peace negotiations and post-conflict reconstruction protect and respect women's human rights and are accountable to the international law applicable to the rights of women and girls. In other words:

> Through SC Resolution 1325, CEDAW becomes clearly relevant to states that are not parties, such as the United States and Sudan, and to the territories in conflict, such as the Occupied Palestinian Territories. Moreover, it reaches beyond governance bodies to all groups participating in the conflict, such as independent armed groups, militias and paramilitaries ... By doing so, 1325 mandates a very broad application of international women's human rights standards, and makes them central to maintaining peace and security.
>
> (UNIFEM 2006c: 8–9)

Thus, in terms of discourse and international legal standards, the security framework has drawn needed attention to women's rights and issues, particularly in conflict and post-conflict situations and it is easy to see the intersection between the human rights approach and the security framework.

While the theoretical links between 1325 and CEDAW are very much there, practically speaking the two seem to operate in separate worlds.[20] The country reporting requirements of CEDAW make it the only human rights treaty-based body dedicated solely to monitoring the rights of women at the national level. Surprisingly, however, CEDAW reporting guidelines, revised in 2003, make no mention or reference to 1325. Further, it was not until 2006 that CEDAW's session report began to make systematic reference to the integration of SCR 1325 in the compliance of State parties to the Convention:

> The Committee urges the State party to ensure that the promotion of women's human rights and gender equality is a central goal of all aspects of the transition process and to raise the legislature's awareness of that important goal. It further urges the State party to give serious attention to the specific needs of women in the post-conflict period and ensure women's equal participation in decision-making, in conformity with Security Council resolution 1325 (2000) on women, peace and security, with direct relevance to article 3, article 4, paragraph 1, and article 7 of the Convention.
>
> (A/61/38 269)

In addition to the three articles mentioned above (3, 4, and 7), SCR 1325 can be directly linked with eight other components of the CEDAW treaty (emphasis added):

- "Affirming that the *strengthening of international peace and security* ... will contribute to the attainment of full equality between men and women" (Preamble, Paragraph 11).
- "Convinced that the full and complete development of a country, the welfare of the world and the *cause of peace require the maximum participation of women* on equal terms with men in all fields" (Preamble, Paragraph 12).

The security framework in practice   53

- "States Parties ... undertake to embody the principle of equality of men and women in their *national constitutions* ... to establish legal protection of the rights of women ... to ensure through *competent national tribunals and other public institutions* the effective protection of women against any act of discrimination ... " (Article 2).
- "States Parties shall take all appropriate measures to *modify the social and cultural patterns of conduct* of men and women, with a view to achieving the elimination of prejudices and customary and all other practices which are based on the idea of inferiority or the superiority of either of the sexes or on stereotyped roles for men and women" (Article 5).
- "States Parties shall take all appropriate measures ... to suppress *all forms of traffic in women and exploitation of prostitution of women*" (Article 6).
- "States Parties shall take all appropriate measures to ensure to women, on equal terms with men and without any discrimination, *the opportunity to represent their Governments at the international level and to participate in the work of international organizations*" (Article 8).
- "States Parties shall grant women equal rights with men to *acquire, change or retain their nationality* ... " (Article 9).
- "States Parties shall accord to women equality with men before the law ... in civil and political matters, a legal capacity identical to that of men and the same opportunities to exercise that capacity. In particular, they shall give women equal rights to conclude *contracts and to administer property and shall treat them equally in all stages of procedure inn courts and tribunals*" (Article 15).[21]

From constitutional rights to judicial rights in tribunals, to the rights of victims of trafficking or prostitution, to the rights to nationality and movement to the right to participate in UN activities and the right to property, it is easy to see how these articles are critical to women in the complex and multidimensional nature of post-conflict societies. The articles seem particularly relevant to the mandate of SCR 1325 and the multifaceted nature of UN Security Council peacekeeping operations. Still it took five years for CEDAW to refer to the three articles in SCR 1325 that were "directly" relevant to the convention. Although this is problematic, it is not surprising given the bureaucratic pace of the UN system and the overworked nature of the CEDAW committee. In surveying all country reports submitted to CEDAW after 2000, only nine of 166 reports even make reference to SCR 1325 (approximately 5%) and only one of those countries—Bosnia Herzegovina—had been on the Security Council agenda previously.[22] It seems imperative, then, to better link these rights as already articulated in CEDAW with the work of holding countries accountable to their commitments to 1325.[23]

What is more striking is that most of my interviewees for this research emphasized the need to create some form of accountability mechanism or enforcement structure for SCR 1325,[24] yet no one made the explicit link to utilizing the CEDAW reporting mechanism already in place.[25] Those working on SCR 1325 have repeatedly called for some sort of reporting structure, enforcement procedures, or

54   The security framework in practice

incentive program to establish some level of accountability.[26] But from all accounts, CEDAW mechanisms, such as the country-reporting system and/or individual complaint procedure have not been considered as part of this response. And while CEDAW as an enforcer is certainly a flawed concept itself, it has still been operating in this realm for more than two decades. This begs the question: why not improve existing institutions and accountability mechanisms? As one long-term UN official articulated, "We should not be inventing new terms that would weaken other terms that we have fought for decades to create" (interview, 2006). This gap in legal accountability highlights a tension between a security approach and a rights-based approach to the protection and empowerment of the world's women, as they seem to operate in two separate realms within the UN system.[27] Moreover, it reflects the institutional disconnect among the various UN agencies working on women's rights. This lack of integration continues to cause problems and even competition for resources and has recently become the latest focus of UN reform.[28] At the end of 2006, the Secretary-General's High-Level Panel on System-Wide Coherence released its official report, "Delivering as One," recommending the establishment of one dynamic UN entity focused on gender equality and women's empowerment.[29] Throughout 2008, ongoing discussions within the General Assembly resulted in considerable support for new gender architecture within the UN, where at the final meeting of the sixty-second session member states adopted by a consensus a resolution that officially moves the gender architecture discussion into the next GA.[30]

In the end, one must recognize that the multilateral, multidimensional approach of the UN system is both its strength and its weakness; it allows for multiple entry points for influence and change while at the same time creating an uncoordinated and large bureaucracy. While it could be argued that separate systems—CEDAW and 1325—are a good way to try to crack the system from different angles, it is critically important not to duplicate the efforts of the women's movement or to create competition among those working towards similar goals. Despite the institutional disconnect in terms of legal apparatus, SCR 1325 has managed to have an impact operationally for women on the ground and it is to this analysis that we now turn.

Procedures, Partnerships, and resources

The final and most important level to measure the success or progress of securitization of women's rights is at the operational level. Turning language and laws into reality on the ground is an entirely different beast and an area where many opportunities have been missed. The failure to fully implement SCR seems to be a common theme of the recent anniversary meetings of the passing of the resolution.[31] To be sure, however, there are areas of noted improvement particularly within DPKO, a more traditional security arena. As Alain Le Roy, Under-Secretary General for DPKO stated at the 2008 Security Council open debate, SCR 1325 "has changed the way we do business in peacekeeping" (SC/9487). These gains, or best practices, can be largely in terms of procedural changes.

The security framework in practice   55

By looking at DPKO missions that started after 2000, as well as those started in the late 1990s whose mandates extended significantly into the twenty-first century, one can see significant procedural shifts in terms of the planning process, training programs, and staffing structures (see Table 3.1). More specifically, all eight missions established after 2000 incorporated SCR 1325 in the mission mandate, created a gender affairs office (or at least the position for a gender adviser) for the mission, and integrated some form of gender training for peacekeeping personnel once in mission. Further, there is even some evidence that women are being incorporated into the peace process, at least in an ad hoc way.

This means that gender-based concerns and women's rights have become at least part of the peacekeeping efforts in East Timor, Liberia, Côte d'Ivoire, Burundi, Haiti, Sudan, Darfur, the Central African Republic, and Chad. Simply put, these indicators of DPKO activity represent procedures and practices that did not exist before.[32] For example, gender advisers and gender advisery offices were not existent prior to 2000, and they now have a dual role in supporting gender mainstreaming within peacekeeping missions as well as externally with government counterparts and women's organizations in the host country. They have even been established now in missions that began before 2000, after the fact. DPKO has also established a Gender Adviser at its headquarters (on a full-time basis in 2004) as well as gender-sensitive training packages for peacekeepers prior to and during their service.[33] Gender training is become a more standard procedure in peacekeeping missions, and trainers often introduce SCR 1325 in their in-mission training programs as a useful entry point to establishing their mandate from the Security Council to conduct such training (Lyytikäinen 2007: 12). Mandates, gender units, and training programs, then, become factors in terms of the allocation of mission funding, and funding is always an issue when it comes to mainstreaming gender.[34] Furthermore, these data illustrate a move from an ad hoc consideration, at best, to a more systematic consideration of gender perspectives by the Council in peace missions.

In addition to these more systematic changes within DPKO, several states have made important gender-sensitive contributions to UN peacekeeping operations as a direct result of SCR 1325. In 2007, the first all-female unit of UN peacekeepers was created and sent to Liberia as part of India's contribution to the mission there. In 2008, Sweden followed suit by providing an all female police contingent to the peacekeeping mission in East Timor. Ghana, the seventh largest contributor to UN peacekeeping operations (as of December 2008) reported the highest level of women peacekeepers—12 percent of the total number of military personnel (just over 400 women). While inserting women personnel certainly does not guarantee gender sensitivity in UN peacekeeping operations, there is much anecdotal evidence to suggest that female UN personnel are perceived as more accessible and less threatening in the eyes of the local population, particularly women.[35] Along these lines, DPKO also disseminated a policy directive on *Gender Equality in UN Peacekeeping Operations* in 2006 and submitted an *Action Plan on 1325* for 2008–2009, reiterating the necessity of increasing women's civilian and military roles in field missions.[36] The mere fact that DPKO is now reporting

Table 3.1 Gender components of UN peacekeeping operations since 1325

	1325 in Founding Mission Mandate	Gender Adviser or Gender Affairs Unit	Gender Training (in mission)[a]	Design of In-Country National Action Plans on 1325	% of women as signatories to or mediators in peace negotiations
Kosovo* UNMIK 1999–present	No	Yes	Yes	No	0 (1999)
Sierra Leone* UNAMSIL 1999–2005	No	Yes (Youth & Gender Office)	Yes	No	0 (2000)
Democratic Republic of the Congo* MONUC 1999–present	No	Yes[b]	Yes	Yes	0[c] Accra (2003) 2% North Kivu 5% South Kivu (2008)
East Timor UNTAET/UNMISET 1999–2002/2002–2005	No[d]	Yes	Yes	No	–
Ethiopia & Eritrea* UNMEE 2000–2008	No	No[e]	No	No	–
Liberia UNMIL 2003–present	Yes	Yes	Yes	Yes	0[f] (2003)
Côte d'Ivoire UNOCI 2004–present	Yes	Yes	Yes	No	0 (2003)
Haiti MINUSTAH 2004–present	Yes	Yes	Yes	Yes	–

Burundi ONUB 2004–2006	Yes	Yes	No	0[g] (2000)
Sudan UNMIS 2005–present	Yes	Yes	Yes	0 (2005)
Timor-Leste UNMIT 2006–present	Yes	Yes	Yes	0 (2006)
Darfur UNAMID 2007–present	Yes	Yes	No	0[h] (2006)
Central African Republic & Chad MINURCAT 2007–present	Yes	Yes	No	0 (2008)

* These missions were established prior to the adoption of SCR 1325 in 2000. Gender advisers/units and training were all established after 2000.

– Information not available.

Notes

a This column includes "code of conduct" training on sexual exploitation and abuse to peacekeepers as well as "gender mainstreaming" training aimed at sensitizing missions on the various gender dynamics within the local population.

b The mission in the DRC is one of the few to have gender on their peacekeeping webpage (http://www.monuc.org/news.aspx?newsID=726).

c Of those who were part of negotiating teams at the peace negotiations in Accra, 12% were women.

d The second East Timor mission (UNMISET) also did not include reference to SCR 1325.

e This mission did have a gender focal point. Other long-standing missions, including Cyprus (UNFICYP), Georgia (UNOMIG), Middle East (UNTSO), Syrian Golan Heights (UNDOF), and Western Sahara (MINURSO) also have gender focal points.

f Of the observers and witnesses to the peace negotiations, 17% were women. For more on the remarkable story on how these women established themselves as observers and contributed to Liberian men coming to a peace agreement in 2003 at Accra, see the documentary Pray the Devil Back to Hell (2008), produced by Abigail E. Disney and directed by Gini Reticker.

g According to official sources, approximately 2% of those in the negotiating teams were women at Arusha.

h Although there were no women signatories or mediators at Abuja in 2006, 36% of the observers or mediators at Abuja in 2006, 36% of the observers to the negotiations were women and 8% of those in negotiating teams were women.

58   *The security framework in practice*

sex-disaggregated data (as of 2006) on police and troop contributions to their missions reflects an awareness or at least an acknowledgment that did not exist before.[37]

The success of DPKO has largely been a product of increasing women's participation and representation. This is not surprising given that the actions mandated in Articles 1 and 3 of SCR 1325 prioritize the women's representation in decision-making bodies. Greater integration of female decision-makers and gender-sensitive units and training has the potential to alter social processes and political structures different from those currently being produced by the male-dominated system (MacKay 2003). Bringing new and different perspectives to the changing security environment might even lead to new "policies, activities, and institutional arrangements" as well as "new opportunities for dialogue" (King 2001: Foreword). On the other hand, we must remember that achieving a critical mass of women as a percentage of their male counterparts in positions of power does not necessarily lead to manifest improvements. As Childs and Krook (2006: 21) maintain, "growing ranks of critics … suggest that the time has come to examine the usefulness of this concept for understanding women's legislative impact, as higher proportions of women do not always translate into gains for women as a group." SCR 1325 is somewhat too simplistic on this notion, glossing over the complexity of these debates. As one UNIFEM official argued:

> And maybe I am just being an academic, but a lot of the work on gender, peace, and security, is based on this essentialist assumption that women are naturally peaceful and that they have a natural contribution to make to peace-building—AND where is the evidence? … Where is the proof that women make such a big difference in peace? And really people don't like hearing that, at all. People don't question their assumptions about women … I mean where is the evidence that women and politics make a difference—there is none. I have looked at that question, and I have analyzed this statistically for every single country of the world. Do women make a difference with reproductive rights policy—actually, they do. There is a tiny impact on abortion rights, tiny. Do women bring a lowering maternal mortality rate? Which is the one thing you would think, feminists or not, nobody likes dying at childbirth that's really not fun. Wouldn't women try to improve that? The answer is generally, no. Women can agree on things, of course. But the thing is, there are institutional constraints. What's the institutional kind of ground that you operate from and what does it allow you to do?
>
> (UNIFEM official, 2006)

Despite the skepticism of this UN official (who at the time of the interview had only been with the UN for one year), many spoke in support of the additive gains made using 1325 in the context of SC peace operations. One official from DPKO upon just returning from Burundi remarked:

> What I saw was 1325 gave a very strong mandate to the constitution. That allowed our gender adviser to influence the making of the constitution …

The security framework in practice 59

that allowed her to work with the Burundians to ensure that there were gender provisions within the constitution. Major! Second, in the process of articulating the electoral role, she [the gender adviser] was instrumental in ensuring a quota—a 30 percent quota—for women in all electoral lists in the elections board in every single province. So in every single province in Burundi, out of five, you had a minimum of two women in the electoral board—the one that oversaw the elections in every province. And there was a 30 percent quota of women candidates in every single part of this. The result of this—Burundi is right now number nineteen for women in parliament. I think the US is only sixty-four. That tells you something.

(DPKO official, 2006)

Despite the inward focus of these procedural changes for DPKO, these shifts have opened up political space for women and gender equality issues in transitioning political systems. In many ways, DPKO has become the most operational gender entity in the UN system. It has a significant gender staff at UN Headquarters as well as one of the few UN agencies to have gender-designated staff in the field.[38]

In addition to political space, the security framework has also allowed for some freeing of resources for women's rights programming in local communities. In a phone interview, a UN official currently working in Sudan pointed out that in Abuja, money was made available by the Canadian government "to make sure women could be sitting at the peace table when the Darfur peace agreement was being negotiated that was not available before" (UNIFEM official, 2006). These examples from Burundi and Sudan are just two of many that point to the ways in which SCR 1325 and the security framework more broadly creates opportunities for resources and new strategic partnerships between state and non-state actors. Overall, many interviewees working in the field perceived 1325 as a useful tool for mobilizing support and creating spaces for women's participation in conflict and post-conflict situations in ways that had not occurred before.

But as anyone who has worked on women's issues can testify, right procedures, more resources, and strategic partnerships do not necessarily translate into gender skills necessary for effective action. Beyond the lack of accountability, the lack of capacity is the other glaring obstacle to operationalizing SCR 1325, and it is not clear whether or not the security framework works toward building capacity, or blinds us to its absence. Many interviewees referred to the fact that the UN simply does not have the skills, experience, and expertise needed to effectively participate in the security arena from a gender-sensitive perspective. The knowledge and skills needed to be gender sensitive and to be aware of the unique challenges that men and women face in post-conflict societies are not natural for most; gender advisers require skills training and development. Simply being a woman, for example, does not make one a gender expert. Further, bringing gender advisers into peacekeeping missions and increasing women's presence in post-conflict reconstruction efforts requires simultaneous institutional reforms that support these individuals in a systematic and legitimate way. One UNIFEM official, in

60   *The security framework in practice*

referring to security sector reform as part of the 1325 mandate, explained the lack of capacity as:

> First, we really need to look at what it means to recruit women to the military and police, especially through disarmament processes where ex-female combatants would get jobs in the police and the military which they should but they don't. And the second, a much more important angle, is gender-sensitive institutional reform to the military and police which is a completely different thing—so it makes very little difference whether you have women there or not. It's about things like introducing zero-tolerance sexual harassment, seriously punishing immediately any kind of sexual exploitation or abuse, changing policing and public security policies to make public and private life safe for women—it is a huge, gigantic change. So this is something that we have been promoting recently, but frankly the quality of the analysis—feminist analysis available on security sector reform—first of all, you barely find it and secondly the quality is very poor because there's not enough evidence of what's worked because there is not enough operational.
>
> (UNIFEM official, 2006)

So while the security framework opens political space and creates different sorts of opportunities, it is often in areas that women's movement is only beginning to establish a presence and the tools necessary to really implement the principles of 1325. Operationally, SCR 1325 has been a mixed bag, but this is also the area—particularly in terms of opening up new issue areas for discussion and creating opportunities for new strategic partnerships—with the most potential for change.

Operationally, legally, and rhetorically there has been some significant progress and many missed opportunities for women's activism to affect the security agenda through SCR 1325. This security framework has meant changes in the language that the SC uses and in the procedures that it follows. But it has fallen short in terms of establishing legalist sorts of accountability mechanisms and the full capacity to really implement the resolution in an effective, systematic, and comprehensive way. These limitations and obstacles can largely be understood by examining the nature of the security framework embedded in SCR 1325 and the implications of this framework for broader goals of the women's movement.

The limitations of 1325 for security and for women

Many frustrated feminists have written off SCR 1325 as another example of lack of political will where rhetoric will never be met by reality. And while this critique certainly has its place, there is much more going on with this resolution and securitization process being used by women within the UN system that deserves further consideration, particularly in terms of the long-term goals of the women's movement.

First, much of the "progress" made in terms of integrating gender-sensitive language and procedures in SC activity, especially in the realm of peacekeeping

The security framework in practice 61

operations, have been policies that increase the number of women involved in existing structures and institutions. Gender advisers and advisory units serve as focal points for UN operations to bring the security concerns of women and women's rights into the peace process, not necessarily gender issues, such as the role of masculinity in continuing violence after conflict. This is problematic at a number of levels. First and most obviously, these separate units or offices designated to women tend to further marginalize those groups in their attempt to ensure that they have some access to the mission. As Sandra Whitworth (2004: 131) cites work done by the NGO *Kvinna till Kvinna* in Kosovo:

> a separate gender unit tends to result in local women's NGOs liaising with the unit, while other local political actors—the majority of whom will likely be men—deal with UN officials in the mainline departments and offices, the majority of whom are also men and who often enjoy more direct access to the chief of the mission.

At a deeper level, this additive approach only serves to make the existing structures and system more effective rather than to really transform the way the UN does security. This additive strategy resembles the often criticized WID approach of the 1970s in terms of integrating women into liberalizing development policy. This strategy, though focused on armed conflict, emphasizes the inclusion of feminine women into the existing structure, further contributing to the naturalization of the UN discursive practices around war, peace, and security.

These problems underlie the fact that the security framework is based upon the difference argument that women are especially vulnerable victims in war and especially adept as peacemakers in post-conflict situations. This instrumental argument makes 1325 a problem-solving tool rather than a critical means to challenge prevailing practices. Whitworth (2004: 133) argues:

> Rather than view UN practices toward women and gender as somehow inconsistent, a more critical engagement with these issues demonstrates that the knowledge claims being produced within the UN have *made possible* certain practices, including the apparently inconsistent treatment of gender itself. Because gender analysis is seen most frequently as a problem-solving activity, the meanings given to women, peace, and security confirm a number of "stories" produced within the UN, including what counts as armed conflict, how those conflicts impact women, who the appropriate actors are in resolving conflicts, and where women fit in terms of response.

Thus, 1325 is merely a matter of working women and gender, as though they are the same, into business as usual.

This is particularly problematic for the women's movement as the securitization language—in the context of SCR 1325—seems to simultaneously open and close doors of opportunity. The resolution has paved the way for changing practices and policies within DPKO, broadening mandates of SC country-specific

62   The security framework in practice

resolutions, focusing and refining existing human rights law, creating new political spaces and leverage to local women's groups in post-conflict situations, and further developing strategic partnerships with UN donors in terms of gender programming. At the same time, it has limited the kinds of questions and challenges that women's activism can make at least for the time being.[39] SCR 1325 does not, for example, allow for questions about the appropriateness of sending men trained to be soldiers out into the world as peacekeepers or if peacekeepers should be soldiers at all. It also does not allow the women's movement to question the militaristic working assumptions of the SC. And although 1325 does allow recognition of collective individual security needs—those of women—it still relies upon the state to establish and maintain security at all levels of society. This is what one UNIFEM official referred to as "the ways in which 1325 has stifled creative thinking on the part of local women's groups working for peace" (interview, 2006). It is important, therefore, to be aware of some of the trade-offs made in using the security framework to make an instrumental argument for the promotion and protection of human rights.

Conclusion

In the end, SCR 1325 is certainly flawed, but it is an instructive case for exploring outcomes of the security framework for promoting and protecting women's rights. Much of the progress associated with 1325 reflects an additive and integrative approach to the international security agenda rather than a transformative and deeply critical approach to the way that the UN does security. Women's concerns, problems, and rights are still largely an afterthought, rather than an internalized and institutionalized change. But as the Women in Development movement of the 1960s and 1970s demonstrates, this might be the only entry point for marginalized groups seeking real change.

Thus, not all hope is lost. SCR 1325 has opened space for potentially transforming the security agenda. The "Women's Participation and Gender Perspectives in Security Council Resolutions Checklist" is an empirical example of an attempt to transform the process from within, to really internalize gender-sensitive decision-making processes. This checklist, if used, has the ability to influence the creation of peace operations and the development of law binding resolutions from the very beginning because it aims to reorient the thinking of SC members in ways that make gender more integral to every question that they might ask about a given country-specific resolution.[40] Further, even adding women to the existing system does have the potential for real, integral change, particularly over the long term. So it is a logical place to start.

Discourse continues to be critical; language can influence attitudes, beliefs, and ultimately behavior. Part of the success in securitization is that the actual definition of security is dependent upon its successful construction and acceptance in the discourse. This is an ongoing project. Furthermore, much more work is needed to understand the relationship between a rights-based approach and a security-based approach. This includes an in-depth look at the conceptual links

The security framework in practice 63

between human security and human rights. As one interviewee with over twenty years UN experience told me, "the network of those involved in initiating the women, peace, and security movement—both NGOs and UN agencies—utilized a bandwagoning strategy by building their case upon the mainstream human rights movement" and this link requires further analysis (interview, 2006).[41]

Overall, the security framework does seem to have some positive impacts for women's rights activism. Through SCR 1325, the framework has served as an organizing and mobilizing force to bring women, particularly for those suffering and working toward stability in war-torn regions of the world. It has allowed women to be the focus of Security Council debate for the first time in the fifty years since its inception. It has created new or improved upon existing strategic partnerships with donor countries, troop contributing countries, UN agencies, and the countless non-governmental and grassroots organizations working to improve women's lives. In some cases, it has even created opportunities for resources and funding that might not have otherwise been available.

Despite these gains, one must proceed with caution. The security language has the potential to be limiting and exclusionary, confirming warnings from securitization theorists, such as Ole Wæver. The framework tends to ignore the bigger issues of militarism and coercion that continue to guide international interaction. And it can often rely upon essentialist assumptions about gender roles that can lead to justification of a return to an oppressive status quo. One must be wary of the security language as a new and more politicized name for the already established human rights regime. In this sense, both academics and policy-makers must ensure that the language builds upon the accountability mechanisms, organizational capacity, and international norms that have long been evolving for international human rights. SCR 1325 is a tool; it must be seen then as one of many means and not an end.

Notes

1 For the full text of Resolution 1325 and related documents see http://www. peacewomen.org/un/sc/1325.html.
2 Some of the most recent translations include Fijian, Hindi (in Roman Script), Montenegrin, Pidgin (Papua New Guinea), Pidgin (Solomon Islands), Rotuman (Fiji), Slovenian, and Tongan. See www.peacewomen.org.
3 Jennifer Klot, one of the architects of SCR 1325, rightfully maintains that the resolution is already limited in its location within the UN SC. She argues, "Although 1325 represents the broadest political interpretation of gender issues ever reflected within the peace and security agenda as defined by the UN, it does not by any stretch of the imagination refer to the entire issues of women, peace, and security. ... 1325 is as specific and narrow as the SC's mandate ... its actions focus mainly on conflict situations and of these, only a limited number of countries make it on to the agenda (i.e. not countries such as Nigeria, Zimbabwe, Algeria, Colombia or Guatemala)" (2002:18–19).
4 As Carol Cohn argues, "my method derives its strength from the juxtaposition and layering of many different windows ... [and] is of necessity partial, in a variety of ways" (2006: 93).
5 For more speeches using this framework, see the collection at http://www. peacewomen.org/un/6thAnniversary/Open_Debate/index.html.

64   *The security framework in practice*

6 It is important to note here that this was not the first time the SC took up a "non-traditional" security issue. Starting in the late 1990s, the SC began holding thematic debates, as opposed to country-specific discussions, on issues, such as civilians and children in armed conflict and the HIV/AIDS crisis. The SC's work on children makes an interesting comparison with women's issues in the SC and is the focus of the next chapter.

7 For more on the monitoring of Security Council activity in terms of 1325, see *1325 Resolution Watch* by Peacewomen.org at http://www.peacewomen.org/un/sc/1325_Monitor/thematicindex.htm.

8 As Cynthia Enloe argues, "*In*attention is a political act" (Enloe, 2000: xxi).

9 Cynthia Enloe was one of the first International Relations scholars to demonstrate the many ways the state can actually threaten women's security rather than enhance it.

10 This cooperation versus cooptation tension is explored more in depth in Chapter 6 with the case of DDR in post-conflict societies.

11 For more an excellent analysis of the positive and negative normative and policy implications of the security framework for those with HIV/AIDS more generally see Stefan Elbe 2006.

12 This backlash after conflict whether under the rubric of nationalism, fundamentalism, or order has long been the aftermath for women in post-conflict situations, as pioneering feminists such as Cynthia Enloe have long been arguing.

13 For the numerous problems with this conflation, see Carver 1996.

14 For Enloe's original articulation of this see "Womenandchildren: Making Feminist Sense of the Persian Gulf War." *The Village Voice* 25 Sept. 1990.

15 This grouping has another insidious implication. When political actors claim to fight for their "womenandchildren," they not only take away women's agency, but they use their helplessness to justify violence.

16 Chapter 5 of the UN Charter states, "The Members of the United Nations agree to accept and carry out the decisions of the Security Council in accordance with the present Charter" (Article 25). This legally obligates all UN member states to implement SC resolutions. Although there are no enforcement mechanisms attached here, SC resolutions still carry significant weight. "Nevertheless, the existence of human rights standards contributes in important measure to the recognition of rights. They provide a focus for efforts to obtain recognition of rights; to enhance respect for them; and to induce compliance with international obligations that have been assumed" (Martin and Carson 1996: Preface). Still, compliance and enforcement continue to be huge obstacles, particularly for women's rights, as the next section will demonstrate.

17 While these national action plans can be seen as a result of SCR 1325, this group of countries has long been sympathetic and supportive to the UN's work on women's rights. Thus, it is not surprising that they were the first to develop such national policies, but SCR 1325 did give these countries the international mandate and organizing framework to put the policies into place. Austria, Switzerland, Liberia and Iceland have also recently published and released national action plans on 1325. These documents can be accessed at http://www.un.org/womenwatch/ianwge/taskforces/wps/national_level_impl.html.

18 As of December 2008, 185 countries are party to the convention. For a list of these countries, see http://www.un.org/womenwatch/daw/cedaw/states.htm.

19 Zwingel (2005) writes that "as of the year 2003, only 27 per cent of states parties have never been late in submitting [progress] reports. 44 per cent of all states parties had submitted their last report eight or more years ago"(p. 407).

20 One exception here comes out of Rwanda, where NGOs have reported using SCR 1325 and CEDAW together to lobby for quotas of women in its parliament and judiciary. For more on this, see http://www.globaljusticecenter.net/publications/Global-Justice-Now.pdf. It is worth noting that elections in Rwanda in 2008 brought the percentage of women in the lower house to 56.3%, the highest in the world.

The security framework in practice 65

21 While other articles could be included here, such as those dealing with non-discrimination in terms of education, employment, health care, marriage and family law, and rural needs, these articles are arguably more indirectly relevant to the scope of SCR 1325 in terms of conflict and post-conflict situations.

22 The nine countries that referenced SCR 1325 in their country reports include Austria (2002), Bosnia Herzegovina (2005), Canada (2007), Columbia (2005), Netherlands (2005), New Zealand (2006), Norway (2007), United Kingdom (2007), and United Republic of Tanzania (2003).

23 Further analysis of CEDAW and the security framework can be found in the following chapter.

24 The main instrument for implementing 1325 in the UN system is the Action Plan of the Inter-Agency task Force on Women, Peace and Security. The Action Plan is a compilation of current and planned activities by 22 different UN system entities. The Inter-Agency Task Force has no monitoring system to ensure these actons are taken. No indicators have been developed to track progress, no measurement or data collection systems agreed, not even a regular reporting mechanism that is tied to the Action Plan developed. It is impossible therefore for the SC or any other intergovernmental body to hold any of the UN agencies involved accountable for implementing this Action Plan.

25 Suggested accountability mechanisms include the designation of a SC member as a focal point or SC working group on women, peace, and security, performance measures and required reporting procedures for national governments, and the requirement of national action plans on 1325.

26 The only mechanism developed by the SC to track its implementation has been the annual open debate on women, peace and security. Since the adoption of Security Council Resolution 1325, the SC has held five public sessions with Arria formula meetings each with a specific theme from 1325. As a result of these open debates, the Council has adopted four presidential statements and has issued one press release noting the progress made, and challenges remaining in the implementation of the resolution.

27 Chapter 4 further explores CEDAW and its connections with UNIFEM as well as the tension that exists between a rights-based approach and a security approach with SCR 1325.

28 Thus, it is critical to take the internal politics of international organizations and broader networks seriously. Recent research on theories of bureaucratic politics to international society are useful here (Barnett and Finnemore 2004). Cooley and Ron (2002), for example, have argued that bureaucratic decision-making in the transnational sector is driven at least as much by short-term concerns with organizational survival as by normative commitments. Similarly, social movement theories have long pointed to the power relations that exist within networks (Weldon 2006).

29 In short, this means consolidating the three existing UN entities into an enhanced and independent gender entity, headed by an Executive Director with the rank of Under Secretary-General, appointed through a meritocratic competition demonstrably open to those outside the UN. For more information, see http://www.un.org/events/panel/resources/pdfs/HLP-SWC-FinalReport.pdf.

30 For more on what is at stake in terms of reform and the NGO campaign push for such action, see GEAR (Gender Equality Architecture Reform) Campaign. Center for Women's Global Leadership. http://www.cwgl.rutgers.edu/globalcenter/policy/unadvocacy/gea.html

31 It is worth noting here that both state and non-state actors focused their concerns on implementation gaps and obstacles at the last three anniversary meetings for 1325, which includes October 2006, 2007, and 2008.

32 These indicators in Table 3.1 only tell part of the story. As Sandra Whitworth (2004)

66   *The security framework in practice*

points out in her research, it is one thing to establish a gender affairs unit, it is quite another thing to allocate such a unit the basic funding that it needs. So while aggregated data is useful for understanding generalized trends, such an approach must not be the end, but rather the means for directing future research questions about the quality of these mechanisms for applying the principles of SCR 1325 on the ground.

33 For a more detailed analysis on these "achievements" for specific country missions, see Hudson N.F. (2005).

34 While funding is always a challenge for gender mainstreaming efforts (and peacekeeping more broadly), several interviewees indicated that donors have been "quite generous" when it comes to gender issues, and in some cases gender advisers have had to return money to donors (via DPKO) because the gender advisers lacked the capacity on the ground to get the funds spent within the time frame allowed.

35 For more on this, see Lloyd (2006).

36 For more information see http://www.peacewomen.org/resources/Peacekeeping/ DPKO/policy_directive.pdf and http://www.un.org/womenwatch/ianwge/taskforces/ wps/actionplan20082009/pdfs/DPKO%202008-2009%201325.pdf.

37 For the most up-to-date information on these statistics, see http://www.un.org/ Depts/dpko/dpko/contributors/gend.html.

38 DPKO currently has a staff of five within its gender unit. In contrast, the Office of the Special adviser on Gender Issues (OSAGI) only has two staff members devoted to work on peace and security. Furthermore, while UNIFEM has regional offices, it does not have a field presence in conflict and post-conflict zones the way that DPKO does

39 In recent years, numerous scholarly panels (International Studies Association Conference panels are of particularly note) have been dealing with these concerns and raising these more fundamental questions about the continued militaristic and state-based approach to security by the UN. Many of these scholars, including Carol Cohn, Sandra Whitworth, Anne-Marie Goetz, among others, also work in the policy arena. And so this limitation certainly has potential to change.

40 The Checklist was actually documented for the most recent joint mission to Darfur. See http://www.peacewomen.org/un/ngoadvocacy/1325Tools/checklist.pdf for the document.

41 These questions are also addressed in Chapter 4.

4 Women and children

Comparative frameworks and strategies within the Security Council

> The key is the accountability issue. On children and armed conflict, not only have you got six resolutions, six, but each one of them strengthening parts of the original one. There is a working group. There is a champion within the Security Council, which is France. There is a SC working group which is seized of this matter at all times and has to make sure that all resolutions pay attention. There is a Special Rapporteur [Representative] to the Secretary-General on children and armed conflict and she is probably the most brilliant person for this job—Radhika Coomaraswamy—who was before that the one on violence against women. And she is allowed to name names. She is allowed to say the LRA are persecuting children, bombing schools and hospitals. Now, we're not allowed to do that. 1325 does not empower us or anybody in UN to say the following armed parties or governments are abusing women's rights, are condoning sexual violence as a military practice, as a weapon of war. We're not allowed to say that. If we could, could you imagine the newspaper reports, the outrage from governments, the shame, the embarrassment? Some states and parties would move to stop these practices, but we're not allowed to do that.
>
> UNIFEM Official, December 2006

Security Council Resolution (SCR) 1325 has had some notable successes, particularly in terms of procedural shifts within the United Nations Department of Peacekeeping Operations as discussed in the previous chapter. But as the resolution's eighth anniversary events, speeches, and meetings held in October 2008 demonstrated, Security Council member states continue to lack political will and a genuine internalized commitment toward its implementation and full realization on the ground.[1] One does not have to go far to find instances where the rhetoric falls short of reality, where procedures have not produced desired outcomes. Given how recent cases, such as the US-led invasion in Iraq or the deficient UN peacekeeping option in Darfur, have challenged the SC's legitimacy and authority, these inconsistencies and inadequacies in holding member states accountable to SCR 1325 are not surprising (Glennon 2003).

In many of my interviews, however, it was surprising how many individuals mentioned the relative success of SC resolutions on children and armed conflict

68 Women and children

in recent years. As the opening quote illustrates, there are now six resolutions that address issues concerning children and armed conflict. Each resolution builds upon the previous one by further articulating and defining children's rights during and after conflict, and more importantly the SC's role in protecting and promoting such rights. The adoption of these resolutions benefited significantly from the office of the Special Representative of the Secretary-General (SRSG) of the Children and Armed Conflict, a high-ranking and well-supported professional position within the UN Secretariat, which was established in the late 1990s. (D'Amico 1999).[2] The resolutions have also mandated an ongoing and systematic role for the Secretary-General on the issue, by requesting the Secretary-General submit an annual report explicitly identifying parties who commit certain grave violations against children's rights. Moreover, these resolutions established a number of accountability mechanisms, including a SC Working Group made up of member states and a monitoring and reporting procedure pushing state and non-state actors toward compliance.[3]

This trajectory of addressing the problem of children and armed conflict within the Security Council raises important questions about SCR 1325 and the place of women's concerns and gender equality within the Council more broadly. Why are there such significant differences between the SC actions on children and armed conflict and its more limited action on women in armed conflict? How can the WPS agenda be understood as part of the Council's very gradual and flawed shift to include humanitarian concerns within its mandate? Given that women and children are most often perceived as vulnerable groups in armed conflict and are almost always categorized as interchangeable, a comparison of the processes and outcomes of the two (as separate groups) in the context of the UN security arena is in order.[4] This chapter explores the ways in which the security framework, strategies, and activism surrounding children and armed conflict have differed from that for women. Does the security framework used by women activists challenge the way the SC "does security" in unique ways? In other words, do women face different structural and institutional barriers in gaining access to the Security Council when compared to other marginalized or vulnerable groups? Answering these questions not only sheds light on the meaning and practice of security within the UN, but also points to important strategies and mechanisms for the marginalized to find entry points into the mainstream.

In order to address these questions, this chapter begins with a brief historical discussion of how the Security Council began to take up and debate thematic issues such as civilians, children, and women in armed conflict.[5] By then exploring the history of the six SC resolutions on children and armed conflict specifically, this process tracing provides unique insight into what the process surrounding "women, peace and security" was lacking and the different institutional obstacles that women in the UN face. The third section compares and contrasts the two. The last section explores the evolutionary nature of Security Council resolutions and whether or not more is actually better. This part of the analysis utilizes a simple coding inventory that illustrates how SC resolutions

Women and children 69

develop over time in terms of the language, accountability mechanisms, issue articulation, linkages to legal frameworks, and overall implementation practices. This section incorporates SCR 1820 (2008) into the analysis to better understand how this most recent resolution on WPS fits into the picture. The conclusion then evaluates the similarities and differences between the processes children and women engage in for accessing and influencing the SC agenda, as a closer look into the case of children provides unique insight into the obstacles that women and gender equality continue to face, particularly in terms of the most recent resolution on women, peace, and security (SCR 1820).

The Security Council and non-traditional security issues

During the Cold War, international humanitarian issues including civilians, women, and children were not considered "security" concerns and were therefore not a part of the Security Council's agenda. According to Thomas Weiss, "no resolution [even] mentioned the humanitarian aspects of any conflict from 1945 until the Six Day War of 1967" (2004: 38).[6] This first resolution to mention humanitarian concerns was Security Council Resolution 237, relating to the Middle East whereby the Security Council recommended "to the Governments concerned the scrupulous respect of the humanitarian principles governing the treatment of prisoners of war and the protection of civilian persons in time of war contained in the Geneva Conventions of 12 August 1949."[7] This weak reference to international humanitarian law characterized much of the 1970s and 1980s when "the Security Council gave humanitarian aspects of armed conflict limited priority" (Baarda 1994: 140).

From this historical perspective of Security Council action, or more appropriately inaction, the 1990s emerge as a watershed for Council activity. During the first half of the decade twice as many resolutions were passed as during the first forty-five years of UN history, and more importantly, these resolutions contained "repeated references to humanitarian crises amounting to threats to international peace and security, and they repeated demands for parties to respect international humanitarian law" (Weiss 2004: 38). This trend is what Weiss refers to as the "humanitarian impulse"—when the Security Council began to develop practices recognizing that humanitarian action is permissive under the UN Charter and at times even desirable while simultaneously political and not always obligatory.[8] Further, this impulse is not instantaneous, but rather a gradual and sometimes sporadic process still very much in progress. As Edward Luck notes, "when the Council members met in January 1992, for the first time at the summit level, to address the Council's expanding horizons, they barely mentioned humanitarian concerns" (2006: 84). Nonetheless, their consensus presidential statement at the time recognized that "the non-military sources of instability in the economic, social, humanitarian, and ecological fields have become threats to international peace and security" (S/23500).[9] Thus, the Council began to recognize that security cannot be defined in narrow, militaristic terms alone, and Council activity must reflect this shifting reality given their mandate to promote and protect international peace and security. Despite this recognition, as Boutros Boutros-Ghali's

70   Women and children

An Agenda for Peace (1992) reiterated, the "respect the sovereignty of the state" remained a guiding principle for UN action, and, of course, inaction throughout the early 1990s.[10]

In the context of the massive failures by the international community to protect civilians in Rwanda and the former Yugoslavia, however, by the late 1990s the Council was confronted with a lively debate on "developing international norm[s] in favor of intervention to protect civilians from wholesale slaughter" (Annan 1999: 49–50).[11] In this sense, the Council was pushed to think about sovereignty not just in terms of power and autonomy, but in terms of responsibility as well, a step toward taking this humanitarian impulse more seriously. By 1999, the Security Council undertook a series of meetings to address this issue of responsibility to protect civilian populations during times of war. These meetings coupled with numerous reports, presidential statements and two resolutions on civilians in armed conflict created a recognizable momentum for the global security agenda to more systematically and purposefully include humanitarian concerns, particularly in terms of war-affected populations (Jones & Cater 2001). This momentum pushed the Council to expand its understanding of what constitute threats to international security, establishing jurisdiction beyond actual or imminent international armed conflict.

Thus began what Sheri Gibbings refers to as the "humanizing" of the Security Council (Cohn et al. 2004: 136). From 1999 to 2000, the Security Council adopted a number of resolutions on thematic issues in addition to the traditional approach of resolutions on country-specific conflicts, reflecting a broader view of security and subsequently an enlarged agenda for the Council. It has approved resolutions on civilians in armed conflict (SCR 1265 and 1296), children and armed conflict (SCR 1261 and 1314), women, peace, and security (SCR 1325), the importance of democracy and human rights in establishing peace (SCR 1327), and the role of HIV/AIDS in promoting international peace and security (SCR 1308).[12] It is noteworthy that all of these resolutions occurred in either 1999 or 2000, during Canada's two-year term as a non-permanent member on the Security Council. According to Michael Pearson (2001), Canada introduced the concept of "human security" to the Security Council and pushed that the SC apply elements of human security to Council debates and decisions including resolutions and field missions. This push is most evident in Canada's ability to frame the rights of groups of people particularly vulnerable during conflict as central to the Councils' mission on promoting and protecting international peace and security. As one activist from the Women, Peace and Security network stated, "the Canadian government's campaign on 'human security' was one factor facilitating an institutional openness of the Security Council . . ." to a broader security agenda (Gibbings, as cited in Cohn et al. 2004: 136).[13]

This institutional openness to the concept of human security not only meant the incorporation of humanitarian law, but human rights law and discourse too. For example, during this period the Council for the first time established a working relationship with the High Commissioner for Human Rights. On September 16, 1999, High Commissioner Mary Robinson was able to formally address the

Women and children 71

SC where she spoke during the Council's debate on the Secretary-General's report on civilians in armed conflict. Ms. Robinson urged the Council to consider human rights emergencies as immediate threats to security, arguing that civilians are no longer solely victims of war, but rather instruments of wars—a situation she described as a "strange and terrible state of affairs."[14] This represented an important integration of two distinct fields, where human rights could be framed and understood as humanitarian needs and vice versa. Both were critical in bringing together the Security Council's framework on thematic issues, or what is often referred to as the Council's human security agenda. As Carol Cohn articulates, "I should add that in the Security Council discourse, 'human security' means something different than it does in academia. In the SC, it means making certain aspects of human rights and humanitarian concerns relevant to the peace and security agenda" (Cohn et al. 2004: 136).

It is all too easy to overstate the importance of these thematic resolutions and debates within the Security Council. In many cases, these thematic issues continue to be supplemental rather than integral to the Council's resolutions in the management of crisis and armed conflict. The majority of Security Council Resolutions are still driven by country-specific hard security issues, such as Iraq, Sudan and the Democratic Republic of the Congo. In other words, the Council still tends to address thematic issues in follow-up resolutions to the initial mandates of Council action in country-specific situations.

Nonetheless, the discourse surrounding these thematic resolutions is significant. A long-time analyst of the UN notes, "The Council's thematic resolutions and, more often, presidential statements on these matters have, in essence, provided it, as well as the UN's larger membership, with sort of a normative compass to guide their exploration of new substantive territory" (Luck 2006: 131). Luck goes on to say that these thematic issues are the "Council's excursion into what could reasonably be characterized as norm building or codification of legal standards" (131). These legal standards include both the articulation and implementation of humanitarian and human rights law. Further, many of the thematic resolutions mirror debates and standard-setting occurring in the sphere of transitional justice. The Rome Statute for the International Criminal Court, for example, outlined a definition of war crimes that included rape and other forms of sexual violence and the recruitment and use of children in conflict as soldiers and otherwise (Askin 1997, 2006; Spees 2003). Thus, the criminalization of these issues not normally considered part of the mainstream security agenda provided an influential backdrop for the process of including both women and children in the Council's activity.[15]

Interestingly, while women and children appear to have made some inroads into the agenda of the Security Council, they have done so largely as separate groups. This split is particularly interesting given that numerous documents coming out of the UN during the 1960s and 1970s considered women and children to be one and the same.[16] This categorization of the two groups is by no means limited to the UN; as noted in the previous chapter, Cynthia Enloe refers to this as the "womenandchildren" phenomenon. But at some point the advocacy surrounding

72   Women and children

these two vulnerable groups took different paths.[17] Many feminist scholars and activists even tout 1325 as significant for "detaching women from 'women and children' and making women visible as active agents" (Cohn et al. 2004: 139). Still, many interviewees in my research referred to the resolution on children as a model for the future goals of the WPS network.[18] Furthermore, one of the key architects on the drafting of SCR 1325 was Jennifer Klot who was at the time the Peace and Security adviser in UNIFEM. Before joining UNIFEM, however, Klot worked on the Graça Machel report on children in armed conflict, which was a major turning point for raising awareness on the relevancy of children's issues to SC activity. Therefore, Klot's experience on what worked to bring children to the Council's attention was key to framing women's issues. This overlap is what Charli Carpenter (2005: 300) refers to as "issue-alignment" where networks take cues from other issue networks on what works in successfully framing a particular cause. Several interviewees supported the applicability of this concept by referencing the progress made by those working on "children and armed conflict" as a positive example for the WPS network to follow.

What is most important to take away from this brief historical narrative of non-traditional security issues on the Council's agenda is that these issues are a relatively recent occurrence. Although humanitarian concerns and human rights standards were slow to become a part of the SC's agenda, they seem to be more generally accepted now at least in terms of language and procedure. Joanna Weschler (2004: 55) argues:

> Today, nobody any longer seriously questions the relevance of human rights to the Council's work and the need for human rights information and analysis at every stage of the Council's action. However, this acceptance has come gradually and haltingly ... Perhaps most important for the gradual acceptance of the relevance of human rights to the work of the Security Council has been the realization that in order to achieve lasting peace agreements human rights need to be addressed.

Weschler rightly recognizes here that the human rights discourse within the Security Council has always been framed in instrumental terms, whereas the framework linking humanitarian law and norms uses language that is largely protection-based. Responsibility seems to bridge the gap between the two, but the different starting points (humanitarian versus human rights law) illustrate some important strategic differences between those advocating for children and armed conflict and those advocating for women in armed conflict. While there is certainly overlap, illustrating this distinction is key. Both rely on instrumental arguments, but the security frameworks utilized appear to have different emphases. The case of children and armed conflict is firmly grounded in an approach that bridges humanitarian and human rights discourse in a way that WPS does not. In order to understand this foundation, I now turn to an analysis of the structural and institutional factors leading up the six resolutions in order to understand just how those surrounding WPS differ.

Women and children 73

Children and armed conflict: a process worth modeling?

While it is clear that SCR 1325 and the resolutions for children and armed conflict were both a product of dynamic, symbiotic relationships between NGOs, the UN and its agencies, and even member states, there are some distinct temporal, legal, and institutional differences that are key to understanding the "success" of children's issues within the Security Council. These differences raise questions about whether or not the process surrounding children and armed conflict can and should be emulated by women working in (and on) armed conflict. A comparison of the six resolutions on children and armed conflict to the two resolutions on women requires not only a look at the resolutions themselves, but at the legal and institutional structures that laid the groundwork for these resolutions. Since the process leading up to SCR 1325 has been well documented and discussed in Chapter 1, this section will focus specifically on children while keeping the discussion closely tied to that of women.

For those who study and advocate for children's rights at the global level, the Convention on the Rights of the Child (CRC) is most often the fundamental starting point.[19] This was not, however, the first international document committed specifically to the rights of children. The first attempt to frame such norms preceded the UN with the 1924 Geneva Declaration of the Rights of the Child, drafted by Eglantyne Jebb, founder of Save the Children.[20] Although this declaration was only five paragraphs in length, it covered children's rights in terms of food, health care, delinquency, shelter, emergency relief, work, and exploitation. Thirty-five years later following the UN's Universal Declaration of Human Rights (UDHR),[21] the UN General Assembly adopted the Declaration on the Rights of the Child (1959).[22] While the link between the two documents is clear—the 1959 declaration even cites the 1924 declaration in its preamble—comparing the two documents also demonstrates how "normative standards related to the child had evolved in thirty-five years," particularly in terms of the latter declaration's articulation of education- and work-related rights and protection from exploitation (Ensalaco 2005: 11).[23]

Also, during the 1950s the international community saw the emergence of the UN Children's Fund (UNICEF). First established in 1946 with General Assembly Resolution 57(I) as a temporary fund for children in emergency situations, UNICEF became a permanent part of the UN system in 1953 officially recognizing that the special needs of children do not end with war.[24] While much has been written on the significant development of UNICEF as a UN body,[25] two points are worth mentioning here as they contributed to UNICEF's unique role in the CRC, laying the groundwork for its continued role with the SC resolutions. First, starting in 1979 with the International Year of the Child, UNICEF began publishing its annual report, *The State of the World's Children*. According to Michael Longford, these reports have provided the international community with sound evidence and "compelling arguments in favour of stronger measures [to protect children's rights] than mere 'declaration'" (1996: 220).[26] Thus, the organization was "well-equipped" to participate in the drafting of the convention. Second, and

74   Women and children

not unrelated, was the development of a program referred to as "Children in Especially Difficult Circumstances (CEDC)," which included working and exploited children and children in war zones. As Joel Oestreich notes, staff working on CEDC "perceived that these issues were related to the goals of the draft convention, and by the late 1980s the organization was actively, if indirectly, trying to shape provisions of the convention to fit its own desires" (1998: 185). Thus, the issue-related focus of the CEDC program created a relevant entry point for UNICEF into the CRC process.

UNICEF's activities, many of which were directed through the UN Commission on Human Rights and an ad hoc network of NGOs, played an important role in the ten-year process of drafting the convention (Gerschutz and Karns 2005). The adoption of the CRC was groundbreaking on a number of fronts,[27] but it was particularly significant in institutionalizing UNICEF and establishing a legally based, structural relationship (between UNICEF and the CRC) that has only strengthened with time. The CRC is the only human rights treaty to specify a UN agency in the implementation process, and it is the only treaty to have given the Committee the power to obtain information from sources other than States Parties. Article 45 states:

> In order to foster the effective implementation of the Convention and to encourage international cooperation in the field ... the specialized agencies, UNICEF, and other United Nations organs shall be entitled to be represented at the consideration of the implementation of such provisions of the present Convention as fall within the scope of their mandate. The Committee may invite the specialized agencies, UNICEF, and other competent bodies as it may consider appropriate to provide expert advice on the implementation of the Convention . . .

Thus, the CRC not only designates a specific role for UNICEF, but allows non-state actors to participate in the bilateral reporting process between the Committee and State Parties. "This provision provides NGOs with a platform in the international arena" where they can "contribute to the jurisprudence of the Convention" through Committee meetings and reports (Breen 2003: 458). Furthermore, the provision has paved the way for the CRC to become the "unofficial constitution" of UNICEF, framing the organization's mission in terms of "rights rather than services," which has required "considerable rethinking of how that organization does business and of its relationship with host states" (Oestreich 1998: 185, 187).

This is what Oestreich coins the "UNICEF/CRC" model that has allowed for both institutions "to take a more active role in human rights promotion than standard setting and fact finding" (1998: 193). This model is based on a symbiotic relationship that has given both bodies an institutional home and direction. He maintains, "The Convention serves UNICEF's purpose as much as UNICEF serves those of the Convention. Where UNICEF claims that the CRC legitimizes and contextualizes its operations, as often as not it also provides a pretext for expanding

Women and children 75

UNICEF's work well beyond what was originally part of its mandate" (191). It was this model that allowed UNICEF and CRC to maintain an institutional presence even after the initial optimism of the post-Cold War political environment fizzled.[28] This model created structural safeguards and access points that kept children's rights on the agenda of the General Assembly (GA), moved it to the desk of the Secretary-General, and then eventually pushed its way onto the agenda of the Security Council through its permanent home in the Special Representative of the Secretary-General on the Impact of Armed Conflict on Children.[29]

The process by which the position of the SRSG was created is as important as the existence of such a high-ranking individual specifically focused on children and armed conflict. In 1992, at the second session of the Committee on the Rights of the Child, the Committee decided to hold its first general discussion on one specific article of the CRC on the topic of children and armed conflict. NGOs participating in the Committee were influential in this decision and thus, participated in the discussion devoted to that topic at the Committee's 38th and 39th meetings (Cantwell 1992; Breen 2003).[30] Following the discussion, the Committee "decided to establish a working group composed of some of its members, entrusted with the task of submitting final proposals at the next regular session of the Committee, scheduled for January 1993" (CRC/C/10 para 76). From the working group's 1993 oral report, the Committee recommended:

> to the General Assembly, in accordance with article 45 (c) of the Convention, that it request the Secretary-General to undertake a study on ways and means of improving the protection of children from the adverse effects of armed conflicts; for this purpose, the Secretary-General might wish to invite the cooperation of relevant specialized agencies, other United Nations organs, non-governmental organizations and the International Committee of the Red Cross.
>
> (CRC/C/16 I)

Following this recommendation, the GA adopted resolution A/RES/48/157 requesting the Secretary-General to appoint an independent expert to undertake a comprehensive study on the impact of armed conflict on children.[31] Graça Machel was appointed and after intensive research and field work, she submitted her report, entitled *Impact of Armed Conflict on Children* (A/51/306) to the GA. In short, her 1996 report not only revealed the extent of suffering of child victims of armed conflict, but it also outlined a comprehensive global agenda for action. In response to this report, the GA adopted A/RES/51/77 recommending that the Secretary General appoint a Special Representative to the Secretary-General (SRSG) on the impact of armed conflict on children to follow up on and implement Machel's findings. In 1997, Olara Otunnu was appointed as the first SRSG, and by June of 1998, Otunnu had been invited to informally brief the SC. Later that year the SC held its first debate on children and armed conflict.

What was significant about this whole process was the level of involvement of the Committee, and thus, UNICEF and the group of NGOs that contributed to the

76   Women and children

Committee's work.[32] The push from this confluence of actors led to the appointment of Machel and contributed to her study. They also maintained an active relationship with the GA, particularly through the process of identifying a need for a SRSG. The Committee continues to have a strong working relationship with the SRSG even today. Also, related to this process was the Committee's, UNICEF's, and related NGO's pivotal role in pushing for and in drafting the Optional Protocol to the Convention on the Rights of the Child on Involvement of Children in Armed Conflict.[33] Each of these benchmarks served to further entrench the issue of children within the UN, and UN's work in peace and security more specifically.

In other words, the benchmarks institutionalized (and were institutionalized by) the role of UNICEF and NGOs in this process. UNICEF was the first UN agency to provide official funding and support to NGOs as well as one of the first to grant NGOs consultative status at the UN (Reimann 2006: 50, 56). This long-standing, symbiotic relationship laid the groundwork for a coordinated, inter-organizational approach to addressing the needs and rights of children. These groups began as organizations committed to development and humanitarian services for the world's children, and now they function from a human rights legal and institutional base through their relationships with the CRC Committee, the GA, the SRSG, and the SC. Thus, their security framework can be understood as one that effectively bridges the gap between humanitarian norms and human rights law. This framework pushes then for a modification of Oestreich's UNICEF/CRC model. In looking at children and armed conflict, the model is better understood as a NGO-UNICEF/CRC model.[34] It is from this expanded model, that we can understand the six SC resolutions on children and armed conflict as a particular discourse developing real *institutional force*.

What children can tell us about women

This process and particular institutional model for children and armed conflict is very different from the one surrounding WPS. Although the process leading up to the Convention on the Elimination of all Forms of Discrimination against Women (CEDAW) was similar to the CRC, the drafting and ratifying processes were quite distinct.[35] CEDAW was preceded by a GA declaration adopted in 1967 much in the way that the 1959 Declaration on Children's Rights preceded the CRC. And while gender equality was part of the UN Charter and the UDHR, there was no specific commitment made by UN member states to the rights of women until the drafting of CEDAW in 1979. CEDAW did not receive unanimous adoption by the GA, and although it is now ratified by 185 countries (approximately 90%) the ratification process was not nearly as quick as that for the CRC.[36] And while the timing differences between the two conventions, one during the height of the Cold War and one immediately following the fall of the Berlin Wall, certainly offers some explanation here, much more than temporal factors explain the relationship between CEDAW and the various components of the UN's gender architecture.

Women and children 77

The first world conference on women held in Mexico City in 1975 was significant in laying the groundwork for CEDAW. The Plan of Action adopted at Mexico City by the 133 governments represented there mandated the drafting of CEDAW, and this task became the focus of the Commission on the Status of Women (CSW) during the Decade for Women (1975–1985) that followed. Working groups within the CSW prepared the text of the Convention in 1976, which then went through a process of extensive deliberations with the Third Committee of the GA for the next three years.[37] The nature of the international conferences for women in 1975, 1980, and 1985 and the structure of the CSW, however, differed significantly from the World Summit for Children (1990) that coincided with the CRC becoming international law and the institutional structure of UNICEF. The World Summit for Children was the largest gathering of world leaders (71 heads of state and government and 88 other senior officials) assembled at the UN up to that point in history.[38] None of the world conferences on women have been summits and were, therefore, not attended by world leaders. Further, the CSW is a reporting body that makes recommendations to the UN Economic and Social Council (ECOSOC), arguably one of the weakest and overstretched organs of the UN system. Thus, the CSW was not in a position to push for any sort of institutionalized role in CEDAW.[39] Along these lines, CEDAW does not specify one specialized agency to contribute to its implementation, nor does it allow for "other competent bodies" (NGOs) to participate in CEDAW's committee work. These initial structural shortcomings or disconnects demonstrate just how far women's activism within the UN is from the NGO–UNICEF/CRC model.

The UN Development Fund for Women (UNIFEM) was also part of the CEDAW process, but just barely. The organization was in its infancy during the late 1970s. In 1977, thirty-three countries pledged $3.5 million allowing the GA to establish the Voluntary Fund for the UN Decade for Women (VFDW). Eight years later, with GA Resolution 39/125 the Voluntary Fund became permanent and renamed as UNIFEM. While this permanent status was significant, it was limited in that UNIFEM was established as an entity associated with the UN Development Program. This location of UNIFEM under UNDP's mandate means that UNIFEM has no independent funding base or national chapters the way that UNICEF does (although UNDP has country offices through which UNIFEM can operate). The relative nascence of UNIFEM in terms of drafting and adoption of CEDAW seemed to contribute to the lack of coordination and mobilization of advocates and resources.[40] The drafting of CEDAW largely took place in 1978 and 1979, just as VFDW was getting off the ground. In General Assembly Resolution 39/125 (1984) making the Fund for Women a permanent agency, the text makes a very weak reference regarding the Fund's relevancy to CEDAW. It states, "As appropriate, the activities of the Fund may be drawn to the attention of the Committee on the Elimination of Discrimination against Women" (GA 39/125 1984: para 14).

As of 2008, UNIFEM continues to lack full autonomy and operates as one of the smallest UN funds.[41] UNIFEM's weak institutional and financial status since its

78   *Women and children*

inception has prevented it from fully engaging in the drafting and more importantly implementation of CEDAW. As many of my interviewees reinforced, "resources are severely limited here at UNIFEM. There is just not enough human resources or otherwise to be as engaged in CEDAW as we need to be" (UNIFEM official, 2006). In short, although UNIFEM operates as a fund as UNICEF does, UNIFEM was not given a specific role in the Convention the way that UNICEF is in the CRC.[42] Furthermore, UNIFEM has been unable to bring the sort of systematic evidence and statistical reporting to the Committee the way that UNICEF does with it annual reports. In this sense, UNICEF was better equipped in that the fund had been around longer, had autonomous operational status, and was better resourced.[43]

The evidence and work that is being done on women's rights and gender equality is spread out among the various organizations dedicated to women's rights and gender equality within the UN system. Currently, there are several agencies focusing exclusively on women's issues that are under-staffed and under-resourced and competing amongst each other for funding.[44] The noticeable disconnect between CEDAW's committee work and UNIFEM's programming is reflective of the fragmented and often counterproductive gender architecture of the UN system.[45] As one UNIFEM official lamented regarding the implementation of SCR 1325 throughout the UN system:

> So what I am saying is that behind 1325 there is a vast, complex architecture of evidence, argument and advocacy which is still in its infancy ... the quality is very poor because there's not enough evidence of what's worked because there is not enough operational.
>
> (Interview, 2006)

This criticism of the UN's gender architecture and the lack of comprehensive information-sharing and evidence-based research stand in sharp contrast to the long-term, systematic data collection by UNICEF, *the* agency for children within the UN.[46]

From these financial, structural, and capacity-driven challenges for those advocating for women's rights and gender equality within the UN, it is not surprising then that CEDAW committee did not push for an independent expert to undertake a comprehensive study of the impact of armed conflict on women the way that the CRC committee did for children through the GA. Even with the passage of SCR 1325, there was no SC or GA support for such a report, and UNIFEM was compelled to sponsor its own independent expert's assessment (OSAGI official, 2006). While SCR 1325, "*Invites* the Secretary-General to carry out a study on the impact of armed conflict on women and girls, the role of women in peace-building and the gender dimensions of peace processes and conflict resolution," and "*further invites* him to submit a report to the Security Council on the results of this study" (S/1325/2000), there is a significant difference between an independent expert's assessment and a SG report in terms of critical analysis.[47] The fact that the UN SC and GA did not sponsor a comparable report by an independent expert on women in armed conflict reflects how the

UN's rhetorical commitment to gender equality is not followed through with policy implementation. This also explains why the SG has not established an office for an SRSG on women and armed conflict as was done for children.[48]

In many ways, the process of codifying children's rights within the UN and getting such issues on the agenda of the SC highlights the unique temporal deficiencies and institutional obstacles that women face. It also demonstrates what children's advocates seem to do well, particularly in terms of bridging the gap between development services and security responsibilities within the UN system. This bridge seems to be largely dependent upon linking the humanitarian demands to the human rights framework in terms of discourse, legal mechanisms, research and analysis, and of course, policy-making. Tracing the process on children and armed conflict, especially in terms of the NGO-UNICEF/CRC model, highlights how such inter-agency coordination allows for such bridges to be built and how fruitful these bridges can be. This model should be seen as part of the ongoing and interactive "process of political globalization which has involved a symbiotic relationship of mutual growth and interdependence among states, IGOs, and NGOs" (Reimann 2006: 63).

This process should also be understood as evolutionary, where the international community continues to improve upon existing policies and approaches. It is a learning and building process. Thus, the last section of this chapter takes a closer look at the six resolutions on children and armed conflict and how these resolutions have developed over time, one building on the other. Such an analysis will allow us to better understand where women stand and just how far "WPS" have to go in terms of implementation and accountability.

Content analysis of Security Council Resolutions

From 1999 to 2005, the UN Security Council adopted six resolutions on the thematic issue of children and armed conflict. Comparing and contrasting these resolutions, one can easily identify the ways in which the Council has been increasingly progressive with each resolution by outlining more detailed measures to protect the rights of the child during and after conflict. According to the Institute for Defense Studies and Analysis (IDSA) this series of resolutions has meant "stronger enforcement of international standards" signifying "a calibrated attempt to attach prominence to the children and security discourse within the Security Council's peace and security agenda" (Podder 2006: 2). To better understand this evolution as well as its comparison with the now two SC resolutions on women, this chapter now turns to a discourse coding scheme developed to analyze the content of these SC resolutions.

Methodology

In order to more systematically analyze the six resolutions on children and armed conflict, I created a simple coding scheme that identified five categories of linguistic change. The schematic clusters words and phrases from the resolutions'

80   *Women and children*

Table 4.1 Content analysis for Security Council Resolutions

Category of change	*Selected code words/phrases referenced*
Substantive details	child protection advisers (CPAs); country-specific situations (or resolutions); small arms; recruitment of children; child soldiers
International legal precedent	UN Charter; the Convention on the Rights of the Child (CRC); the Geneva Conventions; Rome Statute; violation of international law
The protection-based approach	protection of children; child-protection comprehensive strategy (or framework or assessment); international norms
Security framework for effective argument	maintenance of international peace and security; long-term consequences for durable peace, security, and development
Accountability mechanisms and procedures	development of action plans; compliance; implement/implementation; monitoring and reporting mechanism; role of governments; responsibility of states; targeted and graduated measures against non-compliant actors; specification on Secretary-General report

text into themes as a heuristic tool, rather than an objective measure.[49] As Table 4.1 indicates, these categories identify change in terms of the details for substantive issues, the links to legal documents as a means of establishing precedent, the development of the protection-based approach for action, the utilization of the security framework to make an effective argument, and the implementation of accountability mechanisms and procedures. As will be explained below, several of these categorizations are based on interviews with UN officials and their notions of what was important language in SC resolutions. Other categories attempt to define the way in which these resolutions frame the issue of children and armed conflict. None of the categories are designed to be mutually exclusive or comprehensive in terms of explanatory values. Their purpose is simply to illustrate various ways that SC resolutions develop over time.

Analysis of inventory

The language, content, and approach of SC resolutions on children and armed conflict clearly changes from the first one in 1999 to the most recent one in 2005 (see Figure 4.1). Overall, the coding reveals upward trends in the development of accountability mechanisms and the protection-based approach as well as in the substantive details. Further, framing the protection of children's rights as an effective means for the promotion and protection of international peace and security (the security framework) remains a constant in all six resolutions. Somewhat counterintuitively, Figure 4.1 indicates that the latter three resolutions make fewer connections to international legal documents and treaties as compared to the first three resolutions. One UN official explains this downward trend by pointing out how well the first three resolutions establish the legal precedent needed for the

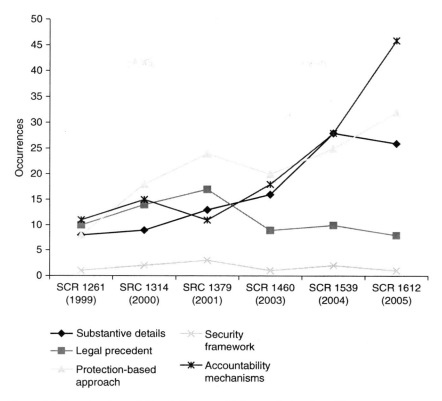

Figure 4.1 Security Council Resolutions on children and armed conflict.

Security Council to act and how repeating those international legal obligations in the latter three resolutions was not perceived as necessary (Interview, 2008).

For example, the first resolution, 1261 (1999), clearly identifies the issue of children and armed conflict as a global priority, to be addressed by the SC rather than by regional or national bodies alone. While this resolution does not invoke Chapter VII of the UN Charter, it does squarely situate this issue within the mandate of the SC by expressing, "its grave concern at the harmful and widespread impact of armed conflict on children and the long-term consequences this has for durable peace, security, and development" (S/RES/1261 para 1). The resolution also frames this issue in terms of protection and contextualizes that framework with numerous references to international laws and legal institutions. It also contains three main substantive recommendations which continue to develop throughout the entire series of resolutions: protecting children from sexual abuse during armed conflict; acknowledging the linkages between small arms proliferation and the continuation of armed conflict; and including children in disarmament, demobilization, and reintegration (DDR) programs.

82   Women and children

Security Council Resolution 1314 (2000), the second of the six, is significant in that it urges member states to sign and ratify the Optional Protocol to the UN Convention on the Rights of the Child on the involvement of children and armed conflict, which had just been adopted in May 2000. In terms of accountability, this is the resolution that really begins to engage in implementation discourse and strategy. It also builds upon the protection approach and the legal precedent of the first resolution. It even makes reference, albeit indirectly, to Chapter VII of the Charter and the responsibilities of the SC to intervene in matters that threaten international peace and security. Paragraph 9 maintains that

> the committing of systematic, flagrant and widespread violations of international humanitarian and human rights law, including that relating to children, in situations of armed conflict may constitute a threat to international peace and security, and in this regard reaffirms its readiness to consider such situations and, where necessary to adopt appropriate steps.
>
> (S/RES 1314)

While building on the protection framework and legal precedent of the first two resolutions, SCR 1379 (2001) takes the significant step of requesting the Secretary-General to attach to his annual report a list of the parties to armed conflict that recruit or use children in violation of international law in situations already on the Council's agenda, empowering the SG to name names as a means "to ensure the compliance by parties to armed conflict" (para 3d).[50] "This 'name and shame' initiative was the first time that the Council had specifically named abusive parties, and was intended to hold violators accountable for their actions" (Becker 2003: 4). UNIFEM refers to this as an "answerability mechanism" because it enables the SG to expose perpetrators (UNIFEM 2008: 98) This resolution is also the first to reference the need for "monitoring and reporting activities" (para 10c); another important step in establishing accountability.

Of all the resolutions, the fourth one seems to be the least progressive. It is a bit thin in terms of the protection framework and legal precedent, although these two categories are still present. The resolution is, however, significant in that it requested that the SG include the protection of children and armed conflict in his country-specific reports. Making the fundamental connection between the Council's thematic work and its country-specific actions is critical to integrating non-traditional security issues into the mainstream security decision-making. These SG reports are a step in this direction. Also, moving toward integration and accountability is the development of the notion of 'action plans' that emerged in this resolution. The notion of action plans emerges here and is significant because it moves in the direction of time-bound targets—an essential component to establishing compliance and accountability. Lastly, as Figure 4.1 demonstrates, SCR 1460 indicates some progress in terms of the details, particularly in terms of recruitment and use of children in armed conflict and provisions mandating child protection advisers.[51]

Women and children 83

Building upon previous resolutions, SCR 1539 (2004) calls upon parties listed in the SG's report for the use of child soldiers to prepare concrete action plans to stop the recruitment and use of children in wars. With this fifth resolution on children and armed conflict, the SC more specifically outlines a monitoring and reporting process; the resolution requests the SG to "devise urgently" an action plan for a comprehensive and systematic monitoring and reporting mechanism which would put in place a procedure for the systematic collection and channeling of information from the field through relevant bodies in the UN system. As seen in Figure 4.1, this resolution represents significant development in terms of accountability mechanisms, specific substantive detail, and the protection-based discursive approach.

Security Council Resolution 1612 (2005) is by far the most progressive resolution to date, as it "has broken new ground in terms of the institution of practical measures towards the ending of impunity of violating parties" (Coomaraswamy 2006: para 6). The resolution creates two important enforcement mechanisms: a monitoring and reporting procedure to document specific violations by state and non-state armed groups,[52] and a Working Group of Security Council members dedicated to processing and following-up on these reports. The former is a Secretariat procedure for collecting, organizing, and verifying information into reports that are then passed along to the Working Group. The monitoring and reporting mechanism has been utilized in all the situations listed in the annexes to the Secretary's General's seventh report on children and armed conflict (A/62/609-S/2007/757), including most recently in Afghanistan and the Central African Republic, where parties have been listed for the recruitment and use of children in 2007. The mechanism is located within the UN country teams in the field (with the support of UNICEF) to encourage the collection of first-hand information about the parties involved in recruiting and using children in armed conflict.[53] From this monitoring mechanism, the Working Group issues conclusions based on the reports, transmits letters, and appeals to parties engaged in violations, and reviews progress in the development and implementation of action plans by parties to armed conflict (Coalition to Stop the Use of Child Soldiers 2008). The Working Group meets bi-monthly with all fifteen members and is chaired by a permanent member of the Council; with all of this work being done by member states of the Security Council, the Working Group brings a certain level of legitimacy and authority in locating the issue of children and armed conflict into the context of the international security agenda.

SCR 1612 also led to the first actions by the SC to apply "targeted measures" against individuals specifically for recruitment and use of children as soldiers.[54] Along these lines, since SCR 1612, the Council seems more willing to include the issue of child soldiers in country resolutions. Resolution 1698 on the Democratic Republic of the Congo, adopted in July 2006, contains the landmark decision to extend the scope of possible sanctions to political and military leaders and individuals recruiting and using children in armed conflict in violation of international law. And although this monitoring and reporting mechanism is far from a streamlined

84   *Women and children*

process, it does indicate a move to a "new phase" in terms of accountability and implementation. According to a recent report from the *Coalition to Stop the Use of Child Soldiers*:

> Although the Monitoring and Reporting Mechanism is still in its early stages of development, it has already proved itself to be extremely valuable, by engaging a range of UN agencies and partners in more systematic documentation of abuses and by providing the Security Council more timely and comprehensive information to inform its action. It [SCR 1612] has also helped move the children and armed conflict agenda into a *new phase* of development; whereas in the past, the focus on children and armed conflict has been addressed as a general thematic concern, the new country reports are now helping the Security Council to focus on individual country situations and the appropriate measures that should be taken in each specific case.
>
> (2006: 2, emphasis added)

Along these lines, the Working Group has piloted country reports in seven countries: Burundi, Côte d'Ivoire, Democratic Republic of the Congo, Somalia, Sudan, Sri Lanka, and Nepal. In May 2007, the Working Group published the first two reports on grave violations being committed against children in Somalia and Uganda.[55] This type of country-specific monitoring and follow-up by UN Member States is a major advancement in expanding the Security Council's agenda to include one of the most vulnerable populations in the world. The violation framework of SCR 1612 is simple and focused. As one Member State official stated, "It is very difficult to argue against child soldiers, even for some of the narrowminded, middle-aged folks of the Security Council" (Interview 2008). Even so, it still took five SC resolutions to get to this point, a point that addresses only one of many issues (child soldiers, primarily) that children in situations of conflict face.

Overall, the analysis finds evidence of several trends when looking at the sequential SC resolutions for children and armed conflict. Most importantly, the content analysis of children and armed conflict illustrates the potential for moving this thematic issue into a new phase of implementation and action on the ground. And while the SC activity on this issue is certainly a work in progress, SCR 1612 represents a substantial step forward. A report from the Radhika Coomaraswamy, the SRSG on Children and Armed Conflict noted:

> It is important to stress that the practice of monitoring and reporting on grave child rights violations is not a new initiative. Over the past several years in particular, the United Nations system and NGO partners have gained valuable experience in monitoring and reporting, which forms the basis of the current efforts to strengthen this critical practice.
>
> (A/61/275 para 39)

As this chapter demonstrates, change within the UN system is gradual and imperfect. It took six resolutions over the course of seven years for the Council to develop implementation procedures and accountability mechanisms for children and armed conflict. From this perspective, having only two resolutions on women in armed conflict—an equally vulnerable group and certainly a group with more participation rights in post-conflict reconstruction—is grossly inadequate. As Figure 4.2 illustrates, the norm development and building process for women in armed conflict does not even compare to that of children.[56] Although using the security framework to make the case that women can effectively contribute to the establishing of peace and security is comparatively well established in the text of SCR 1325, the resolution is notably weak in terms of accountability mechanisms and connection to legal precedent. Thus, it is no surprise then that one interviewee strongly called for:

> A couple more resolutions in the SC backed by serious accountability mechanisms—backed, by which I mean reporting, naming names, review, exposure, asking for explanations. That is what accountability is. And imposing consequences for failure to meet obligations under a binding resolution and the consequences should be sanctions, or other forms of consequences.
> (UNIFEM official, 2006)

There is no SC member that serves as a focal point for SCR 1325 or a working group on WPS. The only mechanism to track the implementation of 1325 (at the

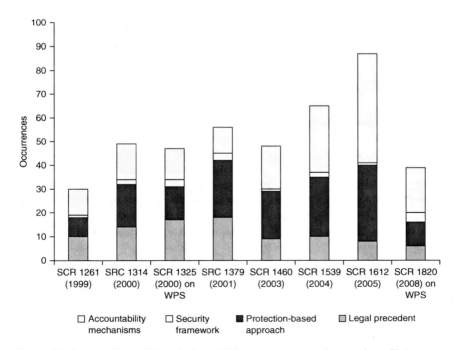

Figure 4.2 Security Council Resolutions children vesus women in armed conflict.

86   Women and children

time of this writing) is the annual open debate on WPS held every October. As a result of these open debates, the Council has adopted numerous presidential statements and press releases—many documents with no teeth.

With the security framework as a constant, Security Council Resolution 1820 seems to make some progress towards increasing accountability and implementation (see Figure 4.2). The text of the resolution emphasizes the implementation of SCR 1325, particularly in the context of executing training programs for UN peacekeeping personnel, troops, and police and enforcing a zero-tolerance policy for sexual exploitation and abuse in UN peacekeeping operations. Accountability is also enhanced with the resolution's request to the Secretary-General:

> to submit a report to the Council by 30 June 2009 on the implementation of this resolution in the context of situations which are on the agenda of the Council … which would include, inter alia, information on situations of armed conflict in which sexual violence has been widely or systematically employed against civilians; analysis of the prevalence and trends of sexual violence in situations of armed conflict; proposals for strategies to minimize the susceptibility of women and girls to such violence; benchmarks for measuring progress in preventing and addressing sexual violence; appropriate input from United Nations implementing partners in the field; information on his plans for facilitating the collection of timely, objective, accurate, and reliable information on the use of sexual violence in situations of armed conflict, including through improved coordination of UN activities on the ground and at Headquarters; and information on actions taken by parties to armed conflict to implement their responsibilities as described in this resolution . . .
>
> (S/RES/1820 para 15)

As noted in several interviews, this request for a report is important because it creates momentum throughout the UN system around the resolution especially in terms of awareness-raising. Furthermore, the report specifies what information is still needed to make the resolution more concrete, and therefore, more achievable. As one UNIFEM official argued, "The language of 1820 is already much stronger than 1325 … it's [1820] even a little adventurous. It actually calls upon the UN and its members to 'debunk myths that fuel sexual violence'" (interview 2008). With this more radical language and emphasis on prioritizing the creation and collection of solid information, many see SCR 1820 to be a critical next step in fully realizing the vision of SCR 1325 via sound and enforceable policy.

Beyond accountability, however, SCR 1820 makes fewer references to legal precedent and to a protection-based framework as compared to SCR 1325.[57] While both resolutions make equal references to "protection" and to "participation" of women during and after conflict, SCR 1820 places much less emphasis on the "rights" of women and actually refers to women as "victims" in ways that 1325 does not.[58] This finding supports the concerns that several prominent women's rights advocates within the UN system have expressed. A DPKO official argued that 1820 "takes away from 1325 in that it remarginalizes already marginalized women" and fails to address the fact that "sexual violence stems from women's lack of empowerment" (Interview, 2008). An official from OSAGI adds to this that SCR 1820 is "diversion of resources" because it creates "duplication and competition" for those "doing gender" at the UN, particularly in the context of 1325 (Interview, 2008).

While duplication and competition are valid concerns (as demonstrated in Chapter 3), most UN officials that I interviewed believed that 1820 was the next step in making 1325 a reality—maybe not a sequential step or even the most ideal step, but an important building block in the WPS agenda nonetheless. As one DPKO official pointed out, "sexual violence is a real indicator for political stability" and therefore is one way to implement SCR 1325 on the ground. For some, agreeing on basic indicators, the way UNICEF and the SC established grave children's rights violations and abuses, is a critical step in creating a database and really institutionalizing a resolution (UNIFEM official, 2008). What is also clear here is that the trend for SC resolutions on WPS will likely not be the same as those for children in armed conflict. In addition to differences with regard to framework and legal precedent, the WPS network faces significant obstacles in creating any sort of accountability mechanisms similar to those established under SCR 1612. Several interviewees, including Member State officials, acknowledged the tremendous amount of extra work that 1612 has created for an already overstretched Council.[59] One UN official maintained, "1612 prevents anything similar in terms for 1325—the mere word of another 'mechanism' is problematic for most, if not all, Security Council members" (Interview, 2008). In other words, Security Council members are not likely to commit themselves to another work-intensive accountability mechanism in the near future for 1325 or 1820.

Conclusions

Just as Chapter 3 found SCR 1325, even the notable success stories have their caveats. Despite the progress made on the issue of children and armed conflict by the UN, the overall decline in use of child soldiers is still very low, and "persistent violators" of children's rights continue to be cited in the SG's reports (Coalition 2006: 2). As one interviewee who had experience working with both UNICEF and UNIFEM argues, "In the sense that those resolutions [on children] have been around longer, yes, sure there are more mechanisms for accountability and monitoring. But do children really have any better protection? No, I'd say they are all equally unprotected" (interview, 2006). And while this is true to an extent, it is also true that "phase one" is now at least in place for protecting children. This is significant, as this is where change must start. Radhika Coomaraswamy, the SRSG for Children and Armed Conflict, articulates this process of creating a dialogue and mechanisms within the UN system in terms of phases in her most recent report to the GA, saying:

> Important advances on the children and armed conflict agenda have created a
> *strong impetus for the application of international standards and norms to*

88 *Women and children*

deliver tangible protection for children in situations of armed conflict. *Concrete measures* are being undertaken to ensure accountability of and compliance by those parties who commit grave child rights violations. It is imperative that the momentum that now exists is maintained and that the gains that have been made for children *are consolidated and further strengthened.*

(A/61/275 Summary, emphasis added)

What is most interesting about this first phase, particularly as it compares to women, is that the framework used by governmental and non-governmental advocates for children relies heavily on a protection-based framework, more so than on any sort of instrumental, value-added argument. Thus, it engages the mainstream security discourse using a language that is protection-focused and grounded within international legal norms and human rights standards. The successful engagement with the SC agenda, however, cannot be understood as a product of language alone. As this chapter has demonstrated, much of the success for this non-traditional security issue was a result of the long-term institutional presence of UNICEF, the structural and normative weight of the Convention on the Rights of the Child, the inter-agency coordination largely led by the SRSG on Children and Armed Conflict, and the timing of how these factors came together and reinforced one another. In this sense, the issue of children and armed conflict has demonstrated that progress with the SC is not impossible particularly when the necessary institutional and legal mechanisms are in place.

SCR 1325 and the WPS network frames women's rights and gender equality as both a matter of protection *and* a matter of what women bring to security and to peace processes across the globe. Many of my interviewees emphasized the latter as the component that makes SCR 1325 so radical. It is this recognition of women as agents and equal partners in establishing security and maintaining peace that sets this resolution apart from other UN documents, resolutions, and declarations on women. This functional or instrumental argument, as argued in Chapter 3 presents certain opportunities as well as some drawbacks, and from this case study of SC resolutions on children it is clear that this framework is not a sufficient factor for engaging a traditional security arena, like the Security Council. Those advocating for children in situations of armed conflict benefited not from a value-added framework, but rather from a protection approach that links humanitarian discourse with the human rights law. This raises important questions about the strategy of the WPS network and how it might be better to justify their cause in terms of women's rights rather than what the international community stands to gain by including women in the security arena. Although SCR 1820 maintains the security framework, it certainly narrows the focus of SCR 1325 by referring to "women's rights" and "gender" dimensions significantly less. Given the Children and Armed Conflict model and trend towards focusing (and narrowing) the campaign to child soldiers, this shift in focus from 1325 to 1820 as strategic move by advocates of WPS is not too surprising.

Returning to the questions posed at the beginning of the chapter, it is still not clear whether or not the inadequacies of Council action on women's issues are

Women and children   89

unique. The Security Council seems to be riddled with inconsistencies for both traditional and non-traditional security issues. It deals with conflict situations in a very ad hoc way, and is not well-equipped to address any issue systematically. What is clear from this case study, however, is that as much as women have gained in the UN system, they do face some unique structural and institutional barriers that children do not. These barriers and gaps are certainly linked to cultural and attitudinal ideas about women's role in society that are so deeply entrenched in all parts of the world.

Further, women and the security framework of 1325 present a more fundamental challenge to the way that the SC defines and does international security. Issues related to children and armed conflict, for the most part, allow the Council to maintain its practices and approaches, preserving the status quo. WPS and 1325, on the other hand, have a much greater potential for changing how the SC defines its work and mandate. By going beyond just considering the special needs of women, SCR 1325 demands that women be included in SC decision-making processes and procedures from the very beginning. This sort of inclusion is bound to shake things up, and this is a critical difference between these two cases. Advocates for children are not seeking a voice for children in the same way. Women as agents present a greater challenge to the existing power structure as they seek to alter who acts as the producers of knowledge—who defines security and what constitutes a threat to international peace and security.[60] As one UN official stated, "Women's human rights do not give you the warm fuzzies like children do" (interview 2008). From this perspective, it is no surprise that women have had a much harder time establishing themselves within the security arena. Women, as non-traditional security actors, have the greatest ability to change this distinction between what are considered traditional and non-traditional security issues.

Notes

1 Several interviewees in and around the UN spoke of the "apathy" and "fatigue" felt at the 2008 anniversary events given that the call for implementation continues to repeat itself as the theme for each anniversary since SCR 1325's passage in 2000.
2 For a comprehensive and informative website on this office and its mandate, see http://www.un.org/children/conflict/english/theoffice40.html.
3 These mechanisms and support procedures will be discussed in more detail below.
4 While there is certainly significant overlap in the two processes, particularly in terms of the rights of the girl child, the origins, language, institutional structures, and outcomes are quite different as the subsequent analysis will show. Cynthia Price Cohen (1997) demonstrates how these divergent paths go all the way back to the development of the two relevant conventions: the Convention on the Rights of the Child and the Convention to Eliminate All Forms of Discrimination Against Women.
5 It is important to note that the first section of this chapter does discuss in general terms the three SC resolutions on civilians in armed conflict (S/RES/1265, S/RES/1296, and S/RES/1674) as they are significant in detailing out the broader context of thematic issues on the Council's agenda. While there is certainly some overlap and a need to more systematically compare the process of civilians with children and with women, this analysis is restricted to a comparison of the latter two. An in-depth look at civilians, and more specifically refugees and internally displaced persons, is beyond the scope of this project.

90   Women and children

6 For more on the Security Council and the implementation of international humanitarian law, see Bourloyannis 1993.
7 For text of Resolution see http://www.un.org/documents/sc/res/1967/scres67.htm.
8 Here I find Weiss's notion of "humanitarian impulse" more convincing and reflective of reality than Edward Luck's more idealistic concept of the "humanitarian imperative."
9 This report can be accessed at http://www.securitycouncilreport.org/atf/cf/%7B65BFCF9B-6D27-4E9C-8CD3-CF6E4FF96FF9%7D/UNRO%20S23500.pdf.
10 While in *An Agenda for Peace*, Boutros Boutros-Ghali also commented that "the time of absolute and exclusive sovereignty ... has passed," the system's commitment to state sovereignty remained in tact as he failed to draw any major doctrinal conclusions from this observations.
11 Secretary-General Kofi Annan's 1998 report (S/1998/318) was actually one of the first to address "protection of civilians" as a "humanitarian imperative" within the context of explaining the cause of conflict and the promotion of durable peace. The full report can be accessed at http://www.securitycouncilreport.org/atf/cf/%7B65BFCF9B-6D27-4E9C-8CD3-CF6E4FF96FF9%7D/UNRO%20S1998%20318.pdf.
12 For more analysis comparing these thematic resolutions to the more conventional, state-based resolutions, see Wallensteen and Johansson (2004).
13 In an interview in 2004, Carol Cohn emphasized the importance of the Human Security Network (HSN) in this process. The HSN is a governmental network led by Canada, along with a few other "like-minded countries." Cohn specifically stated, "I think that the member state Human Security Network was important in at least one sense, though. Before the Human Security Network existed, so-called 'human security' concerns were seen as analytically and organizationally separate from the Security Council; they were seen as solely within the domain of ECOSOC and the Commission for Human Rights. The Human Security Network legitimized the inclusion of human security into the conceptualization of the Security Council's work; I have been told that without that step, the thematic resolutions (children and armed conflict; civilians and armed conflict; and 1325) could not have happened" (Cohn et al. 2004: 135).
14 For Robinson's speech, see http://www.un.org/Docs/sc/pvs/pv4312e.pdf.
15 For example, women's inclusion in the peace and security field was certainly augmented by the historic "Akayesu judgment" delivered by the Trial Chamber of the Rwanda Tribunal in Arusha, Tanzania in 1998, which was the first explicit recognition of rape as being both an instrument of genocide and a crime against humanity. This landmark conviction was built upon the precedent established by the International Criminal Tribunal of the Former Yugoslavia where rape was first articulated as a crime against humanity in its 1993 statute. While this process of establishing rape as a war crime was a separate from the WPS activism surrounding SCR 1325 described in this chapter, the security-based discourses adopted by both were certainly tangential given the parallel international legal arguments being made (interview 2006).
16 See for example, General Assembly Resolution 3318 (XXIX) "Declaration on the Protection of Women and Children in Emergency and Armed Conflict" (http://www.unhchr.ch/html/menu3/b/24.htm).
17 This split will be discussed in more detail below.
18 Along these lines, several interviewees talked about the need for more SC resolutions on WPS. Subsequent resolutions to better articulate and implement SCR 1325.
19 This is largely attributed to the scope and focus of the CRC. "The CRC, extrapolating from the basic principles enunciated in the earlier declarations, contains forty-one substantive articles covering a range of issue-areas, including those not specifically addressed in the earlier conventions but clearly deducible from their principles" (Ensalaco 2005: 13). From these issue-areas, it is clear that the CRC views children as the subjects rather than the objects of rights, where protection accompanies respect for his or her views and participation in family, cultural, and social life in accordance with his or her evolving capacities (CRC Article 12).

Women and children 91

20 This document is available at www.crin.org.
21 Children were briefly mentioned in Article 16 and 25 in the 1948 Universal Declaration of Human Rights, but only in very broad terms.
22 For the full text of General Assembly 1386 (XIV), see http://www.un.org/documents/ga/res/14/ares14.htm.
23 For a graphical depiction of these evolving norms, see Table 1.1 in Ensalaco (2005: 13).
24 This permanent and independent status, separate from UN Development Programme (UNDP), has allowed UNICEF to become one of the largest UN funds with an annual budget of $2 billion.
25 See for example, Black 1996 and Jolly 2001.
26 In this context as well as in terms of the Graça Machel Report, it is important to point out the importance of report-writing in the UN system. Reports are often the catalyst for UN action and for focusing the international community's attention on a particular issue. One Member-State official remarked in an interview (2008), "nothing progresses without a report on it."
27 In addition to the unique role the CRC established for UNICEF in the advocacy and implementation of children's rights, the convention was significant on a number of other fronts as well. It had the largest number of signatories on the day it was opened for signature, and it went into force more quickly than any other human rights treaty. It is the most widely ratified treaty in history; only the United States and Somalia have not yet ratified it. It is also the only treaty to use gender-specific pronouns, disaggregating rights according to sex. For more information see Cynthia Price Cohen and Per Miljeteig-Olssen, 1991. *Status Report: United Nations Convention on the Rights of the Child*, 8 N.Y.L. Sch. J. Human Rights 367.
28 In 1990, those advocating children's rights witnessed an extraordinary confluence of permissive factors that facilitated the international community's momentum on articulating and operationalizing the rights of the child, not the least of which was the end of the Cold War. It was a time of hope and optimism that meaningful international cooperation was within reach. In September 1990 for example, only weeks after the CRC entered into force, 71 heads of state and another 88 governmental representatives came together in New York City to participate in the World Summit for Children and issue a declaration and a plan of action.
29 Special Representatives to the Secretary-General can exercise great influence, as public advocates and institutional coordination and focus. Mingst and Karns maintain that "these officials can be highly influential in building awareness of issues and calling attention to specific problems such as child soldiers and violence against women. They may criticize countries openly, as a special rapporteur has done on torture in China, or work more quietly to foster constructive dialogue" (2007: 75). Their semi-autonomous, semi-permanent status affords them a certain level of authority, legitimacy, and flexibility.
30 The following NGOs contributed to the General Discussion: Friends' World Committee for Consultation, Institut Henri-Dunant, International Catholic Child Bureau, International Council of Voluntary Agencies, and International Save the Children Alliance.
31 The mandate of the GA Resolution specifically, "Requests the Secretary-General to appoint an expert, working in collaboration with the Centre for Human Rights of the Secretariat and the United Nations Children's Fund, to undertake a comprehensive study of this question, including the participation of children and armed conflict, as well as the relevance and adequacy of existing standards, and to make specific recommendations on ways and means of preventing children from being affected by armed conflicts and of improving the protection of children and armed conflicts and on measures to ensure effective protection of these children, including from indiscriminate use of all weapons of war, especially antipersonnel mines, and to promote their physical and psychological recovery and social reintegration, in particular, measures to

92 *Women and children*

ensure proper medical care and adequate nutrition, taking into account the recommendations by the World Conference on Human Rights and the Committee on the Rights of the Child; Requests Member States and United Nations bodies and organizations, as well as other relevant intergovernmental and non-governmental organizations, including the Committee on the Rights of the Child, the United Nations Children's Fund, the Office of the United Nations High Commissioner for Refugees, the World Health Organization and the International Committee of the Red Cross, to contribute to the study requested in paragraph 7 above" (A/RES/48/157 para 7–8).

32 See Breen (2003: 460–465) for a specific list of recommendations made by various NGOs to the Committee.

33 For more on the process leading up to the Optional Protocol, which was open for signatures in 2000 and entered into force in 2002, see Breen (2003).

34 This model is supported by expanding literature on the growth of and the relationship between IGOs and NGOs, in terms of the source of such growth, the many functions of these organizations, and the outcomes of this rapid growth and deepening relationships (see for example, Hertel 2006; Bob 2005; Smith 2000; Passy 1999; Boli & Thomas 1999, Keck & Sikkink 1998a; Finnemore 1996). The top-down structural and normative argument on the emergence of NGOs recently outlined by Kim Reimann (2006) is particularly applicable here and will be taken up in more detail in this chapter's analysis and conclusion.

35 Even the different titles given to these two conventions are worth noting as they seem to suggest a difference in terms of their scope.

36 During this time, there was also a unanimously passed GA resolution (1972) outlining a program of action to employ more women within the UN system (A/RES/2715(XXV)). Further, GA Resolution 3010(XXVIII) declared 1975 as International Women's Year. Both resolutions, however, were very narrowly cast and not particularly radical even in normative terms.

37 For more on the role of the CSW, see http://www.un.org/womenwatch/daw/cedaw/history.htm.

38 For more on the Summit and its outcome documents, see http://www.unicef.org/wsc/.

39 On the other hand, UNICEF, which reports to the General Assembly, utilized the CRC to put forth its agenda and push states along the path it desired (Oestreich 2007).

40 Furthermore, CEDAW's emergence in the late 1970s and early 1980s seemed to label it as a development document, separated temporally and institutionally from the security side of the UN. Until 1993, with the World Conference on Human Rights in Vienna, CEDAW even largely operated outside of mainstream human rights activity within the UN. At Vienna, those advocating for women's rights and gender equality fought to frame women's rights as human rights. For more on this rights-based framework, see Bunch (1990).

41 UNIFEM in combination with Division on the Advancement of Women and the Commission on the Status of Women have a total budget of $65 million. Compare that with UNICEF's $2 billion annual budget or even the Population Fund's (UNFPA) $400 million annual budget.

42 In a number of interviews, it became clear that UNIFEM has never felt ownership of CEDAW the way that UNICEF does with the CRC.

43 For example, the first issue of World's Women was not published until 1991.

44 These agencies include the United Nations Development Fund for Women (UNIFEM), the International Research and Training Institute for the Advancement of Women (INSTRAW), the Secretary-General's Special adviser on Gender Issues (OSAGI), and the Division for the Advancement of Women (DAW), which is where the CSW is housed.

45 It is worth noting here that the CEDAW committee is headquartered in Geneva, while UNIFEM's base office is in New York City.

46 Many interviewees referred to the problems that the current chaotic state of the UN's gender architecture presents for those working for women's rights and gender equality.

Women and children 93

Reforming the current structure into a more independent, more authoritative central UN agency for women has been subject for international negotiation since the 2005 World Summit. For more on different reform proposals being put forward, see http://www.cwgl.rutgers.edu/globalcenter/policy/unadvocacy/gea.html.

47 For a more realistic analysis of women in armed conflict see *Women War Peace: The Independent Experts'Assessment* by Elisabeth Rehn and Ellen Johnson-Sirleaf (2002). Then contrast that with the more idealistic, "best practices" approach in the Secretary-General's reports on SCR 1325 (2002, 2004). These and other reports can be found at http://www.womenwarpeace.org/toolbox/toolbox.htm.

48 The GA did establish a Special Rapporteur on Violence Against Women in 1994, but the mandate for this SRSG has been limited in terms of the security framework as the mandate is not focused on women in conflict situations alone.

49 These categories of change have undergone an inter-coder reliability test where experts in the field were asked to match the words and phrases selected with the thematic clusters provided. These tests confirmed the validity and integrity of this coding schematic.

50 These lists have the potential to expand what countries and conflict situations become part of the Security Council agenda. The SG's list is separated into Annex I and II. Annex I lists parties that recruit or use children in situations of armed conflict already on the SC agenda. Annex II lists parties that recruit or use children in situations of armed conflict not on the official agenda. For example, Annex II addresses the conflict situations in Colombia, Myanmar, Nepal, the Philippines, Sri Lanka, and Uganda. Annex II has been controversial among SC members. For many activists, however, this Annex has potential to expand the SC agenda in a positive, more comprehensive way.

51 This is not surprising given the relative success the transnational campaign to stop the use of child soldiers in the late 1990s and the Optional Protocol to the CRC on Children and Armed Conflict entering into force in 2002. For more on this see Geske and Ensalaco 2005.

52 These violations include killing and maiming of children, the recruitment, and use of child soldiers, attacks against schools and hospitals, rape or other grave sexual violence against children, abduction of children, and the denial of humanitarian access for children.

53 Several governments such as Uganda, the DRC, and Sri Lanka seem increasingly willing to work with the UN country teams in developing action plans. In Côte d'Ivoire, the military wing of the rebel New Forces (*Forces Armées des Forces Nouvelles*, or FAFN) and four militia groups have signed a regional action plan to end recruitment of children. For the most update information on these plans, see www.securitycouncilreport.org and http://www.un.org/children/conflict/english/securitycouncilwgroupdoc.html.

54 See S/RES/1572 concerning Côte d'Ivoire's decision to subject Martin Kouakou Fofie to certain accountability measures.

55 These reports can be found at http://www.crin.org/resources/infoDetail.asp?ID=13477&flag=report and http://www.crin.org/resources/infoDetail.asp?ID=13478&flag=report.

56 This figure has a different key than Figure 4.1. I have omitted the substantive categories because the words and phrases in this category are not applicable or relevant to the resolution on women.

57 One interviewee suggested that the dearth of legal precedent referred to in SCR 1820 can largely be understood by looking at the Permanent Member of the SC who sponsored the legislation—the United States. Given the United States' approach to international law, particularly in terms of not being party to CEDAW, the CRC or the ICC, the lack of legal rhetoric in 1820 is not too surprising (interview, 2008).

58 It is worth noting here that none of the six resolutions on children and armed conflict refer to children as victims.

59 This workload and its challenges were publicly acknowledged in the Security Council's Working Group Annual Report. The final paragraph of the document reads, "While all

94   *Women and children*

these developments are positive, they have naturally entailed a significant excess work-load for the Group that may have adversely affected the organization of its activities and prevented it from monitoring the implementation of its conclusions more methodically. It should be noted in this regard that one of the points on which the Working Group experts seemed to agree in their discussions on working methods is the need, in future, to provide the Working Group with more logistical support, particularly Secretariat services in such areas as the preparation of summary records of formal meetings, the preparation of draft conclusions, internal and external document transmission and administrative follow-up of the measures contained in the Group's conclusions, as is done for some of the other subsidiary bodies of the Security Council" (S/2008/455 para58). This report can be accessed at http://daccessdds.un.org/doc/UNDOC/GEN/N08/420/87/PDF/N0842087.pdf?OpenElement.

60 It is important to note here that the CRC does grant children a certain level of agency in terms of rights; however, children as agents have a different relationship with the existing structure than adult women as agents.

5 The United Nations Development Fund for Women

Working its way into the security sector

> The unique identity of UNIFEM calls for flexibility in order to retain its capacity to innovate. This implies the ability to take risks ...
>
> UNIFEM Consultative Committee, 16th Session

> Now, as a consequence of that we have tried very hard and still need to do a lot more work to bring convincing gender analysis into policy language and policy approaches into hard areas of security reform, and I think the most promising one is security sector reform in post-conflict context—so disarmament, shrinking of armies/merging of armies, reestablishing rule of law by some type of police force. And there is a lot of work to be done there and it's only just starting from a gender perspective. No one to my mind has done credible, evidence-based work on how to bring gender equality issues into security sector reform.
>
> UNIFEM Official, December 2006

As the previous chapter maintains, just engaging in the security discourse with traditional security actors such as the UN Security Council does not necessarily guarantee a genuine commitment to women by the international community in conflict and post-conflict situations. Contrasting the case of children with women in terms of SC action illustrates the importance of institutional structures and legal frameworks in establishing and maintaining momentum for these marginalized groups. The impact, however, of securitizing women's rights—or humanizing security—cannot be limited to an analysis of SC activity or lack thereof. Given the intimate relationship between the United Nations Development Fund for Women (UNIFEM) and the Women, Peace and Security (WPS) network and Security Council Resolution (SCR) 1325 in particular, it is critical to take a closer look at historical progression of this organization committed to women's empowerment in global development. Tracing this organization's history provides important insight into "other ways" that women's issues and gender equality concerns can benefit from the security discourse, by working their way into traditional security arenas at least to broaden, if not transform, the ways those arenas define and enact international security policy.[1]

96 UN Development Fund for Women

In conducting the interviews for this research, it became evident that even though the security discourse can be limiting (or at worst, non-emancipatory) in certain contexts, the discourse can create opportunities for new strategic partnerships and fresh insights into longstanding issues. In this sense, the WPS network and the campaign surrounding SCR 1325 has at times served as a permissive variable allowing UNIFEM entry points into "seemingly" unchartered territory—thus, the focus of this chapter. As seen in Chapter 1, UNIFEM has been part of the WPS network from the beginning and has been instrumental in bringing SCR 1325 to local populations. UNIFEM however, was largely created to deal with women's roles and empowerment in development, not necessarily in the realm of international security.[2] This raises important questions about how a *development* fund—one of the smallest development funds at that—came to be involved in the international security arena. In other words, how did the security framework serve as an entry point for UNIFEM into policy circles they had long been excluded from? And what has this language meant for UNIFEM's work?

I explore these questions here by looking at UNIFEM's historical legacy and how this development organization broadened its mandate to include a division deicated to *Governance, Peace, and Security*. I then examine UNIFEM's strategic framework for 2006 through 2009 where, for the first time, security sector reform is defined as a main focus for the organization. By looking at a number of in-country projects, the analysis demonstrates that although Security Sector Reform (SSR) is a relatively new term in UN circles and place of engagement for UNIFEM, the substance of the reforms being pushed for by UNIFEM is not entirely new. While the language, the actors, and subsequent partnerships involved might be new in terms of UNIFEM's usual collaborations, many of the issues being addressed, such as violence against women, are fundamentally the same and are simply being reframed in terms of security. This reframing of older concerns is a tenet of the literature on human security. The chapter ends by contextualizing UNIFEM's initiatives in SSR within this theoretical paradigm, as many of UNIFEM's most recent reports, statements, and publications refer specifically to *women's human security*. In short, this chapter emphasizes the way the security framework has created discursive opportunities despite the structure, by "formulating and articulating a definition or agenda of women, peace and security, creating a space to debate those concepts and demonstrate their importance, and ensuring that the link is made between the lives, needs and experiences of women" (Cohn et al. 2004: 134).

UNIFEM: the product of the development decades

In order to understand the significance of UNIFEM's involvement in the WPS network and SCR 1325, it is important to begin with UNIFEM's mandate and its original, and notably narrower focus on development and the poorest women in society. This story begins in the context of the 1960s with the number of member states in the UN multiplying as a result of decolonialization and with the increasing disillusionment regarding the 'trickle-down' benefits of modernization policies that resonated with many people throughout the developing world.[3] During this

UN Development Fund for Women 97

time, with the publication of the landmark volume, *Women's Role in Economic Development* by the Danish economist Ester Boserup and with the rebirth of the women's movement in the West, the international community began to take notice of women's centrality in productive processes. These key historical factors "interfaced in 1970 to create the 'women and development [WID] concept, and later the movement" (Snyder 1995: 18). While WID had roots in the developing and the developed world, it ultimately found a home in the UN (Jain 2005).[4] In the words of Dr. Lucille Mair, one the founding members of UNIFEM's Consultative Committee (CC), "I give great credit to the United Nations. It helped. It provided the political and organizational framework for the international feminist movement at a fundamental stage of its development" (1986, as cited by Snyder 1995: 18).

Five years after the WID concept had reached the UN's global agenda, a fledgling movement came into being in Mexico City at the 1975 World Conference of the International Women's Year (Antrobus 2004). Delegates were very specific in demonstrating how "the huge amount of productive work performed by women in agriculture, fuel supply, self-help community improvements and the like, remained nearly invisible to most developing co-operation organizations" and therefore, they were effective in demanding more resources for improving women's situations worldwide (Snyder 1995: 26). Specifically, donations from Princess Ashraf Pahlavi of Iran and from the UK allowed for the creation of the Voluntary Fund for the Decade for Women, 1976–1985 (VFDW).[5] As the movement's financial instrument, it was seen as a way "to ensure that women share equitably in the growing prosperity" and "to help women in the poorest countries, and especially rural women … in particular for small innovative 'grassroots' activities" (Summerskill 1975, as cited by Snyder 1995).[6] By the end of 1976, the General Assembly adopted Resolution 31/133 officially establishing VFDW's mandate stating:

> The resources of the Fund should be utilized to supplement activities in the following areas … priority being given to the related programmes and projects of the least developed … countries [and] special consideration should be given to those which benefit rural women, poor women in urban areas and other marginal groups of women, especially the disadvantaged.
>
> (A/RES/31/133)[7]

Thus, began the "development work" of the fund with its focus on the world's most marginalized and deprived women.[8]

General Assembly Resolution 31/133 also created a Consultative Committee (CC) on the Fund, which functioned "as a unique system for intergovernmental guidance" (Snyder 1995: 28). The resolution "requests the President of the General-Assembly to select, with due regard to regional distribution … five Member States, each of which should appoint a representative to serve" on the CC (A/RES/31/133). As the first director of the Fund observes:

> this unusual Committee came to serve as a protective buffer between the fund secretariat and the bureaucracy; it also provided a way for educating

98   UN Development Fund for Women

members of the General Assembly about the work of the Fund and thereby helped raise contributions to it. Technically, the Committee was only advisery; actually, it could mobilize ...

(Snyder 1995: 28)

This committee was instrumental in developing a very dynamic role for the fund, particularly in laying the foundation for the Fund's future work to go beyond development circles, which at the time was constructed in economic terms.[9]

This foundation goes back to the CC's first meeting when they adopted three principles that continue to guide the Fund today. The first principle emphasized decentralization, particularly in terms of regions noting that women's needs and concerns vary drastically from one culture to the next. Regional divisions still guide much of the Fund's work today. The second principle prioritized small field projects in order to give the poorest women in the least developed countries an opportunity. The third and most important standard set forth by the CC was that the Fund would be a *catalyst for change*. These principles were meant to distinguish the Fund from other funds and agencies, to keep the Fund's focus on low income women, and to establish policies and standards that were flexible enough to be able to support innovative and experimental work. Ultimately, this meant funding projects that were likely to attract other sources of support or become self-sufficient in their own right. Over time, the meaning of the term catalyst was broadened in the way that the Fund attracted additional financing, institutionalized projects, partnered with governments and other organizations (governmental and non-governmental), and established programming teams to work in the field providing project and institutional support.[10] In this sense, the Fund earned a reputation "as a participant as well as an adviser, and that was the source of its clout" (Snyder 1995: 37).

This role as catalyst was a defining feature of the VFDW when the General Assembly made it a permanent structure of the UN system in 1984. Eight years after the creation of the VFDW, the international community (despite some resistance) recognized an urgent need to expand the Fund's role as a specialized resource for development. Having found that the initial arrangements for the Fund in the UN Secretariat proved cumbersome at best because the Secretariat was not set up for financial and technical cooperation, the GA gave it a new institutional home. Granting the Fund greater (although not complete) autonomy, it was established as a "separate and identifiable entity in autonomous association with United Nations Development Programme (UNDP), which will play an innovative and catalytic role in relation to the United Nations over-all system of development cooperation" (A/RES/39/125).[11] Thus, the General Assembly prioritized UNIFEM's role as a catalyst in ensuring women's roles in mainstream development activities by supporting projects and programs that were new, innovative, and even experimental. Such a mandate allowed the fund to take risks, create opportunities, and open new doors for women as it began to define itself in coming years. Margaret Mwangola, the Director of the Kenya Water for Health Organization (KWAHO), testified to the fund's catalytic role, "The UNIFEM funding gave us status in the donor community world and has opened doors for us in numerous places, including other UN agencies" (1993, as cited in Snyder 1995: 40).

The 1990s: a time for a broadening agenda

This "door-opening function" is a mechanism that has come to define UNIFEM, particularly throughout the 1990s. This began with UNIFEM's involvement in the campaign to establish, "women's rights as human rights."[12] UNIFEM was critical in bringing Roxanna Carrillo to the Fund as a consultant to write a report demonstrating how violence against women was in fact a development issue, essentially linking the human rights and development frameworks. In her own words:

> I was hired by UNIFEM to lay the foundations and put together an argument—a policy paper that would look at the issues of violence as part of the development framework. At that point, I am talking late 80s, early 90s, when violence was not considered part of the development discourse. Therefore, UNIFEM could not fund initiatives or programs that dealt with violence against women. We were in a more traditional economic development mindset—micro-credit, income generation. That was the predominant discourse. So when UNIFEM hired me, they said we are faced with demands coming from our program countries, from the ground, to address violence against women in various contexts. The question was, how do we make an argument to the member-states and our board demonstrating how these issues are a total betrayal of the mandate of the organization. It's funny to think about— here we are 15 years later, 17 years later to be exact, and for them it was totally unheard of to try to even put $20,000 into a project that women's groups thought was important, even if they were economically deprived, living in the slums, or whatever. It was not something UNIFEM could have even conceived of as part of the funding. So that's how the whole genesis of the work on violence began within a development organization, like UNIFEM.
>
> (Interview, 2006)

In essence, the case was made that when it comes to the many forms of violence suffered by the world's women, women's lack of economic independence—from the global to the local—lies at the heart of the problem. Carrillo's policy paper (1992) with UNIFEM combined with Charlotte Bunch's (1990) seminal piece on women's rights as human rights helped in mandating a broader focus for UNIFEM in the early 1990s.

In addition to UNIFEM's approach to framing violence against women as a development and human rights issue in the early 1990s, the Fund also established African Women in Crisis (AFWIC). This umbrella program was established to facilitate a gender-sensitive response to societies and peoples impacted by complex emergencies in Africa. This meant protecting and empowering women in crisis situations as well as working to place women at the center of the search for solutions (Bagozzi 1997); thus, the dual strategy of protection and participation

100   UN Development Fund for Women

began to emerge.[13] It became clear from the projects that UNIFEM was sponsoring and partnering with, however, that crisis situations were largely defined as conflict and post-conflict situations and that UNIFEM's aim was to highlight the different ways in which women can be empowered to become leaders at all stages of the peace-building process.[14] Sanam Anderlini, a long-time consultant for UNIFEM, states, "Since 1993, the fund has supported a comprehensive programme aimed at cultivating the leadership and peace-making skills of women in all phases of the conflict and peace continuum" (Anderlini 2000: 1–2). Laketch Dirasse, the UNIFEM official who first managed this program, states that UNIFEM recognized the need for a "well coordinated approach to promoting women as agents of reconciliation and peace" (Dirasse 1999: 14).[15] Thus, she maintains that "AFWIC gave birth to UNIFEM's engagement with women, peace, and security" (interview, 2006). Dirasse also emphasizes that security in this context refers to the "security of women's personhood"—a notion that accounts for security at the "individual and bodily" level.[16]

Throughout the 1990s, the UNIFEM/AFWIC umbrella program supported targeted women's peace projects and associations in Mozambique, Ghana, Ivory Cost, Liberia, Sudan, Zimbabwe, Rwanda and Burundi, Senegal, and Somalia (Snyder 2000; UNIFEM 2001–02).[17] According to Secretary-General Boutros Boutros-Ghali, "Through the programme, UNIFEM has formed partnerships with emerging African women's peace initiatives and networks in order to build a strong women-led coalition for peace and development" (A/50/410 1995: 12). Even more, the program organized the Fifth African Regional Conference on Women in 1994 in Dakar, Senegal, which was the regional preparatory meeting for the UN World Conference on Women in Beijing in 1995.[18] At this forum, peace activists from eleven African countries came together in a "peace tent" to call attention to women's traditional peacemaking roles and their rights to participate equally in phases of the peace process (Snyder 2000).[19] These preparatory meetings were significant; "much of what was accomplished in Beijing has been credited to the work of women's NGOs and the delegates from the South, especially Africans who had coordinated prior to Beijing at the regional PrepCom ... " (Schechter 2005: 147). Undoubtedly, the UNIFEM/AFWIC partnership and programming significantly impacted these regional meetings that preceded the Fourth World Conference on Women.

From here the door was open for participants at the Beijing Conference to debate and articulate the links between the development framework, the rights-based framework, and the security framework.[20] Among other achievements, the Fourth World Conference for Women and the resulting Platform for Action symbolized international consensus on the centrality of women's issues and gender equality to maintaining international peace and security. The *Report on the Fourth World Conference on Women* (A/CONF.177/20/Rev.1) refers to security 49 times; some of the highlights include:

- Recognizing that the achievement and maintenance of peace and security are a precondition for economic and social progress, women are increasingly

UN Development Fund for Women 101

establishing themselves as central actors in a variety of capacities in the move-ment of humanity for peace. Their full participation in decision-making, conflict prevention and resolution and all other peace initiatives is essential to the realization of lasting peace (para 23).

- The advancement of women and the achievement of equality between women and men are a matter of human rights and a condition for social justice and should not be seen in isolation as a women's issue. They are the only way to build a sustainable, just and developed society. Empowerment of women and equality between women and men are prerequisites for achieving politi-cal, social, economic, cultural, and environmental security among all peoples (para 41).

- In a world of continuing instability and violence, the implementation of coop-erative approaches to peace and security is urgently needed. The equal access and full participation of women in power structures and their full involvement in all efforts for the prevention and resolution of conflicts are essential for the maintenance and promotion of peace and security. Although women have begun to play an important role in conflict resolution, peace-keeping and defense and foreign affairs mechanisms, they are still underrepresented in decision-making positions. If women are to play an equal part in securing and maintaining peace, they must be empowered politically and economically and represented adequately at all levels of decision-making (para 134).

These important conceptual links served as the underpinnings for the "Women and Armed Conflict" category outlined in the Beijing Platform for Action.[21] It was one of twelve such categories that identified strategic objectives and subse-quent action.[22] The report and the Platform for Action—both approved by governments at the conference—reflect "a new agenda" whereby the interna-tional community "has broken free from the narrow conception of security as something largely measured in military terms" and instead "charting a new path to peace, based on the recognition that the security of individuals is in the long run not to be separated from the security of States" (Finnbogadóttir 1995: 199). UNIFEM, in collaboration with the Commission on the Status of Women and countless NGOs were particularly influential both prior to the conference in the preparatory meetings and during the conference itself (Schechter 2005; West 1999).[23] Thus, UNIFEM was able to articulate in these meetings and outcome documents the language necessitating the organization to broaden its work beyond development and human rights circles, portraying themselves as both relevant and essential to peace and security issues.

UNIFEM officially enters the security scene

As much as UNIFEM's work influenced the issues that emerged and were addressed at Beijing, the conference impacted their mandate as a development fund in significant ways as well. Through AFWIC, Beijing legitimized UNIFEM's already existing work in peace and security, opening the door for

102 *UN Development Fund for Women*

UNIFEM to further engage in the security discourse. Of particular relevance here is the trajectory of General Assembly resolutions reporting on UNIFEM's annual activities. These resolutions not only mentioned the significance of Beijing, but the tone of the resolutions shifted in the mid-1990s by including references to peace, security and conflict in ways that it had not done before.[24] For example, in GA Resolution 50/410 (1995), UNIFEM first reported "peacebuilding and conflict resolution" activity in the context of AFWIC. UNIFEM's Annual Reports also reflect a similar shift in programming from 1993 onward. By 2000, UNIFEM had established a *Governance, Peace, and Security* division.[25] The creation of this unit within the fund was supported by the General Assembly's call for "engendering governance and leadership" as one of the Fund's three thematic areas of concern (A/RES/56/130 2002).[26] By 2005, the General Assembly called attention to the strategic need to address "gender equality in democratic governance and post-conflict countries" (A/60/137).

This wording and designation is significant as it created political space and even a mandate for UNIFEM to work in conflict situations and peace processes from a security and human rights perspective rather than from a development-only framework in the context of emergency situations.[27] Along these lines, Noeleen Heyzer, former Executive Director of UNIFEM, notes the importance of "finding synergy" between three frameworks: human development, human rights and human security. She maintains that these have been "significant forces" in the way in which UNIFEM has implemented its multi-year funding framework from 2000–2003 (2004: 1). Thus, while governance—or political participation—has always been a central tenet of UNIFEM, this synergy enables UNIFEM to take their issues into a different sphere of activism with access to new partnerships and resources. This is the sphere of "post-conflict" situations where great opportunities exist to integrate women and establish gender equality mechanisms as societies attempt to rebuild after violence and destruction.[28]

In other words, for women to be equal participants in post-conflict governance, they must have personal security, and therefore, they must be part of the rebuilding process of society's security institutions. Such logic serves as the backdrop for entering into a discussion of SSR. One UNIFEM official explained the source of its focus on SSR as follows:

> There is the good governance focus in our work, which we are enjoined to take up not only because it makes sense, but because it is part of the development and human security agenda. What this requires is that we pursue gender-sensitive institutional reforms in judicial and law enforcement sectors.
>
> (UNIFEM official, interview, 2007)[29]

Simply put, women cannot be expected to participate in peace talks for post-conflict governance if their physical safety is at risk for doing so. While post-conflict insecurity exists for both women and men, there are gender-specific features that must be examined. For example, gender-based violence, particularly domestic violence, is in many countries at very high levels after conflict (Peters & Wolper 1995).

UN Development Fund for Women 103

More specifically, "domestic violence, nonpolitical rape, and sexual harassment may actually increase in post-conflict periods as returning soldiers, who are overwhelming male, redirect their aggression to their households ... " (Fitzsimmons 2005: 188). Beyond this, there are cases of women being specifically targeted when they espouse counter-cultural notions of women's rights and gender equality. The 2006 assassination of Safia Amajan, head of the Kandahar Women's Department in Afghanistan is one such tragic example. According to UNIFEM these issues break down into two fundamental concerns:

1   The challenges of building public security for women as well as men which requires gender-sensitive security sector reform. Security institutions must not only protect women and prevent gender-based violence, but should be subject to internal reforms to support gender equality.
2   The context of deepening insecurity so prevalent in transitional societies often translates into shrinking public space for women (as well as increasing violence in women's private space).

(UNIFEM 2006b: 5)

These concerns come from the

growing research and anecdotal evidence that one of the sources of human rights abuse in women's lives is the police, the military, and militias from all sides, which serves to perpetuate sexual violence and other forms of abuse including harassment for bribes, etc. It is impossible to ignore this source of trauma—a source which is supposed to be the provider of public safety.

(UNIFEM official, 2007)

Therefore, the need for making gender-sensitive changes to security institutions "arises from our own field experience and indeed directly from the populations affected by our [UNIFEM] work" (UNIFEM official, 2007). UNIFEM's engagement with state security institutions must ultimately be seen as being driven by women's demands on the ground; their ability to be taken seriously in this realm of the UN can largely be attributed to UNIFEM's ability to draw the necessary conceptual and institutional connections between development, rights, and security.

From this historical perspective, one can trace the process of UNIFEM's broadening mandate to create a division on *Governance, Peace, and Security*. As this division's most recent *Programme Framework* (UNIFEM 2005) demonstrates the Fund continues to reshape its catalytic, innovative, and experimental role through its focus on security sector reform. We now turn to UNIFEM's definition, goals, and projects under this umbrella term, Security Sector Reform.

UNIFEM establishes a distinctive role in SSR

Although security sector reform seems to be moving up on the international agenda, it remains a relatively new area of activity for both scholars and

104 UN Development Fund for Women

practitioners.[30] Various components of security sector reform have long been part of post-conflict reconstruction, but it is only recently that this umbrella term has "increasingly shaped development assistance, democracy promotion, security cooperation and post-conflict peacebuilding" (DCAF 2006: 3). With this plethora of issues and actors, it is not surprising that there is little consensus on how to define the concept of security sector reform or on what the priorities for international assistance should be (Hendrickson & Karkoszka 2005).[31]

While security sector reform often remains an ambiguous concept, there does appear to be a certain convergence around the definition put forward by the Organization for Economic Cooperation and Development (OECD). Accordingly, the security sector—or security system—refers to the state institutions and other entities with the role of ensuring security for the state and civilians. As Table 5.1 demonstrates, the security sector shares many features with public service, but is distinct in its capacity and authority to use force. Security forces include both international (external) and domestic (internal) sectors in post-conflict societies. A wide range of activities then constitute reform aimed at improving accountability mechanisms, restructuring the security apparatus for democratic governance, strengthening civilian control, rebuilding training and recruiting programs, eliminating corruption, and balancing resources spent throughout the system. From inflated armies with little or no civilian control to irregular and paramilitary groups to an overabundance of arms in private and government hands to weak or nonexistent internal security forces to an overall lack of legitimacy of the government's control of the police and military, "the remnants of wartime military and security apparatuses pose great risks to internal security" (Schnabel and Ehrhart 2005: 1). "Internal security" must be understood as going beyond establishing security for a state's ruling elite and include the security of all members of society. Thus, the need for a coherent policy approach to SSR is tremendous and complex, and nowhere is this more poignantly evident than in Iraq after the 2003 U.S.-led invasion.

SSR must be understood as having political, institutional, economic, and societal dimensions, and these are all areas where women's issues and gender equality are relevant, even fundamental, but often excluded.[32] Politically, this begins with national discussion about the role of the armed forces in society and how defense policy is made and implemented. The institutional dimensions of SSR refer to the physical and technical transformation of these structures to deal with issues of size, transparency, professionalization, skills training and recruitment. From an economic perspective, SSR must consider the budgets of the various components of the security system, particularly in terms of demobilizing combatants and retraining soldiers. Lastly, SSR must connect with civil society in order to effectively (re)establish the rule of law, trust in the security sector, and overall accountability for all members of society. In each of these dimensions, women have different experiences and unique roles to play in the transformation; further, gender roles and expectations often underlie many of these processes.[33]

UN Development Fund for Women 105

Table 5.1 The security sector

THE OFFICIAL SECURITY SECTOR	Core security actors	International/Regional forces Military/Paramilitary Police Border guards/Customs/Immigration officials Intelligence services
	Justice and Rule of Law	Judicial and penal systems
	Official oversight bodies	Government bodies Ministries of defense, justice, finance, foreign affairs and internal affairs Parliamentarians
ADDITIONAL SECURITY ACTORS	Non-statutory oversight bodies	Civil society organizations Media Donors supporting SSR
	Non-statutory security forces	Armed opposition groups Private security firms

Source: Geneva Centre for the Democratic Control of Armed Forces (DCAF), available at http://www.dcaf.ch/publications/kms/details.cfm?lng=en&id=25482&nav1=4&print=1 (accessed January 15, 2008).

Approaching SSR from this peacebuilding context, UNIFEM finds a logical entry point in terms of the WPS agenda. The former Executive Director of UNIFEM recently outlined the broad terms of this mandate follows:

> UNIFEM has worked in over 20 conflict-affected countries to bring women to the peace table and strengthen their role in peace-building and post-conflict reconstruction. Guided by the Security Council Resolution 1325 on Women, Peace, and Security our work has focused on supporting women's rights and inclusion in constitutional and legal reform and institution-building processes, as well as strengthening women's leadership and participation in decision-making.
>
> (Heyzer 2006a: 1)

SCR 1325 continues to be central and SCR 1820 builds upon this framework. As one internal UNIFEM document entitled, *Draft Concept Note* (2006), SCR 1325 is what makes security sector actors accountable to gender equality standards, and thus, in need of UNIFEM's expertise and support:

> SCR 1325 holds the global, regional, national and local security actors to a new standard of accountability during and after conflict. Because of SCR 1325 it is no longer adequate to devote all efforts to putting an end to visible hostilities without addressing the 'invisible' violence that women and children experience in the form of sexual attacks in conflict. It is no longer adequate to bring all warring parties to the peace table while excluding women who could articulate gender-specific needs for recovery and gendered interests in the peace agreement and in post-conflict governance. No longer will DDR programmes and

106   UN Development Fund for Women

other elements of security sector reform adequately build a secure post-conflict society if they focus only on demobilizing male combatants and re-organizing a masculine army. They must include women ex-combatants and ensure that the *very concept of security after a conflict is transformed* to make public and private life safe for women. These new standards of peace-making and -building must be translated into new standards for accountability systems.

(1, emphasis added)

These are just a few examples of the many UNIFEM documents addressing SSR that are justified in the context of SCR 1325, not the least of which is *UNIFEM's Programme Framework for Governance, Peace, and Security (Phase II)*.

According to this *Programme Framework* (2005), UNIFEM's first phase (2000–2005) yielded certain insights that made SSR a target area for the second phase (2006–2009). The framework maintains that "women's capacity to participate in post-conflict public decision-making is predicated on gender-sensitive reforms in electoral systems, judicial systems, security systems, legislatures, and local councils" (5). Therefore, UNIFEM is currently targeting "institutional arenas that are critical to assuring human security" (6). SSR is one of two arenas where UNIFEM programming will support "institutional reforms to hold police and other security services accountable for maintaining a gender-equal form of public safety" and will include "not only pilot efforts to alter incentive systems, performance measures, and recruitment methods, but strengthening women's participation in the democratic oversight of security forces" (6).[34] This shift in Phase II moves UNIFEM from the demand-side of accountability mechanisms to also influencing the supply-side, in recognition of "the limits of increasing level's of women's participation in peace processes ... if not supported by institutional changes to strengthen accountability for gender equality in peace and security" (7). This means institutionalizing women's participation and making efforts to address women's needs a routine and not random feature of security sector activity.

UNIFEM's programming in SSR is, as noted above, guided by SCR 1325. It is also guided by a human security approach. According to UNIFEM, the human security approach has four components: addressing critical and pervasive threats, embracing human rights, providing protection, and building on people's strengths. UNIFEM's programming here is clearly engaged in a holistic, yet individually focused security discourse that "enables it to link responses to women's security needs in conflict and post-conflict settings to longer-term efforts to address the structural basis for inequities in gender relations and to prevent conflict from doing so" (UNIFEM 2005: 23–24). This discourse has created an effective entry point for UNIFEM to target the policy-making in a traditional security arena. "The shift from state- and military-centric notions of security to a greater emphasis on human security has underscored the importance of governance issues and civilian input into policy-making" (Hendrickson & Karkoszka 2005: 19). UNIFEM has strategically (and rightly) inserted concerns about gender equality and women's rights into policy-guided discussions on human security, particularly in the context of the UN system.

UN Development Fund for Women 107

In short, UNIFEM has recognized that in order to promote women's political, social, and economic rights they must focus on this sector of society, no matter how corrupt and masculinized it is.[35] Security sector reform is often the first order of business when trying to rebuild a society after armed conflict, and as one interviewee argued, women must be integrated at the very beginning of the peace process, "where we have an entry point for the rule of law" (UNFPA Specialist on Women in Armed Conflict, October 2006). SSR provides this access early on in the process into an arena that women in most societies have been excluded from. Further, the security sector has significant influence in setting the parameters of what post-conflict security will be and how the rule of law will be implemented. In other words, there is the potential for a redefining of security at the national level so that gender-based violence, domestic violence, and other forms of "private" violence are taken seriously as public offenses. Further, this potential allows women to be a part of this process in terms of defining and enforcing security. Given women's distinct experiences in general during conflict, their inclusion in SSR has tremendous potential to raise new questions and bring new issues to the negotiations.[36] This has implications for relationships between civilians and security forces as well as the behavior and relationships among security forces at all levels.

Although UNIFEM is engaged in a number of different activities that fall under the umbrella of SSR, not the least of which is the push for gendering disarmament, demobilization, and reintegration programs (DDR), I am concerned here with UNIFEM's recent involvement in reforming local police units.[37] Projects and programming targeting an (re)emerging police force is new terrain for UNIFEM in terms of many of the actors involved. Thus, policing serves as a useful analysis for understanding how the security discourse functions as a door opening mechanism. By examining a handful of UNIFEM country-specific pilot projects for policing, it becomes clear that even though the partnerships and actors involved may be new, the issues and concerns for UNIFEM are very much the same. Successfully addressing long-time issues, such as gender-based violence, in new and creative ways demonstrates the utility of the security framework for UNIFEM's work.

UNIFEM in-country policing projects[38]

As Tracy Fitzsimmons' field research demonstrates, "the ways in which international actors conceive of, train, and supply new police forces in transitional societies create a gendered, if not unequal sense of peace and security" (2005: 188). Police reform has been a recent programming focus for UNIFEM through partnerships with UNDP country offices and DPKO country missions. For UNIFEM, this has meant increasing the number of women officers and improving the police officers' capacities to address gender-based violence.[39] During 2006 and 2007, UNIFEM conducted a series of fact-finding missions on the status of local police departments in a wide-range of post-conflict societies; following these missions, UNIFEM then executed and assessed a number of pilot

108   *UN Development Fund for Women*

projects aimed at police reform in post-conflict societies. While UNIFEM is becoming increasingly aware of the many, complex obstacles in reforming this sector of society after armed conflict, there have been some signs of progress and some stories of success.

One of the most notable success stories has been the establishment of the "Gender-Based Violence Desk Office" at Rwandan National Police Headquarters in May of 2005 (UNIFEM 2007). This Office, launched under the framework of the joint UNIFEM-UNDP Project, serves a number of functions in the emerging police program in Rwanda. First, it is the place where police personnel are specifically trained to address sexual and gender-based violence, in terms of victim empowerment, psychological support, and victim/survivor protection. The Gender-Based Violence Desk Office includes an interview room to enable women to speak in confidence with a trained officer. It also offers a toll-free hotline service for reporting sexual and gender-based violence. UNIFEM has not only provided all of the technical support, but they have funded an ongoing adviser to help the Gender Desk establish itself in the system. The Office works closely with the Judicial Police Unit as well as the Community Police Unit to ensure that judicial and awareness-building projects in the community are sensitized to the many facets of sexual and gender-based violence. As one report indicates, the work has been significant in:

> enhancing the capacity of law enforcement officials to apply human rights standards to cases of violence against women, in a country racked by rape and genocide within recent memory, and where domestic violence is now particularly pervasive in the provinces, according to Rwandan Police.
>
> (Anderson 2007: 1)

The catalytic role of this Gender-Based Violence Desk Office is already emerging. UNIFEM has provided the Office with motorcycles to enable them to respond rapidly.[40] According to Deputy Commissioner of Police Mary Gahonzire, this support "has facilitated quick reporting and response to cases of violence and increased awareness among the police and community of gender-based violence as a human rights issue" (Anderson 2007: 1). With the encouragement of UNIFEM, the Office has also organized seminars and media campaigns to stimulate a broader awareness with civil society at large about the national and international legal standards applicable to all Rwanda police (O'Neill 2007a: 25–26). In a place where violence against women has long been shrouded in silence and shame, these proactive measures very clearly send the message that women's rights are a national priority. "The partnership between the police and UNIFEM ... empowers police to security their [women's] safety and emboldening women to report abuse" (Anderson 2007: 2). This partnership has the potential to construct a post-conflict society that includes sexual and gender-based violence as a threat to security, thus, redefining the notion of security among Rwandans.

Lastly, the Gender-Based Violence Desk Office has facilitated data collection on gender-based crime throughout the country. This has allowed the Rwandan

UN Development Fund for Women   109

Police to then analyze patterns of criminality and better inform decisions on training, deployment, and prevention measures throughout the police department. These measures have even emphasized how gender-based violence is not just a "women's issue" (O'Neill 2007a: 19).

UNIFEM's strategic partnerships have also had considerable success in SSR reform in the police efforts in Kosovo. Building on a long-standing relationship with the Kosovo Women's Network, UNIFEM hosted a "train the trainers" workshop for gender advisers and other security sector actors in Kosovo. Assistant Deputy Commissioner of the Kosovo Police Service, Behar Selemi, attended this workshop and has been a critical gender advocate ever since. Mr. Selemi was the senior commander that led the creation of a Gender Unit in the Kosovo Police Service in 2004. As several interviewees recounted, this type of senior-level leadership has significant value as all other officers immediately understand that they better take the issue seriously.[41] Several referred to this as the importance of establishing senior "buy-in." According to Willian O'Neill's recent fact finding mission:

> Hyseni Shala, Head of the Gender Unit of the KPS echoed this sentiment, noting that his unit, unique to the Balkans, has significant support from senior leadership. He added that the Unit uses Security Council Resolution 1325 as a baseline to plan and gauge activities mainstreaming gender.
>
> (2006: 5)

UNIFEM's ongoing support has had an impact on educating the leadership in Kosovo, creating awareness of 1325 among security sector actors and civil society, and ultimately, establishing UNIFEM's relevancy to Kosovo's efforts in security sector reform. It has even institutionalized this in the form of a Gender Unit that now reaches out to all police stations in Kosovo.

Additionally, UNIFEM in collaboration with the local women's group (Kosovo Women's Network), the Kosovo Police Service, and NATO peacekeepers have created a number of television shows with gender-based themes aimed at increasing public knowledge on the laws and processes concerning gender-sensitive police issues. These include trafficking, domestic violence, child abuse, prostitution, codes of conduct, etc. The shows also work to enhance the public's perception of the police force to gain civil society's trust, respect, and support (O'Neill 2007a: 28). Thus, many of the shows are based upon interaction between the police and the local community.

Although to a lesser extent, UNIFEM has also been active in the security sector reform process in Liberia. For example, UNIFEM has helped form the Task Force on Gender Violence which includes the Liberian National Police, the UN police, other UN agencies, and local NGOs. The Task Force is developing and implementing a strategy to combat gender-based violence and to act as a community watchdog (O'Neill 2007a: 26). UNIFEM has also been involved in the training of new recruits in the Liberian National Police force by preparing a participatory module that explores the meaning of gender and gender-based violence

110   UN Development Fund for Women

and its relationship to the abuse of power. According the O'Neill's fieldwork in Liberia, the course covers a range of issues including "female genital mutilation, trafficking, forced marriages, infection with HIV/AIDS and the physical, psychological, sexual and economic consequences of sexual and gender-based violence" (2007b: 6).

Cambodia and Bosnia and Herzegovina have also seen new models of community policing that hold promise for increasing women's security in a peacekeeping environment. With support from UNIFEM, women's groups sensitized police forces and community leaders about violence against women. As a result, Cambodian police now consider combating domestic violence to be part of their mission—a mandate that did not exist before. And in Bosnia and Herzegovina, where at one time women could only file complaints through a public interview procedure, now have a special team within the police system that allows them to bring charges in a way that ensures privacy and protection.[42] In this sense, UNIFEM has been instrumental in helping to operationalize community policing, one important component of security sector reform. Community policing—collaboration between civil society and the police to identify security risks—holds promise for increasing women's security, particularly when it is conducted in a way that recognizes the cultural sensitivity involved in the reporting and prosecution of gender-based violence. In this sense, UNIFEM has been able to challenge the public-private dichotomy so often assumed in legal systems and law enforcement.

Still, gendering SSR is extremely difficult, and these projects are only beginning to reveal the majority of the iceberg (that invisible 95 percent) that remains below the surface yet supports the entire exposed structure above the water.[43] Those that are most in need of professional, just and informed security sector services are not only those that are the most vulnerable, socially and economically, but they are often the most suspicious of security forces too. So the obstacles are many, and they stem from the security sector systems themselves as well as the hearts and minds of the civilian population. Nonetheless, UNIFEM has begun chipping away at these obstacles and building bridges between these two sectors of post-conflict societies. There are many obstacles to overcome, but they are not insurmountable as these country-level initiatives demonstrate. They are also in line with UNIFEM's key tools: "Technical collaboration and catalytic funding constitute the two primary entry points for UNIFEM partnerships, while its core strategies support a cycle of knowledge, advocacy, action and evaluation to attain women's human rights and security" (DP/2004/5: 15–16).[44]

UNIFEM, the security discourse and theory-building

This narrative provides a number of important insights into the value of the security discourse as a frame and the significance of UNIFEM at an organizational and normative level. Although the analysis does not demonstrate direct causality between the use of security discourse and UNIFEM's increasing involvement in SSR at the country level, it does demonstrate the effectiveness of strategic framing

UN Development Fund for Women   111

as "actors deliberately package and frame policy ideas to convince each other as well as the general public that certain policy proposals constitute acceptable solutions to pressing problems" (Campbell 1998: 381). In this way, the actors are constructing meaning and thus contributing to theory development and application in the field of human rights, international organization, and security studies.

First, the policing projects illustrate how UNIFEM uses the security discourse to engage actors, such as national police forces or troop/police contributing countries, in strategic partnerships to bring gender-sensitive policies and practices into SSR. While relationships with these actors are new for UNIFEM, the gender issues being highlighted into this context are not. Gender-based violence and women's right to participate in decision-making bodies—the substantive focus of UNIFEM SSR activity thus far—are long-standing issues within the organization. They are just being reframed under the security rubric. The growing importance of these relationships was evident on a global scale when UNIFEM and the UN Department of Peacekeeping Operations hosted a conference in Wilton Park in May 2008, which brought together government officials, military and police personnel, UN peacekeepers, and of course, representatives from women's civil society organizations. This unprecedented gathering of "hard core" security sector actors with gender specialists and women from various conflict zones around the world addressed the role that military peacekeepers must play in the prevention of widespread and systematic sexual violence in conflict and post-conflict societies. Of the 70 participants at Wilton Park, 27 came from military establishments (former Force Commanders, army personnel, and staff of Defense Ministries); others included four MPs, four Permanent Representatives, seven DPKO staff, and a number of other UN personnel, peace activists, and academics. Central to the conference was the acknowledgement that sexual violence is in fact a "security problem requiring a systematic security response" (Wilton Park Summary Report 2008: 2). In this context, sexual violence was clearly situated within the security framework as an essential component to military and police work in UN peacekeeping. As Anne Marie Goetz, Director of UNIFEM's *Governance, Peace and Security* Program argued:

Even a few years ago, a gathering like this would have been unprecedented. Yet it is military peacekeepers now themselves that are demanding practical solutions to the types of conflict they encounter in theatre ... Military tactics have yet to catch up to changed realities on the ground. Security policy-makers and security institutions likewise have to catch up to new forms of conflict, and to the implications for their work of the arenas in which wars are fought, the methods used, and the groups targeted. Sexual violence is a matter for the Security Council, because conflict is its core business, and sexual violence is one way in which conflict is prosecuted. Sexual violence is a matter for governance and economic recovery, because it mars efforts to replace the rule of *war* with rule of *law*, and puts half the population out of commission for the important jobs of social, economic and political rebuilding, where a nation needs to call on every able person to pull itself back together.

112   *UN Development Fund for Women*

Post conflict peace, stability, democratic governance, and livelihoods recovery all require women's empowerment, and women's empowerment requires security from sexual violence, and a demonstrable end to the impunity that serves as incentive for continued violence.

(Wilton Park Conference Presentations 2008: 7, emphasis in original)

The argument here not only emphasizes women's rights as essential to establishing lasting peace and security, but also suggests that violence against women is generally new in the changing landscape of armed conflict and is now relevant to traditional security institutions at the national and international level. This repackaging is effective in building new relationships to deal with long-standing issues, as the very occurrence of the Wilton Park Conference demonstrates.[45]

This reframing has allowed UNIFEM to open new doors to older issues, a mechanism similar to Hertel's "backdoor moves."[46] "Backdoor moves" is a mechanism used by subaltern actors to "introduce additional concepts and corresponding policy goals" to an existing agenda without co-opting, stalling or upsetting the process (Hertel 2006: 8). Here, UNIFEM as one of the smallest UN funds representing the most widely marginalized group in the world acts as a subaltern actor in the UN system, particularly in the realm of international peace and security. UNIFEM projects and programming in SSR represent a mechanism that influences "the evolution of normative understandings" in terms of how the UN conceptualizes security and approaches the rights and needs of women (Hertel 2006: 9). Thus, the end result has a broadening effect and offers support for Hertel's notion of "unexpected power."

UNIFEM's activity in SSR also build's upon the organizational dynamics theorized by Craig Murphy. In his analysis, he very briefly discusses UNIFEM and its relationship to the development of UNDP and its programming. He argues, "UNDP's engagement with the Women and Development movement, and the embedding of the UN Development Fund for Women (UNIFEM) within the UNDP, helped shift the locus of the Programme's attention from countries to individuals" (Murphy 2006: 199). UNIFEM's initiatives in institutionalizing gender training in police forces and gender offices and units within these forces are just the most recent example of UNIFEM drawing focus and attention to the needs of individual women in diverse contexts in the developing world. This means firmly establishing women as both victims and agents in a human-centered approach to development *and* security.

Lastly, this human-centered and gender-sensitive approach to SSR offers a way to operationalize human security. As noted in Chapter 2, human security is frequently used by both scholars and practitioners, but not often understood in any sort of concrete way. UNIFEM's approach to and projects under SSR present real ways to "do" human security.[47] First, UNIFEM's human security approach functions as a "political technology" that links "the personal security of individuals and families with the security of the nation itself" (Burke 2002: 3). In theory, human security *links* different initiatives and actors at various levels in strategic partnerships and alliances to "create a horizontal-cross border source of legitimacy that complements traditional vertical structures" (Human Security Now 2003: 142). Community policing can reflect human security in practice when it connects local women's groups to traditionally hierarchical security institutions. These connections provide legitimacy and therefore a more comprehensive approach to achieving security in post-conflict societies. A women's development fund and local police stations in post-conflict societies are unlikely bedfellows, but within the human security framework this collaboration is logical and necessary. As Hampson maintains, the human security approach recognizes that "international order cannot rest solely on the sovereignty and viability of states—that order also depends on individuals and their own sense of security ... safety of the individual is the key to global security" (2004: 350). UNIFEM's police reform projects clearly prioritize the security needs of individuals and bring together various actors from governmental and non-governmental organizations, at the local, national, regional, and global level. This linking is significant as it recognizes the intersection "between the fields of humanitarianism, development, human rights, and conflict resolution" (Uvin 2004: 353). Furthermore, because the process of democratization empowers new actors in these transitional societies, they "must be accounted for in the security framework" (Acharya 2004: 355). Thus, UNIFEM's approach to SSR provides important theoretical and practical insight into operationalizing human security.

Conclusions

While it is clear the gendering SSR has the potential to *broaden* the meaning of security in post-conflict situations, whether or not these programs can genuinely *transform* the meaning of security over the long term remains to be seen. Many critical theorists are skeptical of human security and its ability to really challenge traditional notions of national security. Berman, for example, argues that human security as a:

> discursive concept functions to securitize realms of human life—biological and bare life—not previously subject to security's purview ... and reinvests the state with the authority/purpose with providing security not just to the state but to human life itself.
>
> (2007: 31)[48]

In other words, human security discourse relies upon the same structuring logic of national security, in assuming the state has the primary responsibility of protecting against a given threat. Heidi Hudson adds, "Human security as a universalistic tool of global governance must acknowledge differences in the degree to which the state leads or participates in the process of the protection and empowerment of individuals" (2005: 157). This latter perspective is a bit more optimistic in coupling protection with empowerment. Both critiques, however, highlight the centrality of the state in the human security discourse. While UNIFEM's involvement in SSR certainly relies upon state structures for the security of women, at

114   *UN Development Fund for Women*

same time UNIFEM has also integrated local women's groups into these traditional state security structures. In this way, UNIFEM is certainly reinforcing the power of the state through the partnership, but it is also laying the groundwork for changing state structures over the long run. As these interactions become institutionalized, they have the capacity for transformative change in the rebuilding process of post-conflict societies.

But one must proceed with caution, as feminist theory reveals drawbacks to institutionalization. Feminist security theorists, such as Sandra Whitworth (2004) for example, are skeptical of most gender mainstreaming efforts. She is unconvinced of the efficacy of "gender training" or "gender offices" in the security sector because these institutions are so thoroughly grounded in institutionalized and militarized masculinity that gender training merely dances on the edges, offering little challenge to the overall ideology, structure, and practice of these organizations. What is even more problematic is that gender mainstreaming can create the illusion of progress without any real change. It creates a certain level of complacency where international actors are no longer concerned with women's issues or gender equality because that box has already been "checked."

These critiques are certainly valid and useful in pushing scholars and practitioners to continue to ask the hard questions. On the other hand, when dealing with these issues on the ground, "practical gender interests" rule the day and meeting the immediate and mid-range needs of women in post-conflict situations is simply a success (Peterson & Runyan 1998). The WPS network and SCR 1325 has allowed UNIFEM to (once again) redefine its catalytic role giving it leverage in traditional security circles. While UNIFEM continues to pursue problems like gender-based violence and women's rights to equal participation in all decision-making arenas, the security discourse has reframed these issues making them relevant to a new set of global, regional, national, and local actors. The security discourse has provided the conceptual and practical link for forging strategic alliances with traditional security actors and creating the "appearance of agreement" on the "central normative message"—establishing and maintaining international peace and security (Hertel 2006: 8). The security discourse has also enabled UNIFEM to continue to push UNDP as well as the rest of the UN system to focus on the individual. This focus on individual development and security needs provides a real world example of human security at work. While this security framework and UNIFEM activism has broadened the security discourse, it remains to be seen whether or not this will transform security or if it will just have an additive effect. The former seems to be the ultimate goal. The latter is still remarkable. As UNIFEM's first Executive Director so eloquently articulates, "At the end of the day, the measure of UNIFEM's effectiveness is the degree to which it stimulates others to take on gender equality concerns and turn innovation into mainstream policy and practice" (Heyzer 2004: 1). From gender-mainstreaming in development circles to the security arena, one can not overemphasize the extent to which these framing strategies continue to reflect intense political struggles fought on a daily basis between those advocating for women's rights and gender equality and those engaged in the mainstream.

Notes

1 "Other ways" refers to Craig Murphy's (2006) "A Better Way?" This serves as the sub-heading of his recent book where he explores the organizational history of the United Nations Development Program (UNDP). His comprehensive account outlines how the UNDP *way* of doing economic development is fundamentally better than the alternatives because "it is not just a way of achieving economic development, but also, more broadly, *a way of conducting relations among peoples and nations*" (2, emphasis in original).

2 As will be discussed below, the development framework of the 1970s, the time during which UNIFEM began as a temporary fund, was fundamentally implemented in social and economic terms making very little connection between economic empowerment and peace and security issues.

3 UNIFEM's story here is limited to the activities, documents, and benchmarks that relate to the Fund's involvement in the WPS network. UNIFEM has been and continues to be engaged in many activities that fall beyond the scope of this chapter. For a more comprehensive and detailed look at UNIFEM's history, see Margaret Snyder's account in *Transforming Development* (1995). At the time of this writing no organizational history has been written on UNIFEM after 1995, when UNIFEM arguably underwent some of the institutions most profound changes, as seen below. This research is just a beginning at filling this gap in the literature.

4 According to Jain's detailed account (2005: 53), "Women in the UN helped provide a format in which Boserup's research findings could be disseminated. In keeping with the goals of the UN's Second Development Decade, an Interregional Meeting of Experts on the Integration of Women in Development was held at the UN in 1972, cosponsored by the Commission on the Status of Women and the Commission on Social Development. The meeting was facilitated both by the large presence of developing countries in the UN and the weight Boserup's book carried within influential circles. Boserup wrote the working document for the meeting. The women who organized and attended this meeting would later become key figures in the international women and development movement."

5 These donations also allowed for the creation of the International Training and Research Institute for the Advancement of Women (INSTRAW).

6 Dr. Shirley Summerskill was the head of the UK delegation.

7 For the full text of the GA Resolution, see http://www.unifem.org/attachments/about/resolutions/a_res_31_133_eng.pdf.

8 It is important to note here the UNIFEM's work clearly recognizes that poverty is not simply an economic issue. Some of UNIFEM's work has focused on the environment or on women's representation in decision-making, but these programs were usually gauged in economic development terms Environmental initiatives, for example, were part of creating sustainable food technologies for rural women seeking economic independence and sufficiency. Similarly, increasing women's participation in decision-making was often aimed at mobilizing women's grassroots organizations on the basis of their common employment in formal and informal sector's of a given society's economic system. For more, see Snyder 1995.

9 In reviewing the many projects UNIFEM funded particularly early on, the underlying logic that emerges is one that prioritizes economic empowerment and control over productive resources as a necessary although not sufficient first step in establishing gender equality in women's security and in political participation.

10 For example, during the initial period of its history, UNIFEM took the innovative step of appointing NGOs as executing agents of their projects at a time when NGOs did not have significant institutional relationships with the larger UN system (Jain 2005: 128).

11 For the full text of the GA Resolution, see http://www.unifem.org/attachments/about/resolutions/a_res_39_125_eng.pdf.

116   *UN Development Fund for Women*

12 See Charlotte Bunch's seminal piece "Women's Rights as Human Rights," in *Human Rights Quarterly* (1990). For more on the 'women's rights as human rights' campaign see the edited volume by Julie Peters and Andrea Wolper (1995).

13 As noted in Chapter 1, this dualistic approach is what informs SCR 1325.

14 It is important to note here that prior to the 1990s when the international community referred to women in crisis situations it was often in terms of environmental or natural disaster situations that merited emergency relief.

15 Dirasse also indicated in the interview that she had been part of a local women's peace organization in her home country of Ethiopia prior to her tenure with UNIFEM, further enabling her to make the connections between UNIFEM in New York and its programming on the ground in terms of WPS.

16 This conceptual emphasis on the individual is significant both in terms of UNIFEM's relationship with UNDP and in terms of operationalizing human security. These two points are addressed in more detail below.

17 In conjunction with these efforts in 1994, the issue of women in "peace-building and conflict resolution" emerged on UNIFEM's annual reports and the Secretary-General's annual reports on UNIFEM activity to the General Assembly for the first time.

18 It was in Senegal that the Federation of African Women Peace Network (FERFAP) was created. FERFAP has become "a regional platform through which women affected by conflicts can articulate their priorities and concerns to policymakers and decisionmakers" (CCR 2005: 29).

19 This early programming demonstrates that local women's groups were making an "instrumental" or "value-added" argument from the very beginning of the "women, peace, and security" campaign. Thus, UNIFEM's initial programming was built upon traditional conceptions of women as peacemakers.

20 Given conflict and violence of the early 1990s in the Former Yugoslavia and Rwanda, it became increasingly difficult for the international community to ignore the critical links and interdependency of development, security and human rights particularly in the context of women's rights and gender equality.

21 Much of the language in this category relies upon the security framework as an instrumental argument, and therefore, Beijing's outcome document is often cited as a major building block in the path toward the passage of SCR 1325.

22 It is important to note here that these 12 categories are overlapping, particularly in terms of the "women, peace, and security" agenda. Other areas of action include violence against women, women in power and decision-making, institutional mechanisms for the advancement of women, human rights of women, and the girl child—all of which are relevant to the security discourse. "Women and Armed Conflict" is highlighted here because under this strategy the international community clearly makes an instrumental argument for women's inclusion in the process of establishing peace and security, while still maintaining a rights-based framework.

23 The Beijing Conference was the largest UN conference to date. It was attended by 189 governments. It had 17,000 participants, with 6,000 government delegates and more than 4,000 accredited NGO representatives. The official website of the conference can still be found at http://www.un.org/womenwatch/asp/user/list.asp?ParentID=4001.

24 These General Assembly resolutions include A/RES/50/410 1995; A/RES/51/391 1996; A/RES/52/300 1997; A/RES/53/363 1998; A/RES/54/225 1999; A/RES 55/271 2000; A/RES/ 56/174 2001. See also, A/RES/50/166 1996; A/RES /54/136 2000; A/RES/56/130 2002; A/RES /60/137 2006.

25 Arguably, this division was operating informally prior to 2000, particularly in terms of UNIFEM's activism in bringing women's issues to the Security Council and drafting SCR 1325. But as several interviews confirmed, UNIFEM's *Governance, Peace, and Security* programme formally emerged in 2000 coinciding with the adoption of SCR 1325. For more, see http://www.unifem.org/gender_issues/governance_peace_security/.

UN Development Fund for Women   117

26 The other two areas include strengthening women's economic capacity as well as promoting women's human rights and the elimination of all forms of violence against women.

27 Several interviewees suggested that UNIFEM had been engaged in this kind of work long before the mid-1990s, but the recognition by the broader UN system and the international community more generally really legitimated UNIFEM's work in post-conflict societies.

28 As feminists scholars have long argued, even though this opportunity exists in post-conflict situations the reality is often exactly the opposite. Political, social or economic gains made by women during times of war are often reversed in the name of order and in an attempt to return to 'normalcy'. Much of Cynthia Enloe's (1990; 2000) work explores how women's rights regress after armed conflict.

29 Ambassador Donald Steinberg's experience of peacebuilding in the Republic of Angola [1995–1998] illustrates that any peace process claiming to be "gender neutral" is—by merely making such assumptions—gender-biased. For more, see the Joan B. Kroc Institute for Peace and Justice at the University of San Diego where Steinberg was part of the Institute's Distinguished Lecture Series in 2004. His lecture entitled, "Conflict, Gender and Human Rights: Lessons from the Field," can be found at http://peace.sandiego.edu/events/archives/2004/2004events.html.

30 According to Hideaki Shinoda (2007) at the Institute for Peace Science, "SSR" was introduced by Clare Short, the then UK Minister for International Development in 1998 in a speech at the Royal College of Defence Studies.

31 Security sector reform is sometimes referred to as a security sector transformation as more holistic (and less of a top-down) approach to implementing change.

32 This book embraces an approach to security sector reform that Shinoda (2007) refers to as positive justification in accordance with the doctrine of peacebuidling. It is built on a strategy of establishing a political, economic, and social foundation for sustainable peace. This is not to be confused with the negative justification for security sector reform where the focus is on the intervening international troops and the strategy is driven by the goal of troop withdrawal. The latter is currently the driving strategy for U.S. policy in Iraq. Shinoda argues that while the two justifications do not contradict each, they are not necessarily mutually reinforcing—"the emphasis on one element may distract attention from appropriate and careful examinations of the other" (1).

33 It is important to note here that no international agreements on women (including CEDAW, Beijing Platform for Action or SCR 1325) specifically employ the terms "security sector" or "security sector reform"; they call for gender mainstreaming, equal and full participation of women, and a focus on violence against women within all the specific institutions of the security sector. Additionally, measures to ensure peace and security such as disarmament and reducing excessive military expenditure are repeatedly highlighted.

34 The other target area for UNIFEM in Phase II is Judicial Reform, also referred to as their Gender Justice Program. While this programming is certainly related to SSR, it is distinct in its focus on truth-telling commissions, reconciliation programs, and inheritance and property rights aimed at building women's economic security. This programming is not as clearly situated in the traditional security arena despite some overlap. Further, it is functionally separate within UNIFEM. Although this issue is beyond the scope of this project, it is an area for future research. A cursory reading of the Gender Justice programming indicates some reframing of long-standing issues within UNIFEM (i.e., land rights) in terms of economic security that will make for an interesting comparison with the reframing of issues under SSR.

35 According to one UNIFEM official in an interview, "Our [UNIFEM] interest in SSR reform actually anticipated a UN-system wide reflection on the UN's approach to SSR. This was launched by the last Secretary-General just before he left, as a reaction to the lack of clarity in the UN as to what is SSR and how to ensure better coherence" (interview, 2007).

118   *UN Development Fund for Women*

36 For example, see Boyer *et al.* (2009).
37 See for example, UNIFEM's recent and comprehensive handbook, *Getting It Right, Doing It Right: Gender and Disarmament, Demobilization, and Reintegration* (2004). Beyond DDR programs, UNIFEM has also—in partnership with DPKO—developed gender training programs and strategizing workshops for troop contributing countries. One UNIFEM official (2006) noted that she is conducting "more research on the C-34 (Committee of Troop Contributing Countries) for an upcoming consultation, a relationship that UNIFEM to this point has very little experience but one with tremendous potential" in terms of humanizing security. While these other areas certainly demand more research, they are beyond the scope of this project. But it is an area that I will be pursuing in the near future.
38 Much of the data from this section comes from internal UNIFEM documents that I was made privy to during the course of my interviews.
39 UNIFEM's dual strategy is based on the fact that gender-based violence most often continues and can even intensify after conflict. Second, UNIFEM's experience on the ground as well as several anecdotal studies indicate that increasing women police officers makes police units more accessible/approachable to local women. Fitzsimmons (1998; 2005) research on women in police forces in Haiti and Kosovo demonstrates that women police officers use force less frequently than their male counterparts, are less authoritarian in their interactions with citizens and with officers of lower rank, possess better communication and negotiation skills, and are more likely than male officers to diffuse potentially violent situations.
40 As Noeleen Heyzer summarizes, "In Rwanda, after police said they could not protect women as they lacked vehicles for rapid response, UNIFEM organized an inter-agency response to set up specialized gender desks in police states and provide them with training, hotlines, and motorcycles to reach women in remote districts." (Heyzer 2006b: 3)
41 This is a case where hierarchical power structures have the capacity to work in women's favor once the senior-level link is established.
42 These two initiatives in Cambodia and Bosnia-Herzegovina were highlighted in Rehn and Johnson Sirleaf's report in 2002.
43 For a fuller description of the iceberg analogy from the perspective of a gender analysis, see Peterson and Runyan 1998.
44 This report on UNIFEM's Multi-Year Funding Framework, 2004–2007 can be accessed at http://www.unifem.org/attachments/products/English_MYFF_2004-2007.pdf (accessed April 2007).
45 All conference documents, including the summary report and individual presentations can be found at http://www.unifem.org/news_events/event_detail.php?EventID=175 (accessed February 2009).
46 Charles Tilly (1999) maintains that organizational mechanisms are generalizable, and challenges us to test and clarify such mechanisms in the pursuit of theory-building.
47 Even the organization classifies its activities in gender-sensitizing SSR as a "human-security based approach" (UNIFEM 2006a: 5).
48 It is worth noting that Berman goes on to argue that human security discourse many not only repeat the structuring logic of national security and the primacy of the state, but that it may actually extend and further empower the state in controlling individuals when examining biopolitics.

6 The United Nations Peacebuilding Commission

A litmus test for assessing the status of women, peace, and security

The creation of the Peacebuilding Commission is a major sort of a reference to gender and peacebuilding. The result of which is now we have a gender adviser sitting in the peacebuilding support office. Yesterday, I sat in on the meetings on Sierra Leone. The Security Council has referred Sierra Leone and Burundi to the peacebuilding commission. I have sat on two days of discussion and there were major interventions around gender by the ambassadors seated on the commission. Now, that means Sierra Leone will walk out with $25–30 million to start working on peacebuilding initiatives and a good chunk of that will go to women and gender issues.

Peacebuilding Support Office Official, December 2006

Recognizing the important contribution of civil society and non-governmental organizations, including women's organizations, to peacebuilding efforts ... Reaffirming the important role of women in the prevention and resolution of conflicts and in peacebuilding, and stressing the importance of their equal participation and full involvement in all efforts for the maintenance and promotion of peace and security and the need to increase their role in decision-making with regard to conflict prevention and resolution and peacebuilding ... Decides ... with the view to operationalizing the decision by the World Summit, to establish the Peacebuilding Commission as an intergovernmental advisery body ...

Security Council Resolution 1645/2005; General Assembly Resolution 60/180, 2005

As the last chapter demonstrated, women have been engaged in peacebuilding activities long before the "women, peace, and security" (WPS) network formally materialized and the Security Council adopted Resolution 1325 (SCR 1325) (Anderlini 2000; Meintjes et al. 2002). Nonetheless, women's roles in peacebuilding were officially mobilized and acknowledged at the global level with the passage of this resolution, generally speaking.[1] Although gender issues had been discussed within various global forums prior to this time, particularly in the context of broader development and socio-economic concerns, it was not until

120   *UN Peacebuilding Commission*

2000 that the UN recognized the need to address gender issues in conflict prevention, management, and reconstruction mechanisms. SCR 1325 reaffirms the "important role of women in the prevention and resolution of conflicts and *peacebuilding* and stress[es] the importance of their equal participation and full involvement in all efforts for the maintenance and promotion of peace and security" (emphasis added). The resolution also maintains that "effective institutional arrangements to guarantee their protection and full participation in the peace process can significantly contribute to the maintenance and promotion of international peace and security." Thus, in keeping within the parameters of the security framework, the resolution emphasizes the vital contribution women can make to peacebuilding and argues that their inclusion is an important dimension of making such processes successful and sustainable.[2]

Five years after SCR 1325, the UN established the Peacebuilding Commission (PBC)—a body intended to propose and facilitate integrated peacebuilding strategies for countries emerging from conflict. This intergovernmental advisory committee is the intersection of political, military, humanitarian, development, and other UN actors involved in post-conflict work—a classic cross-cutting agenda. In principle, the PBC's objective is to coordinate these actors to better assist countries during the fragile transitional period from war to a sustainable peace, thereby resolving an institutional gap in the UN system. Established by concurrent General Assembly (60/180) and Security Council (1645/2005) resolutions, the PBC is designed to serve as a forum for both state and non-state actors, stakeholders and donors, with experience in peacebuilding—including those from both the development and the security communities. According to the two resolutions, the "main purpose is to bring together all relevant actors to marshal resources and advise on and propose comprehensive strategies for peacebuilding and post-conflict recovery." In short, the role of the PBC is to provide the space for strategy formulation, sharing of best practices, and to mobilize resources to assist local actors in post-conflict reconstruction efforts.

Given the potential significance of the PBC in post-conflict processes around the world and the commitment of the UN and Member States to SCR 1325 (not to mention Fourth World Conference on Women in Beijing, CEDAW, and the UN Charter—at least in theory), it would seem obvious that the commitments embodied in SCR 1325 should have been factored in to the process of establishing and implementing the PBC. As activist Thelma Ekiyor maintains, "Essentially Resolution 1325 should serve as a monitoring tool for the Commission to gauge its performance on including women" (2006: 3).[3] In other words, the PBC presents an ideal opportunity for the UN to fulfill and implement the principles set forth by the women, peace and security campaign—codified in SCR 1325—in the Commission's design, mandate, and activities. The development of this official peacebuilding structure at the end of 2005, therefore, provides a unique means for assessing the impact of SCR 1325 as a normative framework as well as the role of the women, peace, and security network in the UN system. In other words, the PBC as a case study serves as a window for understanding how security is being operationalized by the UN and what role, if any, the WPS

UN Peacebuilding Commission   121

network has played in this most recent attempt to restructure its peace and security agenda. This chapter takes a deeper look at processes leading up to the PBC as well as its first eighteen months of activity to gain insight into how women's activism has impacted the UN's security agenda and what this new body has meant for women's rights and gender mainstreaming—the broader goals of the global women's movement.[4]

It is important to note that the PBC has only been operational since the end of 2005; so the organization is still trying to get its feet on the ground in terms of UN procedural growth and development. Thus, this case study analyzes the work of the organization from its establishment in December 2005 until the summer 2007. Even though the PBC is still in its institutional infancy, it is distinct in its mandated role to bridge the security and the development bodies within the UN. It is at this formative stage in its institutional development that the consideration of women and gender concerns are so critical, meriting a closer examination.

Furthermore, the PBC must be seen as part of broader efforts to reform the UN, reflecting a shift in thinking about the relationship between security and development that has gradually been taking shape since the end of the Cold War. From the Millennium Development Goals to *In Larger Freedom* (A/59/2005), theorizing and policy-making around the so-called "security-development nexus" has grown markedly in recent years.[5] Building on the insights of critical security studies and the ongoing experience of international involvement in peacebuilding, the logic of this approach is to explore how the security and development agendas are linked through peacebuilding as well as the tensions that can arise between the two agendas when they undermine rather than reinforce one another, particularly in the context of women's rights and gender equality. As one former UN employee argued, ". . . the [Peacebuilding] Commission was intended to address all of these cross-cutting issues and tensions ... as the intersection and interdependence of development and security is no where more glaringly obvious than in post-conflict reconstruction" (interview, December 2006). Women have been at the forefront in terms of bridging this divide—by identifying the overlap as well as the contradictions—for more than thirty years. This activism goes back to the UN Decade for Women (1975–1985) where women established the theme, "Equality, Development and Peace." With SCR 1325, the women's movement has identified the way that security concerns underscores and unifies these three areas of concern. Thus, the WPS network is just the latest effort to draw attention to the interconnectedness between these issues at both the conceptual and practical levels. By placing women in this broader framework of UN reform, this chapter illustrates the major attitudinal and structural obstacles that women face in challenging how the UN defines and pursues international peace and security and linking that pursuit to broader development goals in the context of the UN peacebuilding agenda.

By conducting a gender analysis of the PBC, one can gain a better understanding of the impact that SCR 1325 and the WPS network has had in establishing a normative framework for action in the UN system; therefore, shedding light on the meaning of security as the UN settles in to the twenty-first century. Such a

122   *UN Peacebuilding Commission*

case study also illustrates the ways that the security discourse as a strategy has created new entry points for the broader women's movement in the context of international peace and security. This chapter analyzes the process leading up the establishment of the PBC as well as the PBC's first year and a half of work to better understand how "women, peace, and security" have been able to impact this new body in how it defines and "does" peace and security. By looking at the PBC's work developing in Burundi and Sierra Leone, one can begin to see what the PBC means at the national level. But before evaluating the inclusion of women and a gender perspective into the mandate, the first year of the PBC, and its two existing country programs, one must begin by examining the historical development of the UN's work in peacebuilding. It is to this evolution that we now turn.

The 1990s and the need for peacebuilding

The proliferation of intra-state conflict combined with the effects and demands of globalization, the spread of HIV/AIDs, the increase in small arms and drug trafficking, and mass movement of refugees and internally displaced people that surfaced in the aftermath of the Cold War pushed the international community to rethink the causes and consequences of instability, violence, and insecurity. "Against the backdrop of these emerging challenges, the UN, unhindered by the ideological obstacles that had constrained action in previous decades, sought to adopt new approaches to 'ending the scourge of war'" (Barnes 2006: 3). The existence of these sorts of complex emergencies meant the UN was forced to re-evaluate its development assistance strategies, its guidelines on humanitarian intervention, and what it meant to enforce and keep peace. Further, the fact that complex emergencies often occurred in failed states only reinforced the notion of an interdependent relationship between conflict, development, and security (Milliken 2003).[6] Such post-conflict situations were the reality confronting the UN. As one UN official recalled:

> you have to understand the context of the early to mid-1990s with the all the civil wars going on around the world. Everyone at the UN and elsewhere was scrambling, trying to figure out what to do. What can be done? What were the capacities?
>
> (interview, 2007)

Thus, the context of the 1990s demanded action based on peacebuilding—a concept that quickly gained currency in the policy and practice of the United Nations.

While there is no universally accepted definition of peacebuilding, most studies begin with UN Secretary-General Boutros Boutros-Ghali's 1992 report entitled, *An Agenda for Peace*.[7] This report is a significant benchmark for identifying the UN's new role in terms of international intervention after the Cold War and potential reform agenda in the years to come. In the report, Boutros-Ghali coined the term "post-conflict peace-building," loosely defined as "action

UN Peacebuilding Commission 123

to identify and support structures that will tend to strengthen and solidify peace in order to avoid relapse into conflict" (1992: para 20).[8] Although this definition seems all-encompassing, his report did distinguish peacebuilding from preventative diplomacy, peacemaking, and peacekeeping; yet, he maintained that they are entirely interdependent processes.[9] Peacebuilding is distinct as a post-conflict framework in its focus on preventing intra-state conflicts from reigniting after the fighting has stopped (Paris 2001b: 33). From disarming and demobilizing combatants and training security personnel to monitoring elections and other good governance reforms to advancing efforts to protect human rights, the report describes a wide range of activities and goals that fall within this intervention framework while still maintaining the fundamental primacy of state sovereignty.[10] Despite this reaffirmation of the state, the *Agenda for Peace* was the first stage in widening the UN peace and security agenda beyond traditional national security discourse towards "more inclusive (and interventionary) approaches focusing on human rights and collective action based on liberal principles" (Barnes 2006: 4).[11]

Boutros-Ghali's subsequent reports were similar in that they continued to put forth grand visions without outlining practical steps to be taken. In *An Agenda for Development* (1994), he made the argument that development was *the* foundational step for lasting peace, acknowledging that addressing conflict effectively meant dealing with root causes.[12] Thus, peace and development could not be achieved without the other. The *Supplement to the Agenda for Peace* (1995) went on to make socio-economic, cultural, and humanitarian problems relevant to conflict and post-conflict resolution, further articulating the development-security nexus. These reports contained plenty of rhetoric without any sort of operational guidance.

These efforts toward operationalizing a UN approach to peacebuilding and linking the development and security fields, however, is best understood as "definitional haze" where grand ideas seriously lack concrete recommendations in terms of strategies, time frames, roles, and responsibilities (Bhatia 2003: 11). Since the publication of the *Agenda for Peace*, the UN has been struggling with questions of sequencing, resources, and spheres of jurisdiction as seen in the peace operations in Namibia, Cambodia, Angola, Kosovo, and East Timor. As Christine Chinkin argues, "the linkages between human rights, democracy, and the rule of law (including international law) as the ideological basis for peacebuilding are implicit—but they are not explicitly spelled out" (2004:27). Thus, by the late 1990s the UN had been repeatedly criticized for its weak capacity to coordinate the complex and multifaceted demands of post-conflict societies.[13]

Still Boutros-Ghali's grand visions set the stage for Secretary-General Kofi Annan to launch an ambitious reform agenda in 1997.[14] In response to growing disillusionment and criticism of the UN ability to meet its overarching goal of peace and security given the peacekeeping disasters of the early and mid-1990s, one of the "core areas" that Annan identified for reform was the need to develop the UN's institutional capacity for preventative diplomacy and post-conflict peacebuilding (UN 1997: para 63–66). In order to operationalize the goal, Annan commissioned a group of high-level experts to make specific and realistic

124   UN Peacebuilding Commission

recommendations on how to improve the performance of UN peace operations. The panel of experts produced the *Report of the Panel on United Nations Peace Operations*, most often referred to as the Brahimi Report in 2000.[15] Importantly, the report points out that United Nations peace operations to date "did not *deploy into* post-conflict situations but tried to *create* them," despite the fact that the mandates, resources, institutional structures, and coordination mechanisms that were in place were both inadequate and inappropriate for such efforts (UN 2000: viii, emphasis in original). According to the report, peace operations not only demand political, financial, and military support, but a sound peacebuilding strategy as well. Such a strategy is defined as a process of "reassemb[ling] the foundations of peace and provid[ing] the tools for building on those foundations something that is more than just the absence of war" (2000: para 13).[16] Overall, the Brahimi report concluded that UN peacekeeping has largely been a failure because of the lack of clear, strong, and sustained political, institutional, and financial support.[17] The report argued that the UN must stop behaving as though its peacekeeping function is a temporary, ad hoc affair and begin embracing it as a core activity that is properly institutionalized and strengthened through permanent capacities. Peacebuilding necessarily and logically fell into this call for change.

The next high-level panel report known as *A More Secure World* (2004) took this notion of reforming the UN's approach to peace and security even further and recommended that the Security Council under Article 29 of the Charter establish a Peacebuilding Commission. The report identifies peacebuilding as an institutional deficit in the UN system and the need for a coherent doctrine and coordinating mechanisms that allow the many different actors involved in peacebuilding operations to work in the most effective and organized way possible. This translates into UN actors coordinating with other UN actors as well as with other intergovernmental bodies, such as the World Bank and the International Monetary Fund, with international non-governmental organizations, such as the Red Cross or Human Rights Watch, and with local actors at the state, non-state, and grassroots level. As Cutillo rightly points out, "it has been widely recognized that peacebuilding activities so far have been undertaken by a multitude of actors in absence of an overall political strategy" (2006: 1). The creation of the PBC is an attempt to address some of these shortcomings. According to a 2006 report from the NGO Working Group on Women, Peace, and Security:

> Not only is it a recognition of the many different kinds of knowledge and activities required for building peace, it is also a recognition of the fact that, in any post-conflict situation, there are a tremendous number of different actors involved in the peacebuilding process—not just warring parties, but the rest of society; not just the warring country or countries, but also others in the region, and those that act as donors in the peacebuilding process; not just the UN, but organizations, financial institutions, development agencies, and non-governmental organizations ... it is also indicative of the need to coordinate, involve and ensure communication between all of the actors and elements of societal reconstruction throughout the process. Finally, the

UN Peacebuilding Commission   125

establishment of the PBC can be seen as recognition of the need to learn from the experiences of peacebuilding and to retain, add to, and disseminate that knowledge for future efforts.

(2006: ix)

But the creation and work of the PBC should not just be analyzed from this lessons-learned, policy perspective. It must also be rooted in a normatively based, theoretical discussion that allows for broader deductions about the present and future direction of international peace and security as defined and pursued by the UN. In reviewing both academic and policy-related research on peace operations in general, Roland Paris has found that most literature operates as a technical, how-to guide completely lacking any sort of "macrotheory" that uses peace missions "as windows into the larger phenomena of international politics" (2001b: 28). This dearth of theoretical insight is problematic as it tends to shield the political nature of peacebuilding from closer scrutiny, ignoring the underlying power dynamics, conflicting interests, and hidden agendas that operate under the technical language of donor reports, inter-agency coordination, and funding cycles.

From a theoretically informed perspective one can contextualize the ambitious and radical nature of the idea of peacebuilding itself. As Michael Barnett (1995) argues, this shift in the character of UN peace operations is a reflection of changing ideas about meaning of international order based upon the constitutive norms of the "international society" approach in international relations theory. Peacebuilding seeks to bridge security and development at and between the international level and domestic levels in order to offer an integrated approach to understanding and dealing with the full range of issues that threatened peace and security. From both a practical and theoretical perspective, the transformative potential of peacebuilding is profound for countries emerging from war as well as for the broader international community as well. Michael Doyle maintains that "successful contemporary peacebuilding not only changes behavior but, more important, also transforms identities and institutional context ... more than reforming play in an old game, it changes the game" (2001: 544). Many remain skeptical, however, about just how much "change" the PBC represents. Along these lines, the presupposed interdependence between security and development is often more a matter of conjecture rather than knowledge grounded in empirical evidence.

One way to assess the extent to which "the game is changing" is to examine how SCR 1325 has been implemented in the context of the PBC's work. This analytical lens provides critical insight because the incorporation and integration of women and gender concerns into the peacebuilding approach would illustrate a significant departure from the traditional parameters and rules of the game. A gender perspective puts into focus the political nature of the game, recognizing the many obstacles that a truly transformative peacebuilding approach must still overcome. The next section will evaluate the role of women and gender in the conceptual and practical development of UN peacebuilding before turning to the actual PBC's mandate and its first year of work.

126　*UN Peacebuilding Commission*

Women's peacebuilding, gendered peacebuilding

Although the UN's approach to peacebuilding has been expanding and shifting since the end of the Cold War, the role of local women in building peace continues to be largely neglected (Mazurana & McKay 1999).[18] It is reasonable to argue at the outset, that the various actors involved in this developing notion of peacebuilding showed little concern or sensitivity to the role that women play in peacebuilding and to the gendered nature of all activities of post-conflict reconstruction. In the *Agenda for Peace*, women only appear once and that is in the context of being lumped together with children as the "more vulnerable group" in society (1992: para 81). There is no mention of gender. Further, gender is not mentioned as one of the "essential components" to effective peacebuilding in the *Brahimi Report* in 2000, although the word does appears eight times in the 74-page report. Seven of those references addressed the need to ensure "fair geographical and gender distribution" in terms of staffing and leadership positions in UN operations, and once was to stress the importance of UN personnel being sensitive to gender and cultural differences (A/55/305–S/2000/809).[19] While focusing on a gender balance in terms of personnel recruitment and leadership roles in UN peacebuilding, such an approach barely scratches the surface when it comes to integrating gender into the work of peacebuilding.

This lack of attention to women *and* gender issues is not surprising given that the notion of simply gender balancing the UN system is far from realized.[20] For example, the high-level panels appointed by the Secretary-General to access peace operations and current threats to international peace and security were made up of predominantly male members, despite Annan's repeated call for greater gender equality within the UN system.[21] Increasing women's participation at the highest levels of the UN continues to be a major challenge and focus of the most current reform efforts.[22]

Although women and gender issues were largely left off the reform agenda, NGOs working on women, peace, and security did manage to impact the language of the report of the Secretary-General's High-Level Panel on Threats, Challenges, and Change in one important way. This 2004 report, which first proposed the creation of a peacebuilding commission, did emphasize the need for a peacebuilding commission to work toward "great consultation with and involvement in peace processes of important voices from civil society, especially those of women, who are often neglected during [peace] negotiations" (71). This reference to consulting with local women' groups resulted from the constant efforts from the NGO Working Group on Women, Peace, and Security in conjunction with UNIFEM and The UN's Methodist Women's Division who worked effortlessly to lobby Member states to insert such wording (NGO Working Group on Women, Peace and Security 2006).[23]

Overall, the impact of the WPS network on the development of UN peacebuilding efforts can best be categorized as initiatives aimed at increasing women's participation at UN headquarters and on the ground (governance-based) and those focused on integrating gender awareness, gender training, and gender sensitivity

UN Peacebuilding Commission   127

into all policies and practices (gender-mainstreaming). The former can be seen as meeting practical, more immediate interests of women, while the latter is more strategic, long-term gender goals.[24] These categorizations, although interconnected, allow for an understanding of what women and gender mean for and from a peacebuilding perspective.

The former emphasis on women and governance arises from numerous studies and policy reports indicating that women on the ground are already engaged in peacebuilding activities. The problem lies in the fact that these activities and initiatives are often invisible to the broader international and national community because women have little power and presence within formal political structures and the nature of their initiatives do not fit mainstream approaches. Thus, the aim is to include women's groups, such as the Mano River Union Women Peace Network (MARWOPNET) who have already been working towards establishing peace in Liberia and Sierra Leone (Fleshman 2003).[25] This additive approach to peacebuilding often relies upon notions of women peacebuilders that emphasize women's tendencies to emphasize psychological, relational, and spiritual processes (McKay 2004: Mazurana & McKay 1999). In a study based on a dialogic workshop with South African women leaders, de la Rey and McKay (2006) revealed that women's definition of peacebuilding is based on a relational process that promotes reconciliation and meeting basic human needs. Consequently, their activism can take unconventional forms such as demonstrations, petitions, door-to-door campaigns, and other forms of grassroots mobilization efforts (Anderlini 2000). Thus, the research on women peacebuilders focuses on this "difference argument" where women are found to contribute to peace and security in unique and positive ways (Karamé 2004). From this perspective, consultation with and the inclusion of local and regional women's groups is a significant area of concern for the UN's peacebuilding institution. As McKay (2004: 167) argues, "A major goal of women's peace-building is to call attention to women's and girls' oppression, marginalization, and threatened security, and to establish a peace-building agenda that involves women as key actors." In this sense, women's participation in decision-making bodies is framed and presented as an untapped resource that could significantly contribute to the process—another illustration of the security framework.

But testing the impact of the WPS network on the PBC cannot stop there. The aim of this movement goes beyond gender balancing and improving women's participation in arenas of governance. It also includes the more integrative aim of gender mainstreaming where gender roles (both male and female) are recognized and scrutinized in terms of the causes of conflict and the path to peace.[26] This means that in developing peacebuilding programs and policies, it is critical to analyze the potential effects on both women *and* men as they experience the erosion of security differently (Nakaya 2003). Gender-mainstreaming cannot just focus on including women and on participation issues. It must also target men and explores notions of masculinity and femininity as their intersection is critical to understanding obstacles to a lasting peace, acknowledging that no peacebuilding policy or program is gender-neutral. Planned action ranging from distributing

128   *UN Peacebuilding Commission*

humanitarian aid to demobilizing and disarming combatants to repatriating refugees to establishing a judicial system, all have gendered impacts. As the NGO Working Group on Women, Peace and Security articulates:

> In every aspect of reconstruction—from rebuilding roads to rebuilding political structures—every decision taken, every project funded, and every policy implemented will have a gendered impact. The impact may be to reinforce the status quo, or to change it, but no matter whether peacebuilders *consciously* analyze the gendered effects of their program or not, they are *de facto* making decisions about gender.
>
> (2006: 18)

Thus, each and every peacebuilding initiative needs to be (and is mandated to be) aware of and address the ways that such efforts affect men, women, and the relationships between the two. This understanding of gender-mainstreaming goes beyond *widening* who participates to really *transforming* the internal processes at a personal and organizational level. This means asking questions about how the international community defines and deals with violence and how violence is gendered. Are non-public and unorganized forms of violence, such as domestic forms of violence, adequately addressed in peacebuilding programs? Are gendered shifts in demographics, such as the frequent influx of female-headed households accounted for in planned action? This means questioning whether the goals of *re* -integration, -settlement, and -construction are equally desirable conditions for all members of society. In short, gender-mainstreaming involves questioning and challenging social structures and institutions that seem natural to understand how men and women experience them differently and how such groups of varying class and race experience them differently.

Indeed, focusing on civil society organizations, such as women's groups already engaged in conventional and not-so-conventional peacebuilding activities becomes a critical component of the PBC's work. Further, the extent to which gender—understood as men and women, masculinity and femininity—is integrated into processes and programs of the Commission must also be accessed. The marginalization of women and naturalization of gendered causes and effects in peacebuilding continue despite the numerous, interdisciplinary studies that demonstrate how women have different peacebuilding interests and how all peacebuilding efforts have gendered consequences.[27] From this perspective, the chapter now turns to the PBC—its mandate, its eighteen months of its existence and its two existing country programs—to analyze the way in which WPS and SCR 1325 interact with this institutional development to the UN's approach to security.

The PBC and its mandate

Acting on the High-Level Panel's recommendations in *A More Secure World*, UN Secretary-General Kofi Annan proposed the establishment of a

Peacebuilding Commission in his March 2005 report. The report, entitled *In Larger Freedom: Towards Security, Development, and Human Rights for All*, Annan argued that peacebuilding was an institutional gap within the UN system as demonstrated by the fact that roughly "half of all countries that emerge from war lapse back into violence within five years" (A/59/2005 para114). Despite some valid critiques of the reliability of this statistic, one cannot deny that the UN as a whole needed to do a better job supporting countries in their pursuit of enduring peace, particularly after peacekeeping missions left. The creation of the Commission was part of a package of reform proposals presented for negotiation and approval at the September 2005 General Assembly's High-Level Plenary Meeting, also know as the World Summit. The PBC was one of the few proposals that received almost unanimous support at the meeting. "The establishment of a Peacebuilding Commission is regarded by many as the most prominent achievement of the September 2005 World Summit at the United Nations" (Cutillo 2006: 1). The Summit was followed by a series of negotiations during the General Assembly's sixtieth session—a process that led to the joint General Assembly and Security Council resolutions establishing the PBC in December 2005. These two resolutions established the PBC as a double subsidiary, something new and innovative in the UN system, and while such a status has allowed for some flexibility for the PBC and its working methods, it clearly reflects the ongoing pushing and pulling within the UN between the GA and the SC, between "the Global South" and the "Global North," and between development and security in its post-conflict work.

In short, the PBC was designed to work on the strategic level rather than the operational level. More precisely, the four main objectives of the Commission are to:

- propose integrated strategies for post-conflict peacebuilding and recovery;
- help to ensure predictable financing for early recovery activities and sustained financial investment over the medium to longer-term;
- extend the period of attention by the international community to post-conflict recovery; and
- develop best practices on issues that require extensive collaboration among political, military, humanitarian, and development actors.

Furthermore, the concept of national ownership in peacebuilding processes is recognized as central to the work of the Commission. According to a *Draft Concept Note on the Design of Integrated Peacebuilding Strategies*:

given the fundamental importance of national ownership to the sustainability of peacebuilding efforts, the elaboration of an integrated peacebuilding strategy ... for a country on the agenda of the PBC should be firmly vested with the national government and supported by the UN and other concerned stakeholders (civil society, private sector, donors, and other international actors).

(PBSO 2007: 1)[28]

130　UN Peacebuilding Commission

While recognizing that "stakeholders" extend far beyond national governments is a significant step, many non-state actors were critical of the document because it did not outline *how* such actors were to be included in the process.

As an organization, the PBC operates in terms of three subcommittees: the Organizational Committee (OC), the County-Specific Committees, and a Working Group on Lessons Learned (WGLL). There are thirty-one members of the Commission ranging from key UN bodies to member states to important groups of member states. They include seven members selected by the SC (including all five permanent members); seven members elected by the GA; seven members of the Economic and Social Council (ECOSOC); five top providers of assessed contributions to UN budgets and of voluntary contributions to UN funds, programs, and agencies; and five top providers of military personnel and civilian police to UN missions. The Country-Specific Committees also mandate a role for the World Bank, the International Monetary Fund, the relevant UN country team, and relevant neighboring countries and regional organizations with an interest in the country in question.

To ensure the Commission's capacity to carry out its mandate, the UN has also established a Peacebuilding Support Office (PBSO) to serve as a focal point for analysis and strategic planning; the PBSO assists the PBC by conducting research and analysis, drafting reports, and supporting communication and outreach with the range of stakeholders involved. The PBSO is located within the UN Secretariat under the Executive Office of the Secretary-General and staffed by experts in the various aspects of post-conflict reconstruction. The third component of the peacebuilding architecture is the Peacebuilding Fund (PBF), launched in October 2006 as a standing multi-year fund aimed at ensuring the immediate release of resources needed to support post-conflict stabilization and capacity-building initiatives. Provision of funding from the PBF is not limited to countries on the agenda, but funds may be allocated by the UN Secretary-General to similar at-risk countries emerging from conflict and war. As of January 2009, the voluntary fund has donor commitments totaling US\$=283.8 million and of that, has allocated US\$=121.9 million, approximately. Although the fund is small (especially compared to the need), it is significant in its potential to shift the United Nations' current financing method away from the Secretary-General asking for support with hat in hand every time there is a crisis (Lehrer 2005). An immediate reserve to draw from as post-conflict crises arise could shift how the game works possibly allowing for more thoughtful and sustained involvement by the international community in peacebuilding efforts.

From this brief description, the PBC and its supporting structures have the potential to be a real entry point for the WPS network and the implementation of SCR 1325 in peacebuilding efforts. The formal documents establishing the new peacebuilding architecture put forth many principles, such as a more long-term, comprehensive approach to security, that certainly overlap with the WPS agenda. A closer look at the Commission's mandate and its first year of work reveal, however, a much more complex story of some luck, dogged persistence by certain organizations, and many missed opportunities.

The PBC, women, and gender—one year on

To understand how women's activism has been able to insert itself in the PBC's first years, analysis of several basic indicators is merited. Language, gender balancing, and civil society access constitute three distinct but interconnected ways for examining the influence of women on the Commission and the implications of the security framework in the peacebuilding context for establishing and developing women's rights and gender equality. These indicators also provide insight into the content of the country-specific meetings for Sierra Leone and Burundi where language, PBSO staff and civil society have substantially influenced the work of these in-country programs.[29]

Language

Despite various efforts from state and non-state actors, the concurrent GA and SC resolutions that established the Commission made no specific reference to SCR 1325.[30] They did, however, contain language reflective of the spirit of SCR 1325 and the overarching agenda of the WPS network. For example, the preambular paragraphs recognize the "important contribution ... of women's organizations to peacebuilding efforts" and the "important role of women in prevention and resolution of conflicts and peacebuilding." They specifically called upon the PBC to "integrate a gender perspective in its work" and "consult with civil society, non-governmental organizations, including women's organizations, as appropriate." Further, using the discourse of the security framework, the resolutions reaffirm, "the important role of women in the prevention and resolution of conflicts and in peacebuilding, and stressing the importance of their equal participation and full involvement in all efforts for the maintenance and promotion of peace and security ..."[31] Compared with other UN entities dealing with peace and security matters, the inclusion of this language is significant in its own right.

As many critics of these formal documents have rightly pointed out, however, the language does not establish any sort of mechanism to monitor or enforce the integration of a gender perspective or consultation with women's organizations on the ground. They did not institutionalize any means for ensuring women's participation or representation in the PBC or its work, and this constitutes a missed opportunity for the UN to really "gender-sensitize" its peacebuilding efforts. Thus, implementing a gender perspective and accounting for the role of women in this process is largely left up to motivated and influential individuals in the UN system. In this sense, the members of the PBC, and more importantly, the appointed staff of the PBSO merit a closer look as they bear the responsibility of carrying out the Commission's ambitious mandate.

Gender balance

Given the value placed on women's participation in SCR 1325, it is critical to assess the gender balance and the role of certain individuals within this new

132   *UN Peacebuilding Commission*

institutional body. Gender-balancing goals are the most realistic for the newly created PBSO, as it was conceptualized to be a small office of highly qualified and experienced staff members with the ability to provide the strategic analysis, operational planning, and technical support needed by the Commission.[32] In this regard, the GA through its fifth committee[33] has mandated the Secretary-General to ensure that the PBSO has the necessary gender competence to support the integration of gender in the Commission's work "taking into account, inter alia, Security Council Resolution 1325 (2000) and drawing on the appropriate expertise in the United Nations system" (A/60/7/Add.36).[34] Unfortunately, "gender competence" is a vague term and no monitoring mechanisms exist to ensure that some if not all of the PBSO staff are gender-aware and gender-sensitive. Such unenforceable language did not even assure the appointment of a gender adviser or gender focal point within PBSO. Despite this lack of teeth, there are two important PBSO positions, and people in particular, to consider here.

The first is top position within the PBSO and the second-highest ranking position throughout the entire UN system, Assistant Secretary-General. This position is one of significant influence, and so from a gender perspective the PBSO office is extremely fortunate that the Secretary-General appointed Carolyn McAskie as the first Assistant Secretary-General for Peacebuilding Support. McAskie, a Canadian, served as the Special Representative to the Secretary-General to Burundi where she developed a reputation for "strongly promoting gender equality and women's human rights principles within the UN peacekeeping mission in Burundi" (Roberts-Davis 2006: 1). Given her experience in dealing with gender issues, McAskie was an important factor in shaping the PBSO in its most formative years and encouraging the inclusion of gender-sensitive practices and programs from the beginning.[35]

The second position is that of a gender adviser post within the office, something similar to the gender adviser at the Department of Peacekeeping Operations, as discussed in Chapter Three. The gender adviser not only coordinates with gender experts at the country level but with other gender focal points at UN headquarters as well, most especially the one at DPKO (Ekiyor 2006: 4). The General Assembly did not, however, provide for a gender adviser as part of the office's fifteen posts. Toward this end, UNIFEM has since "seconded" a gender and peacebuilding expert, Vina Nadjibulla (NGO Working Group 2006: 11). Nadjibulla, an Afghan native, was part of the NGO Working Group on Women, Peace, and Security during the push for the adoption of SCR 1325. She then was hired by UNIFEM as a program specialist on governance, peace, and security where she further developed her expertise on gender in post-conflict situations. UNIFEM not only initiated the position within the PBSO, but sacrificed a qualified staff member for it. As the last chapter explained, UNIFEM is a tiny fund and such a move was certainly felt by the rest of the staff working in *Governance, Peace, and Security* (UNIFEM official, interview 2006).

Although McAskie and Nadjibulla certainly qualify as being gender competent, the process by which they were appointed was ad hoc, piecemeal, and frankly quite lucky. The PBC lacks any formal procedures to ensure a gender

UN Peacebuilding Commission 133

balance, let alone a staff that is gender competent. This means the PBC and its supporting structures should be equipped with gender training for its staff. Gender training for all staff is critical if the peacebuilding architecture is to avoid the "usual ghettoization" of gender—where gender is represented by one person relieving all other operational components of any gendered responsibilities (Jain 2005). Gender, like peacebuilding, is a cross-cutting concept and cannot be merely one isolated component of it. Furthermore, quantity is as much of an issue as quality. Fifteen staff members with one dedicated to the all-encompassing directive to deal with gender and peacebuilding is hardly adequate. So, in short, the PBC lacks official procedures, monitoring mechanisms, quality training, and sufficient resources to fully integrate a gender perspective into its work.

Mechanisms for civil society access

Although the language specifically mentioned the need to consult with women's organizations, the resolutions failed to establish mechanisms to facilitate a systematic consultation process or to encourage national governments and other actors in the post-conflict field to adopt broader consultation strategies with local women's groups and civil society more broadly.[36] The inclusion of local women's groups enhances the legitimacy and local ownership of the entire peacebuilding process. Further, women's groups are an "important resource for local knowledge and expertise in a number of sectors relating to rebuilding societies after conflict, including the implementation of DDR strategies, encouraging reconciliation, accountability for war crimes, and provision of social services" (NGO Working Group 2006: 23). Despite this, the language concerning civil society's seat—including women's groups—with the Commission is "extremely weak compared to other UN organs" (Wyeth 2006: 3).

This emphasis on the inclusion of civil society is based upon successful precedents of UN peacebuilding efforts. In Guatemala, for example, UN-mediated negotiations established a standing forum, the Civil Society Assembly (ASC), in a framework agreement signed by the warring parties. With funding from bilateral donors, the ASC represented a wide cross-section of Guatemalan civil society, including indigenous organizations, women's groups, business associations, academics, the media, and others that were mandated to discuss the substantive issues under consideration at the official negotiating table. This enabled them to develop and offer consensus-based, non-binding positions in each area and to review and even endorse final draft agreements in the negotiation process. This inclusive process was critical; as one UN official recounted, ". . . the 6-year process involved so many sectors of society that when the agreement was not fully implemented, violence did not erupt. This was because so many people became invested. There was a real sense of ownership" (interview, 2007). So although the ASC's participation declined during the implementation of the peace agreement, these civil society organizations became stakeholders and therefore committed to seeing the process through. In the words of Enrique Alvarez, it "became a historic milestone because of the capacity for dialogue, negotiation, and agreement between different

134   *UN Peacebuilding Commission*

sectors … it is likely that the peace process would have been very different—and probably much less comprehensive—without them" (2002: 6).

The most logical access point for civil society and women's organizations in particular is the PBC's country-specific committees. Although the PBC does not offer a formal seat for such groups, they still "present the best opportunities for civil society organizations and in particular women's groups to participate in the Commission's work" (Ekiyor 2006: 4). NGOs, including women's groups, have been able to establish a working, albeit an informal relationship, with the country-specific committees for Sierra Leone and Burundi.[37]

Country-specific strategic planning: Burundi and Sierra Leone

Six months after the PBC came into being at its second organizational committee meeting in July 2006, Burundi and Sierra Leone were selected as the first cases for the Commission.[38] The first country-specific committee meetings were held in October 2006 and the second were held in December 2006; civil society groups were invited to participate in both rounds. Numerous informal country meetings have been held in recent months. In March of 2007, the PBC conducted a field visit for consultation with local actors in Sierra Leone and did the same in Burundi the following month.[39] A content analysis of the documents emerging from these meetings and visits reveals several significant themes for understanding how women and gender have materialized in this developing security discourse called peacebuilding over the course of 2006 and half of 2007. To trace this process, the bullets below represent the majority of official statements on references to women and gender in country-specific terms since Sierra Leone and Burundi were put on the PBC agenda.[40]

Sierra Leone:
- At the first country-specific committee meeting, Member States explicitly reaffirmed centrality of SCR 1325 for the implementation of peacebuilding strategies.
- Several delegations at the country-specific meetings mentioned the issue of women's employment as part of the peacebuilding mandate.
- Mr. J. Victor Angelo, Executive Representative of the Secretary-General for Sierra Leone, at the second country-specific meeting identified women's participation in democratic institutions of governance as a gap that still exists despite peacebuilding efforts in the country. He also put forth the notion of enhancing women's capacity to participate equally in the political processes of Sierra Leone as an important next step in the peacebuilding process.
- Mrs. Pratt, Executive Board Member of the Network on Collaborative Peacebuilding for Sierra Leone argued at both country-specific meetings for the need to focus on human resource development, including skills and training of youth and economic empowerment of women.
- In July 2006, the West Africa Network for Peacebuilding in partnership with its national network, Network on Collaborative Peacebuilding, organized a

civil society consultation focused on the PBC and its work in Sierra Leone. Gender-mainstreaming emerged as one of eight priorities of civil society. The meeting operationalized this priority in terms of women's legal rights, legislation targeting discrimination, and representation in parliament.

- In an informal briefing with the PBC, Milkah Kihunah, representing Women's International League for Peace and Freedom stressed the importance of women's perspective in the peace process. Giving the example of girl soldiers in Sierra Leone, she emphasized the need for special programs for women and girls.
- In an informal thematic discussion briefing paper on justice sector reform, Ms. Kelli Muddell of the International Center for Transitional Justice, made the case that one of three immediate concerns that the PBC must address in this area is "the growing insecurity of women and children occasioned by early marriage, forced marriage, female genital mutilation, and the increasing incidents of violence against women and children including domestic violence and rape."
- Ms. Muddell also informally briefed the PBC on the gender justice and the Truth and Reconciliation Commission in Sierra Leone.
- In January 2007, the PBSO in partnership with UNIFEM and the Sierra Leone Ministry of Gender and Children Affairs hosted a two-day National Consultation for Enhancing Women's Engagement with the United Nations Peacebuilding Commission, the conclusion of which will factor into Sierra Leone's Peace Consolidation Strategy and the proposals to be submitted to the Peacebuilding Fund. Much of the discussion focused on Sierra Leone's upcoming elections and women's participation in that election as voters and candidates.

Burundi:
- At the first country-specific committee meeting, Member States explicitly reaffirmed centrality of SCR 1325 for the implementation of peacebuilding strategies.
- Also at this first country meeting, several delegations including Burundi, Denmark and El Salvador stressed the need to increase women's participation and representation in decision-making structures.
- In the fall of 2006, the Swedish Centre and the Global Partnership for the Prevention of Armed Conflict organized a series of consultations involving 68 civil society organizations. That report was produced from these meetings articulated the need for a Gender National Policy under the rubric of prioritizing women and children in community recovery efforts. Of the 83 individual participants, only 3 represented a women-specific group.
- At the December country meetings, Ms. Karen Barnes, Gender and Peacebuilding Program Officer from International Alert, pointed the PBC's attention to not only focus on the quantity of women's participation in Burundian decision-making structures, but the quality of such participation as well. She also discussed a report from the Center of Women for Peace in

136 UN Peacebuilding Commission

Burundi that recommended the PBC invite local women to consultations, support the establishment of a truth commission, support the reform of discriminatory laws, and involve more women in security sector reform to better address the women's personal insecurity.

- In February 2007, at informal thematic discussion on promoting good governance, the Chair of the Burundi committee, identified gender issues, "including the impact of conflict on Burundian women (rape, projected decline in life expectancy from 60 to 39 by 2010, discrimination in property and land ownership and participation) and their participation in sustainable peacebuilding efforts" as remaining challenges for the PBC in establishing good governance.

As this list demonstrates, references to women and gender have been emerging from both state and non-state actors at the global, regional, and local levels. At first glance, this list indicates a fairly strong recognition of women's roles in the work of the PBC at the country level and the importance of including women's civil society groups in the peace process. Nadjibullah's involvement in the meetings with women's groups in Sierra Leone, representing the PBSO, is an example of the kind of "engagement in priority-setting processes" that women's groups and civil society more broadly is aiming for (Wyeth 2006: 3). In short, the country field missions have met with civil society organizations, including women's organizations, and gender specialists have presented at both formal and informal meetings.[41] Further, the PBC has been open to input from the NGO community in New York as illustrated with the roundtable, *Enhancing Security and the Rule of Law: How can gender be better integrated into the priorities of the UN Peacebuilding Commission?* (June 5, 2007).[42]

Both the Strategic Peacebuilding Strategy for Burundi (PBC/1/BDI/4, June 22, 2007) and the Sierra Leone Peacebuilding Cooperation Framework (PBC/2/SLE/1, December 3, 2007) identify gender issues as cross-cutting priorities. As emphasized by civil society, gender mainstreaming translates into capacity-building measures in several areas. First, participation emerges as a significant theme throughout. This means that women must be included in decision-making structures at the national level in order to promote good governance, democratic institutions, and legislative and judicial reform. Women's role in peacebuilding also demands women's involvement in economic development, particularly in terms of capacity building for employment. Protection also emerges as a framework for action in the context of women and children as vulnerable groups. All-in-all women's issues have established a certain presence in these deliberations and that is significant—particularly given the institutional shortcomings in the development of the peacebuilding architecture discussed in previous sections of this chapter.[43]

At the same time, these references to women and gender should also be interpreted with caution and skepticism. First, women's issues are largely understood from a governance perspective that emphasizes creating opportunities that allow women to participate in the existing political, economic, and social structures of these post-conflict societies. While this is undoubtedly an important component of the WPS agenda, it is far from adequate. Such a focus really only promotes a widening of the existing institutions and discourses, rather than something more transformative. By not taking the notion of gender seriously, the planned action of the PBC thus far really only adds women rather than challenging the fundamental nature of the peacebuilding approach. Now, certainly as the composition of people participating in UN peacebuilding expands, the potential for more integral change improves greatly. But political and economic structures must be seen as gendered institutions in order for such change to occur and women are only part of this equation. As one interviewee who had been part of the NGO Working Group on Women, Peace, and Security argues, "in some ways women, peace and security and 1325 have lost their comprehensiveness ... it has become a program on women and governance ... losing the potential of really integrating gender into the broader peace and security agenda" (interview, 2007). This highlights one of the main paradoxes of attempting to securitize women's rights and gender equality in the context of peacebuilding practices. In order to engage with the dominant security structures and processes of peacebuilding, it is necessary to "speak the language," thereby dulling the ability to present real, transformative change. As Sandra Whitworth (2004) argues, anything beyond technical solutions and problem-solving approaches is not part of the UN system. Although the existence of the WPS network and SCR 1325 provide useful guidelines for post-conflict contexts, it is not clear that anything other than tokenism results and the "central problem of bridging security and development with a gender-sensitive understanding of security is not addressed" (Barnes 2006: 24). Such language in traditional security arenas does not allow for the possibility, for example, to problematize the "security-development" nexus as inherently flawed in certain circumstances and for certain people.

Moreover, the majority of references made focus on women only, not gender and not men.[44] The terms gender and women are used interchangeably, and this is problematic on a number of levels for both men and women in post-conflict societies. This conflation of terms does not allow the PBC to seriously engage the various constructions of masculinity and femininity in post-conflict societies, and the implications of those gendered roles and expectations on establishing long-term peace and stability. In this way, the policy of gender-mainstreaming as adopted by PBC is fatally flawed given that it only seeks to understand women's relationship to men and to existing institutions. Not only does this raise important questions about how "mainstreamed" gender mainstreaming is, but how "gendered" it really is as well. There appears to be a real need to distinguish between but yet promote both a women-specific approach and a gender-mainstreaming approach so as to avoid one approach rendering the other invisible. The international community has yet to strike this balance.

Conclusion

"As a classical crosscutting issue, peacebuilding does not fit within the exclusive jurisdiction of any single international body" (Cutillo 2006: 2). The same can be

138   *UN Peacebuilding Commission*

said for women's rights and gender-mainstreaming strategies, and although the UN's reform process, in particular the focus on post-conflict peacebuilding, theoretically offered an opportunity for the goals of the WPS network and SCR 1325 to be fully implemented, women's rights and gendered notions of security have yet to become part of the mainstream. Maybe full integration with the mainstream, as is, is not possible. Women's activism as mandated by SCR 1325 has helped to advance women's participation within peacebuilding to a certain degree, and this is a significant achievement. Nonetheless, as Cynthia Enloe (2005: 281) maintains:

> perhaps what was not grasped, and is still not absorbed by the members of those delegations or by the thousands of officials worldwide who found 1325 lying in their boxes, was the genuinely radical understanding that informed the feminist analysis undergirding 1325. That feminist understanding is this: that patriarchy—in all its varied guises, camouflaged, khaki clad, and pin-striped—is a principal cause both of the outbreak of violent societal conflicts and of the international community's frequent failures in providing long-term resolution to those violent conflicts.

Thus, this case study of the PBC illustrates the way that the security discourse has enabled women to broaden the UN's approach to peace and security without necessarily challenging some of its most fundamental premises. Women's inclusion in the security arena is still a product of women's relentless activism at the local, regional, and global level even in the context of peacebuilding. It definitely did not come about on its own, or by the PBC member states. In this way, the security discourse and SCR 1325 has not led to the institutionalization of women's right to participate or the integration of a gender perspective into most of the day-to-day activity of the UN's security processes and practices. The gains that women have made have largely centered on political participation and governance issues and have been the result of intense lobbying by major actors within the WPS network. While such gains are certainly important, they are not necessarily transformative and may even serve to reinforce existing political, economic, and social structures, most especially the central role of the state.

Along these lines, this case raises important questions about the nature and even the desirability of gender advisers or women's groups as mechanisms for empowerment. To a certain degree, such mechanisms reflect the old "add women and stir" approach that dominated global development circles in the 1960s and 1970s. While this approach is still criticized, its emergence is not surprising, nor its use entirely ineffective given how post-conflict societies so severely lack resources and usually operate under major political constraints. In some ways, adding women may be the only place to start when it comes to integrating a "gender perspective." Not unexpectedly, many interviewees prioritized this strategy as the logical and necessary first step in working toward political change. Still, "the gendered nature of peacebuilding interventions requires constant questioning and indeed, significant transformation, of attitudes and structures that may not be

UN Peacebuilding Commission 139

possible through such methods" (Barnes 2006: 25). By no means does adding women lead to change in attitudes or structure, but it may be a way of establishing a basic foundation to be built upon over time. Such an approach will inevitably require the continued vigilance of the WPS network for many years to come.

The tension presented by this additive approach is not all that different from one of the ongoing and fundamental challenges in post-conflict peacebuilding. The PBC was established to institutionalize a long-term, sustained approach by the UN for countries transitioning from war and conflict. Much of the work to this point, however, has been based on the need to act quickly. In other words, the PBC and the Fund most often revert to what is most urgent; the short term wins out.[45] This is similar to meeting the urgent needs of women's rights in post-conflict situations—just get them in the room, bring them to the table and allow them to be part of the process. Meeting these immediate needs is central and is out of necessity, but as this chapter demonstrates, this may present obstacles to truly integrating a gender perspective and achieving gender equality over the long run.

As a case study, the PBC also provides insight into the power politics that still guide the work of the UN and its evolving approach to international peace and security (Rougheen 2006). As Roland Paris (2001b) argues, it is not enough for studies of UN peacekeeping and peacebuilding to analyze the efficacy of UN approaches, but they must situate the UN's approach to peace and security in the larger dynamics of international relations. The PBC is not ideologically neutral and should be seen as a new construction of power relationships. The negotiations leading up to the establishment of the PBC were dominated with concerns about the relationship between the PBC and other key UN bodies, not the least of which was the SC, as well as who would serve on the PBC. It was clear that member states from the "Global South" were concerned about the SC and major donor countries dominating the PBC and its work. These concerns clearly trumped any concerns about gender or SCR 1325 that might have emerged, and they continue to impact the politics of PBC today. Women's rights and gender equality are just one component of this political dynamic, where state power and national security are still predominant despite NGOs ongoing efforts to chip away at state-based notions of security.

Notes

1 There are two notable exceptions here within the context of the UN. The first was the "Women's Contribution to Peace Project," launched in 1996 by the UN Economic, Social and Cultural Organization (UNESCO). This initiative aimed at empowering women and supporting their peace projects as well as gender-sensitizing international efforts by emphasizing non-violent approaches. For more information, see http://www. unesco.org/ccp/uk/projects/wcpinfo.htm. Second, in 1998, the UN Economic Commission for Africa (UNECA) sponsored the *African Women's Report* which recognized that "women in post-conflict situations are not mere passive sufferers and aid-dependent beneficiaries specially vulnerable to abuse, but have been and should be very much part of the solution" (UNECA 1998: v). These programs were relatively small and remained part of an economic approach rather than embedded within the security discourse.

140 UN Peacebuilding Commission

2 It also, however, acknowledges women's *right* to participate (Cohn 2004).

3 At the same time, many argue that the Commission's narrow focus on the post-conflict stage ignores many important elements of SCR 1325, as it is concerned with all aspects of conflict: pre, during, and post. The Commission is only mandated to deal with the latter, and was not created to address preventative or during conflict strategies.

4 Security Council Resolution 1820, although not part of the case study for this chapter, does stress "the important role the Peacebuilding Commission can play by including in its advice and recommendations for post-conflict peacebuilding strategies, where appropriate, ways to address sexual violence committed during and in the aftermath of armed conflict, and in ensuring consultation and effective representation of women's civil society in its country-specific configurations, as part of its wider approach to gender issues (2008: para 11).

5 It is important to note that this nexus exists despite significant resistance, particularly from the United States. Jeffrey Laurenti rightly points out how "Washington resists linking the political and military issues that Americans understand as 'security' with the economic and social issues arising from the deep poverty prevalent in four-fifths of the world's nations. Others think the linkage is obvious. Even the comfortable elites in developing countries are acutely aware they are sitting atop powder kegs, and their personal security, as well as their political stability and security of their regions, is chronically at risk" (2006: 431).

6 A recent study by Collier *et al.* (2003) finds that failed states rarely have the institutional structures and the minimal resources necessary in post-conflict reconstruction. These shortcomings for effective governance and peace building are only exacerbated by the underdevelopment, poverty, and marginalization that exist in these states.

7 For the full text of this document, see http://www.un.org/Docs/SG/agpeace.html.

8 Cheryl de la Rey and Susan McKay (2006) describe this approach to peacebuilding as "typical" and classify it as "post-conflict reconstruction of societal infrastructures and action-based approaches" to peace building.

9 It is important to note here that Galtung (1976) actually introduced the idea that building peace is different from making or keeping peace. In his conceptualization, which is still applicable today, peace building consists of an infrastructure within and between nations that offers alternatives to and removes causes of war.

10 Boutros-Ghali maintains, "The foundation-stone of this work is and must remain the State" (1992: para 17).

11 For a more detailed account of this ideational and programmatic shift see the special issue on recovering from civil conflict in *International Peacekeeping* (2002), especially Sorpong Peou's article.

12 For the full text of this document, see http://www.un.org/Docs/SG/agdev.html.

13 For more on this see, for example, Collier *et al.*(2003).

14 For the full text of this program, see http://documents-dds-ny.un.org/doc/UNDOC/GEN/N97/189/79/img/N9718979.pdf?OpenElement

15 General Lakhdar Brahimi served as chair of this expert panel.

16 It is worth noting here that feminist scholars and activists have long problematized notions of "peace" or "post-conflict" as being male-centered assumptions about the relative "security" experienced by a given society once a ceasefire has been put into place or a peace agreement has been signed. "Post-conflict security" or "stability" often has very different meanings for men and women in a war-torn society, which can blur the line between "conflict" and "post-conflict." For more on this, see Mazurana et al. (2005), particularly the Introduction and Part I.

17 This is perhaps most starkly evident in the fact that roughly half of all countries that emerge from conflict lapse back into violence within five years. For more, see the 2005 report of Secretary-General Kofi Annan, *In Larger Freedom: Towards Development, Security, and Human Rights for All*. Available at www.un.org/larger-freedom/contents.htm.

18 One important exception here is the research of Sanam Anderlini (2007).

19 These references occur on pages 11, 32, 33, 39, 41, 62, 71, and 72.

20 The UN system on the whole continues to fall short of reaching—or even coming to close to reaching—its stated goal of 50–50 gender equality. As of December 31, 2007, women in the UN system constituted 38.4% of all staff in the professional and higher categories with appointments of one year or more; 27% of all staff at the D-1 level and above; and 39.6% of all staff at the P level. At the highest level of Under Secretary-General, women only constitute 17.5%. For more information regarding sex-aggregated statistics of UN personnel, see the Report on the Improvement of the Status of Women in the United Nations System (A/63/364).

21 Of the ten members of the panel that produced the Brahimi report, only two were women. The panel that produced the report *A More Secure World* in 2004 had 16 members, three of which were women. Even Annan's most recent high-level panel on UN-system-wide coherence in areas of development, humanitarian assistance and the environment has only three women out of 15 members.

22 See for example, *Delivering As One*, the report of the High-Level Panel on UN-System Wide Coherence (2006). Available at http://www.un.org/events/panel/resources/pdfs/HLP-SWC-FinalReport.pdf.

23 These groups not only held informal meetings with Member State delegations, but they also produced numerous documents making the case for including women's civil society groups in the process. See for example, "The UN Peacebuilding Commission: A Blueprint for Amplifying Women's Voices and Participation" (2005). Available at www.womenpeacesecurity.org.

24 This insight is based on concepts set forth by V. Spike Peterson and Anne Runyan (1998).

25 The UN Security Council, with Resolution 1478 (2003) has even recognized this specific network in its peacebuilding initiatives in Sierra Leone.

26 The UN has defined gender mainstreaming as "a strategy for making women's as well as men's concerns and experiences an integral dimension of the design, implementation, monitoring and evaluation of policies and programmes in all political, economic and societal spheres so that women and men benefit equally and inequality is not perpetuated" A/52/3/Rev.1.

27 For a comprehensive description of the existing literature, see Porter 2003.

28 For more specifics on the functions, structure and operational principles of the PBC, go to http://www.un.org/peace/peacebuilding/ and http://www.reformtheun.org/index.php/issues/1735?theme=alt4.

29 This chapter does not examine outcomes of country programming because the empirical time frame for this analysis end in the summer of 2007 prior to any project implementation in Sierra Leone or Burundi. A closer look at programming output and implementation will certainly be an important area for future research.

30 Importantly, the Summit Outcome document, in addition to endorsing the establishment of a peacebuilding commission, did reaffirm Member States commitment to implementation of SCR 1325 and to women's role in establishing peace and security. This reference, however, appeared in a different section than that of the PBC and thereby omitting the obvious connection between 1325 and women's role in peacebuilding. This disconnect among Member States at the World Summit helps to explain why SCR 1325 was not specifically part of the resolutions creating the PBC.

31 See UN Security Council Resolution S/RES/1645 (December 20, 2005) and General Assembly Resolution A/RES/60/180 (December 30, 2005).

32 A critical analysis of the actual 31-members states of the PBC is also important, but more difficult to break through as these national delegations have existed prior to the establishment of the PBC and a gender balance would require a reworking of established national delegations to the SC, GA, ECOSOC, and other organizations. Given that the PBSO is starting from scratch, it has much more potential for shifts in the gender balance of the organization.

142   UN Peacebuilding Commission

33 The General Assembly carries out its work through six main committees; the fifth committee is charged with reviewing budgetary and administrative matters.

34 The text of this resolution can be found at http://www.peacewomen.org/un/women_reform/PBC/5thComRes.pdf.

35 McAskie retired in June 2008 and was succeeded by Assistant Secretary-General Jane Holl Lute.

36 In early drafts of the Summit Outcome Document, the PBC mandate included references to the participation of non-Member State actors in the PBC country-specific discussions, such as civil society organizations. This category of participants was dropped, however, in the final document adopted by member states. See *High-Level Plenary Meeting of the General Assembly 14–16 September 2005 Draft Outcome Document*, available at www.un.org/ga/president/59/draft_outcome.htm.

37 According to the annual PBC progress reports to the GA and the SC, gender issues have been considered by the PBC in the Country-Specific Committees. See *Report of the Peacebuilding Commission on its first session*, A/62/137-S/2007/458 (July 25, 2007) and *Report of the Peacebuilding Commission on its second session*, A/63/92-S/2008 (June 24, 2008).

38 Many have been critical of the amount of time it took the PBC to select these two countries. The political-dynamic of this process was highlighted by the fact that it took Member States over five months (from December 2005 to May 2007) to elect the full membership of the PBC's Organizational Committee. Before that, the political haggling over the wording of the resolutions that established the PBC resulted in confusion surrounding its precise role. For more, see Wyeth (2006).

39 Following these two field visits, the UN General Assembly and the Security Council selected the Central African Republic and Guinea Bissau to be added to the PBC's agenda per resolutions 60/180 and 1645 (2005). These two states are not, however, part of this analysis.

40 The data for this section was drawn from documents posted at a number of reputable websites, including www.reformtheun.org, www.securitycouncilreport.org, www.womenpeacesecurity.org, and http://www.un.org/peace/peacebuilding/.

41 It is worth noting here that a majority of the statements on women and gender came from the mouths of women, whether as part of Member State delegations or NGO networks.

42 Specifically, this meeting was organized by International Alert and the NGO Working Group on Women, Peace and Security. At this meeting, a representative from Dushirehamwe (a network of women peace activists) spoke to high-level officials about the fact that women's representation was absent from the Peacebuilding Fund National Steering Committee in Burundi. As a result, Burundian women's organizations were asked to put forward a women's representative for the Steering Committee (interview, 2007).

43 In looking ahead, it will also be important to monitor the work the Working Group on Lessons Learned, which was established by the PBC in January 2007. Although the work of this body extends beyond the temporal limits of the research for this case study, the Working Group has great potential to enhance dialogue and attention to gender issues relevant to the country-committees' agendas in the coming years.

44 One exception here is Ms. Muddell's address to the PBC on gender justice and the Truth and Reconciliation Commission in Sierra Leone. In her statement, she discussed how social structures and gender roles continue to foster a violent society at all levels. She spoke from a critical, feminist perspective that challenged definitions of violence, gender, and security.

45 I am thankful to William Durch for this insight.

7 Women, peace, and security

Not the final analysis

NGOs, UN organizations and sympathetic governments now need to be collaborating to develop long-term strategies, rather than focusing mainly on short-term tactics. Short-term tactics should be part of a larger sustainable plan that includes research, policy development, advocacy, and/or implementation, and is practical and realistic in approach. But a long-term strategy also needs to be framed in the context of building a social movement reaching out to those working on issues of human rights, international law, the environment, globalization, and terrorism-related issues. This could facilitate a paradigm shift in thinking about security.

Felicity Hill and Maha Muna 2004

I spent yesterday with women from the Solomon Islands, Vanuatu, Bougainville and Fiji, who were talking about their actual—not theoretical—experiences of war and their efforts to attain any sort of access to decision-making power. Yesterday, women spoke about being reduced to getting on their knees, literally, outside the discussions they were barred from to beg for the disarmament process to happen in Bougainville. Both policymakers and the women I sat with yesterday have a very "commonsense" response to the idea of being categorized: Whatever the code words let us in! Peace-builder, decision-maker, whatever argument works, let us in! Let us in so we can wrestle with the discussion at least; contest the parameters, and react, in real time, and not after the fact. Let us into the Security Council, into the decision-making fora, into the rooms of the elusive place, let women in. It is the horror experienced daily which is the reason we want to get hold of the steering wheel of the Security Council. It is because the Security Council sets the contours of the political discussion on peace and war on this planet and, significantly, because it mandates actual peace operations.

Felicity Hill 2004

The quotations above were taken from a roundtable discussion of scholar-activists who played significant roles in the drafting, adoption and/or implementation of SCR 1325.[1] The concerns expressed highlight well one of the major tensions that the security framework, as utilized by the WPS network particularly in the context

144   *Women, peace, and security*

of SCR 1325, presents for those working in this field. On the one hand, activists must remain committed to the long-term, comprehensive emancipatory goals of the broader women's movement. This involves being critical of state-based security structures for their gender biases and often contradictory policies that are deeply embedded in their foundational institutions, such as the military and the police. On the other hand, the immediate needs of women in conflict and post-conflict situations often demand strategies and approaches that are not necessarily in line with the more strategic goals and may even work against certain components of the larger project of ending women's subordination worldwide. In many cases, these most urgent needs trump all else. As this book illustrates, the security framework reflects this conundrum. The line between engaging UN security actors and institutions to make feminist critiques and the critique itself being neutralized through engagement with those structures is not always discernable. Employing the security language may be advantageous in the short term, but it also situates many actors in the WPS network in positions where more fundamental critiques challenging the traditional security paradigm become impossible and even unthinkable. So, while the WPS network and Security Council Resolution (SCR) 1325 have facilitated entry points into the corridors of power, we must proceed with caution. "Simultaneously the power structures that we wish to dismantle are the very structures that set the terms of women's entry ... this revolutionary capacity can also be caught *recycling* rather than resignifying the terms of the debate" (Kinsella, as cited in Cohn et al. 2004: 137–8).

Although the case studies in this book highlight the significant problems posed by this underlying tension in securitizing women's rights and gender equality, they also provide insight into theory development as well as avenues for moving forward in terms of practice and policy. My findings are best understood by returning to the three basic questions that were posed in the introductory chapter:

1   How is security defined *and* practiced within the context of international organization?
2   In what ways, if any, has women's activism been able to challenge traditional conceptions of security?
3   What are the implications of the security framework for the broader goals of the women's movement?

From a theoretical perspective, this research proves that state-based conceptualizations of security are still paramount and realpolitik is most often the guiding norm for the international peace and security agenda. Nevertheless, important exceptions exist as a result of the increasing use of the securitization strategy and human security as a conceptual framework for action. Furthermore, women's activism has played a role in challenging traditional conceptions of security. Specifically, through the security framework and SCR 1325, the WPS network has been able to broaden the scope of UN Security Council procedures, thereby expanding the traditional agenda to include unconventional issues and individual-level concerns in ways that have not been done before. Lastly, as the

Women, peace, and security 145

security framework has impacted the international security agenda, so too has it affected the women's groups that utilize such language. In this way, securitization as a strategy has been both beneficial and limiting, reminding those working for women's rights and gender equality in conflict and post-conflict situations across the globe to choose their words (and frames) wisely and to proceed with caution.

Defining international security policy in the twenty-first Century

This project demonstrates that the academic debates on the meaning of security have mirrored those in the policy arena, at least within the context of the United Nations. Although rumblings emerged in the 1980s, scholars and practitioners have increasingly criticized the traditional security agenda for being too narrow, particularly since the end of the Cold War. These critiques have often called for greater breadth and depth in terms what constitutes a security issue and whose security is at stake.[2] Economic, societal, and environmental risks and threats have been compared and contrasted with the conventional preoccupation of military and territorial threats, while individuals, communities, and even ecological systems have been conceptualized as referent objects alongside the state.

And while it is clear that traditional state-based (and militaristic) approaches to security are still central, they have not gone uncontested or unaffected. Human security, as a guiding principle and framework for action, has been at the fore of these discussions and debates regarding the nature and business of international peace and security today. As the case studies here illustrate, human security is not simply a concept for academics to dispute, but one that is applicable to global, national, and local processes. In this sense, these findings diverge from the many critics that find human security to be operationally and practically irrelevant.[3] In short, human security as a discourse "reflects and is working towards changing the all-important contexts in which different conceptions and practices of security are evoked by actors" (McDonald 2002: 292). So although human security, as a framework, was not necessarily a conscious, strategic choice for many activists within the WPS network, the concept supported their objectives and was part of the language that they used to frame their concerns.

In looking at this discourse and the way in which human security was operationalized within the WPS network, we can begin to see common themes emerge that give some definitional parameters to a concept that is often criticized as too vague and all-encompassing.[4] First, human security "seeks to place the individual—or people collectively—as the referent of security" (Newman 2001: 239). The WPS network has successfully focused the international community—at least in an ad hoc way—on the individual security needs of women as a significant collective.[5] This is not only evident in the increased language on women and gender at UN headquarters and within SC resolutions themselves, but also in the increased recognition of women's needs on the ground, as seen with UNIFEM's

146   Women, peace, and security

work in security sector reform. In working with national police in post-conflict situations, UNIFEM has been able to focus the reform of these institutions on the individual and unique security needs of women in those societies. Additionally, this relationship is indicative of another central tenet of human security in terms of newly emerging actors and partnerships. Human security as a discourse creates space for actors usually excluded from agenda-setting process to access the international security agenda and its conventional actors in new and creative ways (McDonald 2002). UNIFEM's relationships with the Security Council, Member States, and even local police units exemplify this aspect of the human security agenda. Lastly, proponents of human security maintain that this encompassing paradigm brings together fields that have traditionally been kept apart—humanitarian affairs, development, and security (Oberleitner 2005). The gaps between these fields has been particularly obvious in UN efforts in post-conflict reconstruction, and as the case study on UN peacebuilding here illustrates, the human security discourse has been part of establishing a common strategic agenda in various realms of UN activity, at least in terms of its mandate and vision. Simply put, human security as a conceptual framework for action on women's rights and gender equality serves as an important bridge between development and security. Just as attention has been "paid to ensuring that development efforts not only do no harm but play a positive role in helping to alleviate tensions, address structural sources of conflict, and promote sustainable peace" (Anderlini 2007: 206), so must the security community be vigilant about its impact on development. Human security in the context of women's rights and gender equality highlights the critical value of the security-development nexus as well as the ways in which harmony between the communities is not necessarily natural, and therefore must be an intentional part of policy-making at every level.

Where this project diverges from most theories on human security is in beliefs about what human security means for the state and the centrality of national security interests. Many proponents of human security see it as an affront, a contradiction, a challenge, or, at least, an alternative to state-based notions of security. Opponents of human security, particularly those from critical security studies, often dismiss it as irrelevant and meaningless.[6] My findings, however, suggest that human security is not only relevant but has significant implications for the nature and practice of national security and the role of the state in international security matters. Human security approaches not only rely upon and reinforce state-based notions of security, but in some ways may expand state control over individual security needs—in this case women. From the perspective of the referent object, the shift from the state to the individual is significant, but it certainly does not challenge the central status of mainstream security institutions. As the case studies illuminate in terms of policy and practice, a human security approach has been reliant upon state-based structures—the UN, the Security Council, peacekeeping operations, the PBC, the Human Security Network, and international and national military and police forces.[7] Such reinforcement strengthens the role of the state, somewhat neutralizing any erosion of state sovereignty that might result from the involvement of new actors and the focus on new issues and referents. In securitizing women's rights, human security, at least in the short term, actually reinforces the primary position of state security institutions and structures.

Another point where this research departs from many theories on human security is the way that human security has been linked and even interchanged with human rights (Suhrke 1999). For example, Ikeda (1996: 170, as cited in Rees & Blanchard 1999) identifies respect for human rights as the essence of human security and Liotta (2002: 474) characterizes human security's focus on individuals rather than nation-states as a "protection of individual liberties and rights." Although the connection between human security and human rights seems logical in theory, this research identifies a number of problems when it comes to practice. When looking at SCR 1325 as a tool, as a mechanism for international law, there seem to be functional and organizational gaps between those working on SCR 1325 and those implementing the Convention to Eliminate All Forms of Discrimination against Women—the international human rights treaty for women. Further, as the comparison with children's rights in the Security Council illustrated, the security framework separates human security from a rights-based approach. This latter approach would have meant framing women's issues and gender equality in conflict and post-conflict situations, for example, in terms of how violence against women constitutes a violation of women's fundamental human right to equality and physical integrity. This means approaching women's issues and gender equality as an obligation to international human rights law, and thereby, legally part of any international peacekeeping or peacebuilding effort. Simply stated, these concerns are a matter of internationally recognized, legally binding human rights as much as they are a matter of security. Such a framework would shift the discussion from how states stand to gain from such efforts in terms of narrow national interest to the *responsibilities* of states to protect and promote women's rights and gender equality.

In short, my findings reveal an institutional gap between those working on WPS and those working on women's human rights in the context of international law. There is a gap where the two are not taking advantage of the overlap and common goals within their work. This is not altogether that surprising given that the security framework relies on the unique contributions that women make to peace processes (rather than on women's inalienable human rights). In this stereotypical model, women are mothers, wives of soldiers, care-givers, and teachers; they are defined in relation to their responsibility for others, and are therefore framed as essential building blocks in the peace and security agenda. While women are essential building blocks in these critical processes, this model does not promote women as rights-holders, per se, and can therefore contribute to further polarizations and discrimination along gender lines as societies work to rebuild after conflict. The security framework focuses in on the interests of states, rather than the responsibilities of states to protect human rights, creating long-term obstacles in any real transformation away from traditional state-based constructions of security to a more human-centered paradigm.

148 *Women, peace, and security*

The impact of women's activism on the security agenda

Although women's activism and their use of the security framework have not fundamentally transformed the international security agenda, they have been able to engage international security actors, altering the process by which international security policy is enacted. For example, Chapter 3 concludes that SCR 1325 has led to rhetorical, legal, and procedural shifts that broaden the security agenda to include women and women's concerns in new and important ways. This shift has translated into increased awareness and sensitivity by those in the international security arena, particularly in terms of how UN operations impact women and men differently. As one UN official noted:

> Yes, I've seen changes, some changes in the last five years. I've seen more acceptance and less laughter. I haven't heard laughter when the gender issue is being raised for some long time. It's now considered bad taste, that is a change, it is being taken more seriously, and I think that is thanks to measures like the resolutions and the ownership [by states].
>
> (Hill 2004–05: 39, emphasis added)

While this indicates a stronger taboo awareness especially in policy-making circles, it also underscores how far the international community has yet to go in integrating and internalizing a gender perspective. Authentic gender-mainstreaming has transformative qualities that would not allow anyone to refer to gender as "the gender issue," as such a categorization still marginalizes, ghettoizes, and underestimates the range of concerns and contributions that a gendered perspective and approach means for the mainstream.

Even widening the security agenda, however, must be seen as indirectly and, at times, directly supporting the principal role of the state in providing security. The emphasis on the Security Council as a legitimate and authoritative security body, the focus on *national* action plans to implement SCR 1325, changes to peacekeeping operations based on *in-country* programs, and the creation of gender advisers and gender affairs offices within existing mainstream security apparatuses reinforces the centrality of the state. UNIFEM's engagement with Security Sector Reform, as seen in Chapter 5, also supports this finding in terms of the Fund's reliance on state institutions, such as the police, for inserting women's issues.[8] The analysis of the Peacebuilding Commission is further indicative of the role of state sovereignty as the organizing principle for the international community, as the PBC's organizational structure is based on voluntary participation of states and country-specific meetings for developing peacebuilding strategies. To this extent, my research supports the neorealist mainstay that the state, as a national unit, is the "standard unit of security" (Buzan 1991: 19).

Nonetheless, changes in the language, procedures, and practices of state-based approaches to security are significant, particularly when these changes mean including references to women and gender concerns. Such shifts are the beginning stages of norm diffusion. This project has demonstrated the significance of

Women, peace, and security 149

the UN, its agencies, and most especially, related non-governmental organizations working symbiotically in the process of norm diffusion. The UN is both an "incubator" and "forum" for norm diffusion with the global outreach to engage thinking and consensus-building on alternative approaches to security (Morphet 2007). Using Finnemore and Sikkink's (1998) process of norm diffusion, we can access how far the norms set forth by the WPS network and SCR 1325 fall have come in terms of four stages: norm emergence, a tipping point of acceptance by a critical mass of relevant actors, a subsequent norm cascade, and then the eventual institutionalization and internationalization. The case studies have shown that there is an overall acceptance by a critical mass of relevant actors of the normative idea that women's rights and gender equality are legitimate concerns to be raised in discussions about international peace and security. While there is some evidence of this norm cascading into national policies for women, peace, and security in gradual and sporadic ways, it is clear that the norm has not yet reached the fourth stage. Women's rights and genuine gender awareness are far from institutionalized and internalized by the security sectors in the UN system.[9] NGOs are still the driving force of SCR 1325 and are continually pushing state actors to move from general acceptance to actual implementation. Thus, diffusion of norms linking women's rights to international peace and security is still teetering somewhere between the second and third phase. There is consensus that women's rights and gender equality are, in fact, legitimate concerns in the realm of international peace and security, but this is not the same as a belief that these concerns are necessarily essential. This is where more hard data is so disparately needed by those within the Council that are friendly to SCR 1325 and the WPS network. As emphasized in a number of the interviews that I conducted, there continues to be a real demand by Member States for *empirical and systematic* evidence (beyond anecdotal narratives) that women are vital components of establishing lasting peace and security. This demand certainly signals the continued importance and reliance upon the security framework for women in the years to come.

In the end, attempts at humanizing security lead to a discourse that is both engaging and limiting, especially when language leads to securitizing women's rights. As scholars from the Copenhagen School tradition argue:

We believe that there are many ways to understand security, and that each will have its merits and its drawbacks. Focusing on any one element will always make some things clearer at the cost of obscuring or distorting others. That is the nature of social theory, and there is no escaping from it.

(Buzan & Wæver 1997: 249–250)

Thus, the framework is just that, a framework, a starting point for change. A former UNIFEM official explains the significance of such a starting point:

a lot of people, people that don't know how politics work particularly in the international arena, they don't see the point of sitting in the corridors of the UN fighting for this language or that framework. But that is what it is about.

150   *Women, peace, and security*

You do that—you engage, you discuss, you argue, you advocate, whatever. Then you have a product that allows, that gives the policy weight, that raises the concerns and issues and then you have the potential to move the system.

(Interview, December 2006)

SCR 1325 and the WPS network must be seen as a means, rather than an end, and it must be one of many avenues being pursued in working toward the goals of the global women's movement.

Securitization as a strategy for women

From the perspective of human security, securitization as a discursive strategy has both advantages and drawbacks. The opportunities and limitations of this instrumental approach have been demonstrated by the case studies and support the warnings observed by the Copenhagen School: security is not necessarily "positive phenomena" and by "working with the assumption that security is a goal to be maximized, critics [potentially] eliminate other, potentially more useful ways of conceptualizing the problems being addressed" (Wæver 1995: 57). "Potentially" is inserted here because although my research identifies limitations, it also finds significant opportunities that securitization creates for marginalized groups such as women.

The limitations, as noted above, include the reinforcement of the primacy of the state in matters of security as they pertain to women's rights as well as the disconnect between securitization strategies and a rights-based approach. Furthermore, the security framework is limited by the essentialist assumptions that it makes about the world's women and the role that they play in conflict and post-conflict situations. Securitizing women's right relies upon the symbolic understanding of women as peacemakers and community reconcilers, and it assumes that these are the only sources from which women draw power and influence. This is not just problematic for women, but for the lack of attention such an approach gives to men and masculinity. Hill argues that the women, peace and security debate:

is potentially revolutionary as it could transform ways of understanding how security conceived, protected and enforced. It could make photos of only male leaders at peace negotiating tables starkly outdated. But for this to happen, the focus has to move from women to men and this still hasn't happened. Perpetually problematizing women, placing women, their absence or their 'victimhood', at the centre of 'the problem' of women, peace, and security fails to notice the problematic role of masculine identities in security discourse and actual wars, or the systematic over-representation of men.

(as cited in Cohn et al. 2004: 137)

In this way, there is conceptual confusion in the use of the term "gender." From "gender-mainstreaming" to "gender advisers" to the UN's "gender architecture,"

Women, peace, and security 151

this book illustrates the many ways that gender continues to be used interchangeably with women. While this conflation is not surprising, it is problematic for those trying to enact policies and programs around these concepts. It was clear in a number of interviews that both policy-makers in New York and practitioners working in the field were not entirely clear on what, for example, specifically constitutes gender-mainstreaming or the mandate of a gender adviser. What is increasingly obvious is that being gender-sensitive is, in fact, a skill set. It does not come naturally, even to women; it involves dedicated training and resources. The uncertainty surrounding how this skill set should be taught, or who should be teaching it remains a substantial obstacle for those committed to SCR 1325 and the WPS agenda.

Still, securitization has created the necessary language and political space that has allowed women entry into traditional security circles. The case studies illustrate how the security framework facilitated strategic partnerships, unlikely engagements, and even resources for the WPS network. In the eight short years of its existence, SCR 1325 has led to the creation of gender advisers, gender affairs units, consultation with local women's groups, and gender training at the national and international level in UN peacekeeping and peacebuilding efforts. These are initiatives that did not exist before, and although they are flawed, they are still significant.

Furthermore, the security framework has served as a mechanism for those involved in the WPS network to reframe old issues as new concerns of the security agenda. As seen in Chapter 5, gender-based violence and women's right to participate in decision-making bodies—the substantive focus of UNIFEM security sector reform activity thus far—are long-standing issues within the organization. They are just being reframed under the security rubric. This reframing has allowed UNIFEM to open new doors to long-standing issues, a mechanism resembling a "backdoor move" (Hertel 2006). Thus, marginalized groups have gained unexpected power because of the broadening effect of this mechanism.

The successes and failures of securitization as a strategy for the WPS network highlight the power dynamics underscoring the international peace and security agenda. In this sense:

> seeing the processes of 'securitization' within the broader understanding of the processes of 'institutionalization' gives us both a better understanding of the processes through which security problems and policies are practically constituted, the forms and exercise of power within those processes, and the kinds of power that formal organizations exercise in those contexts.
>
> (Williams 1997: 289–290)

My interviewees continually reminded me of centrality of power in every aspect of their work; as one UN official stated, "it is simply a political struggle every day here" (interview, November 2008).

152   *Women, peace, and security*

A way forward for WPS

This book presents several significant findings for understanding and analyzing women's activism in international relations. The security framework provides insight into the increasing presence and effect of NGOs in international politics in terms of their role in norm emergence and the agenda-setting process, the shifting dynamics of the global women's movement in the twenty-first century, and the transformative potential of gender-mainstreaming efforts for international security policy. These three indicators highlight the various ways that women's groups have been affected by their strategies.

The story of the WPS network began with the determination and creative work of women's activism largely in the context of NGOs. This is especially true for the emergence and adoption of SCR 1325:

> What makes 1325 unique is not only that it (finally) addresses women, war, and security, or that its scope is expansive and its implementation radical; what makes 1325 unique is that it is both the product of and the armature for massive mobilization of women's political energies.
>
> (Cohn 2004: 8)

These energies have largely come from non-state actors, although groups such as UNIFEM are central. NGOs continue to be the driving force in this process as demonstrated in the last case study on UN peacebuilding efforts and women's pursuit to influence the Commission. Thus, this research supports established literature on the strengthening relationship between transnational advocacy networks and global policy-making (Keck and Sikkink 1998a; Florini 1999; Joachim 2007), as well as the body of work that explores women's strategic use of UN mechanisms (Friedman 1995).

What is more, women's activism has not been isolated in the ivory tower of UN headquarters. The security framework has established a sort of common ground building a bridge between women activists in the Global North and the Global South. For example, 1325 has been translated into 95 different languages, from Danish to Hindi to Krio to Thai to Zulu. There are five pending translations from various Sudanese dialects alone.[10] The document is being used as a tool by local women to give them leverage with ruling parties. In my research, I had multiple opportunities to speak with women activists from Burundi and Liberia who were using 1325 to gain access to leaders and official political processes as well as to educate local women about their rights. According to a women's rights and peace activist from Burundi, "The most important thing is to know how to use 1325 as an advocacy tool ... We have to design a plan of activities around Resolution 1325 to make it more useful and understandable" (Ndacayisaba 2007: 3).

While these findings support the many "bottom up" approaches that explain the rise and role of NGOs, they also point to the increasingly important symbiotic relationships between NGOs and international governmental organizations (IGOs) as well as states. "Top down" theories on the influential role of NGOs have received

Women, peace, and security 153

increased attention by international relations scholars in recent years (Reimann 2006). Scholars, such as, Joachim (2007), Hertel (2006), Carpenter (2005), Smith (2000), and Boli & Thomas (1999), have begun to bridge the gap between social movement theories and theories on international institutions and organizations by emphasizing the role that IGOs and states, in partnerships with NGOs and TANs, have in creating political opportunities structures, resource mobilization, norm-diffusing mechanisms, and normative world cultures. This project lends credence to the validity of these studies and the need for future work to better understand the relationship between NGOs, IGOs, and states in issue emergence, norm diffusion, agenda-setting and policy-making. The WPS network clearly merits further analysis and study along this vein.

Lastly, this book contributes to theories on gender-mainstreaming by better distinguishing the normative and practical implications of broadening versus transforming the security agenda. From Women in Development (WID) to Gender and Development (GAD), the global women's movement was believed to have moved from an additive approach to a more integrative one, where gender was actually mainstreamed so as to transform the very fundamentals of the process from design to implementation. But as far as the security framework as a discursive strategy is concerned, women's organizations are still largely working to simply be incorporated into the process. Many of the "successes" analyzed in this research reflect an "add women and stir approach." This, of course, can be interpreted as the only starting point for women working in a field such as international security, where they have so long been isolated from. There is certainly some validity to the argument that by adding women and women's issues and therefore broadening the security agenda they will eventually have transformative consequences. As the Copenhagen School suggests in theorizing about securitization, it is only in working from the inside out that substantial change in nature and practice of security can occur. Thus, the additive approach becomes the first step for those part of the WPS network as they embody outsider status on at least two important levels. Women's groups involved in transforming the security arena carry a double burden—as women and as non-state actors. From this perspective, the additive approach seems less problematic and very pragmatic.

As feminist scholars remind us, however, genuine change requires proactive engagement with the mainstream in the mainstream, which goes beyond the important steps of inserting women into the process and putting women's concerns on the agenda. In this sense, transforming the mainstream must be seen as a "prerequisite for and an integral element (rather than a consequence) of the full realization of women's human rights and gender equality" (Corner 2004: 15). For the WPS network this requires a return to a debate on the overarching goals of the women's movement and recognizing the difference between securitizing women's rights and humanizing security. This sort of transformation is extremely difficult, but not impossible especially when viewed as a long-term process. As articulated by a UNIFEM official:

154 *Women, peace, and security*

We still really have not seen the women's peace agenda influencing the peace and security agenda as much as I would hope. In fact, the latest reports on militarism, we are still spending more and more on military spending than on humanitarian concerns or economic development. So, clearly we have not had that kind of impact yet. But that is a long-term process. I think in terms of resolving regional conflicts and having women able to have a voice in that, to have their role recognized, these are baby steps. Our long-term agenda of not having war at all, that is a long, long-term process. And we are very far from that."

(UNIFEM official, October 2006)

In the end, this research is "a study of evolution, metamorphosis, and experiment, of failure and success" (Kennedy 2006: xiv–xv). The WPS network continues to utilize the security discourse creating opportunities as well as obstacles and limitations. But these challenges are not a reason to write off this activism or SCR 1325 as just another resolution. Its broadening impact is significant; the potential for transformative change is radical. Such change, however, must not only be framed as a matter of international peace and security, but as a matter of universal human rights, global economic development, and democratic freedom as well.

Notes

1 For the full transcript of this roundtable, see Cohn et al. (2004).
2 The widening–deepening distinction was introduced by Keith Krause and Michael C. Williams (1996).
3 For a summary of this critique, see Paris 2001a.
4 For an overview of this debate, see the special edition on human security in *Security Dialogue* (UN, 2004).
5 This notion of "collective signification"—presenting individual security threats as collective concerns, thereby locating them within the public, political realm—is articulated by the security discourse analysis of Lene Hansen (2006) on the Bosnian War.
6 One important exception here is the work of Jacqueline Berman (2007) who argues that human security works to securitize everyday life in new ways that ultimately expand in the influence and control of the state and its security structures.
7 Even the *Human Security Now* report acknowledges that the "state remains the fundamental purveyor of security" (Commission on Human Security 2003: 2).
8 One former UNIFEM official was of the opinion that UNIFEM, overall, "hurt the comprehensiveness of the women, peace and security movement ... [in so much that] ... UNIFEM has really emphasized the governance aspect and less on the broader peace and security agenda ... and while the former is certainly important, such an approach is missing the radical potential." Further, UNIFEM is still an agency of an IGO, and therefore, "can not be too critical of any member states and this is a problem." (interview, April 2007).
9 Research by Hill (2004-2005) supports this finding in terms of gender norms diffusing in global disarmament policy circles, debates, and treaties.
10 This number is current as of January 2009. For the most updated list see, http://www.peacewomen.org/1325inTranslation/index.html.

Appendix A

Resolution 1325 (2000)

Adopted by the Security Council at its 4213th meeting, on 31 October 2000

The Security Council,

Recalling its resolutions 1261 (1999) of 25 August 1999, 1265 (1999) of 17 September 1999, 1296 (2000) of 19 April 2000 and 1314 (2000) of 11 August 2000, as well as relevant statements of its President, and *recalling also* the statement of its President to the press on the occasion of the United Nations Day for Women's Rights and International Peace (International Women's Day) of 8 March 2000 (SC/6816),

Recalling also the commitments of the Beijing Declaration and Platform for Action (A/52/231) as well as those contained in the outcome document of the twenty-third Special Session of the United Nations General Assembly entitled "Women 2000: Gender Equality, Development and Peace for the Twenty-First Century" (A/S-23/10/Rev.1), in particular those concerning women and armed conflict,

Bearing in mind the purposes and principles of the Charter of the United Nations and the primary responsibility of the Security Council under the Charter for the maintenance of international peace and security,

Expressing concern that civilians, particularly women and children, account for the vast majority of those adversely affected by armed conflict, including as refugees and internally displaced persons, and increasingly are targeted by combatants and armed elements, and *recognizing* the consequent impact this has on durable peace and reconciliation,

Reaffirming the important role of women in the prevention and resolution of conflicts and in peace-building, and *stressing* the importance of their equal participation and full involvement in all efforts for the maintenance and promotion of peace and security, and the need to increase their role in decision-making with regard to conflict prevention and resolution,

Reaffirming also the need to implement fully international humanitarian and human rights law that protects the rights of women and girls during and after conflicts,

156   *Appendix A*

Emphasizing the need for all parties to ensure that mine clearance and mine awareness programmes take into account the special needs of women and girls,

Recognizing the urgent need to mainstream a gender perspective into peacekeeping operations, and in this regard *noting* the Windhoek Declaration and the Namibia Plan of Action on Mainstreaming a Gender Perspective in Multidimensional Peace Support Operations (S/2000/693),

Recognizing also the importance of the recommendation contained in the statement of its President to the press of 8 March 2000 for specialized training for all peacekeeping personnel on the protection, special needs and human rights of women and children in conflict situations,

Recognizing that an understanding of the impact of armed conflict on women and girls, effective institutional arrangements to guarantee their protection and full participation in the peace process can significantly contribute to the maintenance and promotion of international peace and security,

Noting the need to consolidate data on the impact of armed conflict on women and girls,

1   *Urges* Member States to ensure increased representation of women at all decision-making levels in national, regional and international institutions and mechanisms for the prevention, management, and resolution of conflict;
2   *Encourages* the Secretary-General to implement his strategic plan of action (A/49/587) calling for an increase in the participation of women at decision-making levels in conflict resolution and peace processes;
3   *Urges* the Secretary-General to appoint more women as special representatives and envoys to pursue good offices on his behalf, and in this regard *calls on* Member States to provide candidates to the Secretary-General, for inclusion in a regularly updated centralized roster;
4   *Further urges* the Secretary-General to seek to expand the role and contribution of women in United Nations field-based operations, and especially among military observers, civilian police, human rights and humanitarian personnel;
5   *Expresses* its willingness to incorporate a gender perspective into peacekeeping operations, and *urges* the Secretary-General to ensure that, where appropriate, field operations include a gender component;
6   *Requests* the Secretary-General to provide to Member States training guidelines and materials on the protection, rights and the particular needs of women, as well as on the importance of involving women in all peacekeeping and peace-building measures, *invites* Member States to incorporate these elements as well as HIV/AIDS awareness training into their national training programmes for military and civilian police personnel in preparation for deployment, and *further requests* the Secretary-General to ensure that civilian personnel of peacekeeping operations receive similar training;
7   *Urges* Member States to increase their voluntary financial, technical and logistical support for gender-sensitive training efforts, including those undertaken by relevant funds and programmes, inter alia, the United Nations Fund

Appendix A   157

for Women and United Nations Children's Fund, and by the Office of the United Nations High Commissioner for Refugees and other relevant bodies;

8   *Calls on* all actors involved, when negotiating and implementing peace agreements, to adopt a gender perspective, including, inter alia:

   a   The special needs of women and girls during repatriation and resettlement and for rehabilitation, reintegration and post-conflict reconstruction;

   b   Measures that support local women's peace initiatives and indigenous processes for conflict resolution, and that involve women in all of the implementation mechanisms of the peace agreements;

   c   Measures that ensure the protection of and respect for human rights of women and girls, particularly as they relate to the constitution, the electoral system, the police and the judiciary;

9   *Calls upon* all parties to armed conflict to respect fully international law applicable to the rights and protection of women and girls, especially as civilians, in particular the obligations applicable to them under the Geneva Conventions of 1949 and the Additional Protocols thereto of 1977, the Refugee Convention of 1951 and the Protocol thereto of 1967, the Convention on the Elimination of All Forms of Discrimination against Women of 1979 and the Optional Protocol thereto of 1999 and the United Nations Convention on the Rights of the Child of 1989 and the two Optional Protocols thereto of 25 May 2000, and to bear in mind the relevant provisions of the Rome Statute of the International Criminal Court;

10   *Calls on* all parties to armed conflict to take special measures to protect women and girls from gender-based violence, particularly rape and other forms of sexual abuse, and all other forms of violence in situations of armed conflict;

11   *Emphasizes* the responsibility of all States to put an end to impunity and to prosecute those responsible for genocide, crimes against humanity, and war crimes including those relating to sexual and other violence against women and girls, and in this regard *stresses* the need to exclude these crimes, where feasible from amnesty provisions;

12   *Calls upon* all parties to armed conflict to respect the civilian and humanitarian character of refugee camps and settlements, and to take into account the particular needs of women and girls, including in their design, and recalls its resolutions 1208 (1998) of 19 November 1998 and 1296 (2000) of 19 April 2000;

13   *Encourages* all those involved in the planning for disarmament, demobilization and reintegration to consider the different needs of female and male ex-combatants and to take into account the needs of their dependants;

14   *Reaffirms* its readiness, whenever measures are adopted under Article 41 of the Charter of the United Nations, to give consideration to their potential impact on the civilian population, bearing in mind the special needs of women and girls, in order to consider appropriate humanitarian exemptions;

158   *Appendix A*

15 *Expresses* its willingness to ensure that Security Council missions take into account gender considerations and the rights of women, including through consultation with local and international women's groups;

16 *Invites* the Secretary-General to carry out a study on the impact of armed conflict on women and girls, the role of women in peace-building and the gender dimensions of peace processes and conflict resolution, and *further invites* him to submit a report to the Security Council on the results of this study and to make this available to all Member States of the United Nations;

17 *Requests* the Secretary-General, where appropriate, to include in his reporting to the Security Council progress on gender mainstreaming throughout peacekeeping missions and all other aspects relating to women and girls;

18 *Decides* to remain actively seized of the matter.

Appendix B

Resolution 1820 (2008)

Adopted by the Security Council at its 5916th meeting,
on 19 June 2008

The Security Council,

Reaffirming its commitment to the continuing and full implementation of resolution 1325 (2000), 1612 (2005) and 1674 (2006) and recalling the Statements of its president of 31 October 2001 (Security Council/PRST/2001/31), 31 October 2002 (Security Council/PRST/2002/32), 28 October 2004 (Security Council/PRST/2004/40), 27 October 2005 (Security Council/PRST/2005/52), 8 November 2006 (Security Council/PRST/2006/42), 7 March 2007 (Security Council/PRST/2007/5), and 24 October 2007 (Security Council/PRST/2007/40);

Guided by the purposes and principles of the Charter of the United Nations,

Reaffirming also the resolve expressed in the 2005 World Summit Outcome Document to eliminate all forms of violence against women and girls, including by ending impunity and by ensuring the protection of civilians, in particular women and girls, during and after armed conflicts, in accordance with the obligations States have undertaken under international humanitarian law and international human rights law;

Recalling the commitments of the Beijing Declaration and Platform for Action (A/52/231) as well as those contained in the outcome document of the twenty-third Special Session of the United Nations General Assembly entitled "Women 2000: Gender Equality, Development and Peace for the Twenty-first Century" (A/S-23/10/Rev.1), in particular those concerning sexual violence and women in situations of armed conflict;

Reaffirming also the obligations of States Parties to the Convention on the Elimination of All Forms of Discrimination against Women, the Optional Protocol thereto, the Convention on the Rights of the Child and the Optional Protocols thereto, and *urging* states that have not yet done so to consider ratifying or acceding to them,

Noting that civilians account for the vast majority of those adversely affected by armed conflict; that women and girls are particularly targeted by the use of

160   *Appendix B*

sexual violence, including as a tactic of war to humiliate, dominate, instil fear in, disperse and/or forcibly relocate civilian members of a community or ethnic group; and that sexual violence perpetrated in this manner may in some instances persist after the cessation of hostilities;

Recalling its condemnation in the strongest terms of all sexual and other forms of violence committed against civilians in armed conflict, in particular women and children;

Reiterating deep concern that, despite its repeated condemnation of violence against women and children in situations of armed conflict, including sexual violence in situations of armed conflict, and despite its calls addressed to all parties to armed conflict for the cessation of such acts with immediate effect, such acts continue to occur, and in some situations have become systematic and widespread, reaching appalling levels of brutality,

Recalling the inclusion of a range of sexual violence offences in the Rome Statute of the International Criminal Court and the statutes of the ad hoc international criminal tribunals,

Reaffirming the important role of women in the prevention and resolution of conflicts and in peacebuilding, and *stressing* the importance of their equal participation and full involvement in all efforts for the maintenance and promotion of peace and security, and the need to increase their role in decision-making with regard to conflict prevention and resolution,

Deeply concerned also about the persistent obstacles and challenges to women's participation and full involvement in the prevention and resolution of conflicts as a result of violence, intimidation and discrimination, which erode women's capacity and legitimacy to participate in post-conflict public life, and acknowledging the negative impact this has on durable peace, security and reconciliation, including post-conflict peacebuilding,

Recognizing that States bear primary responsibility to respect and ensure the human rights of their citizens, as well as all individuals within their territory as provided for by relevant international law,

Reaffirming that parties to armed conflict bear the primary responsibility to take all feasible steps to ensure the protection of affected civilians,

Welcoming the ongoing coordination of efforts within the United Nations system, marked by the inter-agency initiative "United Nations Action against Sexual Violence in Conflict," to create awareness about sexual violence in armed conflicts and post-conflict situations and, ultimately, to put an end to it,

1   *Stresses* that sexual violence, when used or commissioned as a tactic of war in order to deliberately target civilians or as a part of a widespread or systematic attack against civilian populations, can significantly exacerbate situations of armed conflict and may impede the restoration of international peace and security, *affirms* in this regard that effective steps to prevent and respond to such acts of sexual violence can significantly contribute to the maintenance of international peace and security, and *expresses its readiness*, when considering situations on the agenda of the Council, to, where

Appendix B 161

necessary, adopt appropriate steps to address widespread or systematic sexual violence;

2   *Demands* the immediate and complete cessation by all parties to armed conflict of all acts of sexual violence against civilians with immediate effect;

3   *Demands* that all parties to armed conflict immediately take appropriate measures to protect civilians, including women and girls, from all forms of sexual violence, which could include, inter alia, enforcing appropriate military disciplinary measures and upholding the principle of command responsibility, training troops on the categorical prohibition of all forms of sexual violence against civilians, debunking myths that fuel sexual violence, vetting armed and security forces to take into account past actions of rape and other forms of sexual violence, and evacuation of women and children under imminent threat of sexual violence to safety; and *requests* the Secretary-General, where appropriate, to encourage dialogue to address this issue in the context of broader discussions of conflict resolution between appropriate UN officials and the parties to the conflict, taking into account, inter alia, the views expressed by women of affected local communities;

4   *Notes* that rape and other forms of sexual violence can constitute a war crime, a crime against humanity, or a constitutive act with respect to genocide, *stresses the need for* the exclusion of sexual violence crimes from amnesty provisions in the context of conflict resolution processes, and *calls upon* Member States to comply with their obligations for prosecuting persons responsible for such acts, to ensure that all victims of sexual violence, particularly women and girls, have equal protection under the law and equal access to justice, and *stresses* the importance of ending impunity for such acts as part of a comprehensive approach to seeking sustainable peace, justice, truth, and national reconciliation;

5   *Affirms its intention*, when establishing and renewing state-specific sanctions regimes, to take into consideration the appropriateness of targeted and graduated measures against parties to situations of armed conflict who commit rape and other forms of sexual violence against women and girls in situations of armed conflict;

6   *Requests* the Secretary-General, in consultation with the Security Council, the Special Committee on Peacekeeping Operations and its Working Group and relevant States, as appropriate, to develop and implement appropriate training programs for all peacekeeping and humanitarian personnel deployed by the United Nations in the context of missions as mandated by the Council to help them better prevent, recognize and respond to sexual violence and other forms of violence against civilians;

7   *Requests* the Secretary-General to continue and strengthen efforts to implement the policy of zero tolerance of sexual exploitation and abuse in United Nations peacekeeping operations; and *urges* troop and police contributing countries to take appropriate preventative action, including pre-deployment and in-theater awareness training, and other action to ensure full accountability in cases of such conduct involving their personnel;

162   *Appendix B*

8   *Encourages* troop and police contributing countries, in consultation with the Secretary-General, to consider steps they could take to heighten awareness and the responsiveness of their personnel participating in UN peacekeeping operations to protect civilians, including women and children, and prevent sexual violence against women and girls in conflict and post-conflict situations, including wherever possible the deployment of a higher percentage of women peacekeepers or police;

9   *Requests* the Secretary-General to develop effective guidelines and strategies to enhance the ability of relevant UN peacekeeping operations, consistent with their mandates, to protect civilians, including women and girls, from all forms of sexual violence and to systematically include in his written reports to the Council on conflict situations his observations concerning the protection of women and girls and recommendations in this regard;

10   *Requests* the Secretary-General and relevant United Nations agencies, inter alia, through consultation with women and women-led organizations as appropriate, to develop effective mechanisms for providing protection from violence, including in particular sexual violence, to women and girls in and around UN managed refugee and internally displaced persons camps, as well as in all disarmament, demobilization, and reintegration processes, and in justice and security sector reform efforts assisted by the United Nations;

11   *Stresses* the important role the Peacebuilding Commission can play by including in its advice and recommendations for post-conflict peacebuilding strategies, where appropriate, ways to address sexual violence committed during and in the aftermath of armed conflict, and in ensuring consultation and effective representation of women's civil society in its country-specific configurations, as part of its wider approach to gender issues;

12   *Urges* the Secretary-General and his Special Envoys to invite women to participate in discussions pertinent to the prevention and resolution of conflict, the maintenance of peace and security, and post-conflict peacebuilding, and encourages all parties to such talks to facilitate the equal and full participation of women at decision-making levels;

13   *Urges* all parties concerned, including Member States, United Nations entities and financial institutions, to support the development and strengthening of the capacities of national institutions, in particular of judicial and health systems, and of local civil society networks in order to provide sustainable assistance to victims of sexual violence in armed conflict and post-conflict situations;

14   *Urges* appropriate regional and sub-regional bodies in particular to consider developing and implementing policies, activities, and advocacy for the benefit of women and girls affected by sexual violence in armed conflict;

15   *Also requests* the Secretary-General to submit a report to the Council by 30 June 2009 on the implementation of this resolution in the context of situations which are on the agenda of the Council, utilizing information from available United Nations sources, including country teams, peacekeeping operations, and other United Nations personnel, which would include, inter

Appendix B 163

alia, information on situations of armed conflict in which sexual violence has been widely or systematically employed against civilians; analysis of the prevalence and trends of sexual violence in situations of armed conflict; proposals for strategies to minimize the susceptibility of women and girls to such violence; benchmarks for measuring progress in preventing and addressing sexual violence; appropriate input from United Nations implementing partners in the field; information on his plans for facilitating the collection of timely, objective, accurate, and reliable information on the use of sexual violence in situations of armed conflict, including through improved coordination of UN activities on the ground and at Headquarters; and information on actions taken by parties to armed conflict to implement their responsibilities as described in this resolution, in particular by immediately and completely ceasing all acts of sexual violence and in taking appropriate measures to protect women and girls from all forms of sexual violence;

16 *Decides* to remain actively seized of the matter.

References

Abad, M.C. Jr. 2000. "The Challenge of Balancing State Security with Human Security," Paper presented at the 9th Harvard Project for Asian and International Affairs Conference, Beijing. http://www.aseansec.org/14259.htm, accessed 11 February 2007.

Abirafeh, Lina. 2005. "Lessons From Gender-Focused International Aid in Post Conflict Afghanistan ... Learned?" *Gender in International Cooperation*, 7. Bonn, Germany: Friedrich Ebert Stiftung (FES) Division for International Cooperation, Department for Development Policy.

Acharya, Amitav. 2004. "A Holistic Paradigm," *Security Dialogue* 35(3): 355–56.

Ackerly, Brooke A., Maria Stern, and Jaqui True (eds). 2006. *Feminist Methodologies for International Relations*. Cambridge: Cambridge University Press.

Alvarez, Enrique. 2002. "The Civil Society Assembly: Shaping Agreement," *Accord 13— Owning the Process: Public Participation in Peacemaking*, Edited by Catherine Barnes. London: Conciliation Resources. Paper accessed May 2007 at http:// www.c-r.org/our-work/accord/public-participation/guatemala-civil-society-assembly.php.

Anderlini, Sanam. 2000. "Women at the Peace Table: Making a Difference," NY: UNIFEM. Accessed May 2007 at http://www.peacewomen.org/resources/Peace_Negotiations/WomenattheTable2000.pdf.

Anderlini, Sanam. 2007. *Women Building Peace: What They Do, Why It Matters*. Boulder, CO: Lynne Rienner.

Anderson, Letitia. 2007. "Gender-Based Violence Offices—A Sign of Progress in UNIFEM Partnership with Rwandan Police," *Women's UN Report Network*. Accessed May 2007 at http://www.wunrn.com/news/2007/04_07/04_23_07/042907_rwanda.htm.

Anderson, Mary. 1993. *Focusing on Women: UNIFEM's Experience in Mainstreaming*. UNIFEM.

Annan, Kofi A. 1999. "Two Concepts of Sovereignty," *The Economist*. September 18: 49–50.

Annan, Kofi A. 2005. In Larger Freedom: *Towards Security, Development and Human Rights for All*. New York, NY: United Nations Publications.

Antrobus, Peggy. 2004. *The Global Women's Movement: Origins, Issues and Strategies*. New York: Zed Books.

Askin, Kelly. 1997. *War Crimes Against Women: Prosecution in International War Crimes Tribunals*. London: Martinus Nijhoff Publishers.

Askin, Kelly. 2006. "Holding Leaders Accountable in the International Criminal Court (ICC) for Gender Crimes Committed in Darfur," *Genocide Studies and Prevention* 1(1): 13–28.

Austin, J.L. [1962]1970. *How To Do Things With Words, 2nd Edn*. Oxford: Oxford University Press.

References 165

Austin, J.L. 1971. "Performative-Constative," in *Philosophy of Language,* edited by John R. Searle. Oxford: Oxford University Press, pp. 13–22.

Axworthy, Lloyd. 2001. "Human Security and Global Governance: Putting People First." *Global Governance,* 7(1): 19–23.

Axworthy, Lloyd. 2004. "What is 'Human Security'? A New Scientific Field and Policy Lens." *Security Dialogue,* 35(3): 348–49.

Baarda, Th. A. van. 1994. "The Involvement of the Security Council in Maintaining International Law," *Netherlands Quarterly of Human Rights* 12(1): 140.

Baden, Sally and Anne Marie Goetz. 1998. "Who Needs [Sex] When You Can Have [Gender]?" in *Feminists Visions of Development: Gender Analysis and Policy,* edited by Cecile Jackson and Ruth Pearson. London: Routledge, pp. 19–38.

Bagozzi, Daniela. 1997. "Women in Special Development Situations," *DHA News,* United Nations Office for the Coordination of Humanitarian Affairs—OCHA Online. April/May: 22, article accessed 1 May 2007, http://www.reliefweb.int/OCHA_ol/pub/dhanews/issue22/index.html#toc.

Bajpai, Kanti. 2000. "Human Security: Concept and Measurement," *Kroc Institute Occasional Paper,* no. 19. Notre Dame, IN: University of Notre Dame.

Baldwin, David A. 1995. "Security Studies and the End of the Cold War," *World Politics* 48(1): 117–41.

Baldwin, David A. 1997. "The Concept of Security," *Review of International Studies* 23: 5–26.

Balzacq, Theirry. 2005. "The Three Faces of Securitization: Political Agency, Audience and Context," *European Journal of International Relations* 11(2): 171–201.

Barnes, Karen. 2006. "Reform or More of the Same? Gender Mainstreaming and the Changing Nature of UN Peace Operations," YCISS Working Paper Number 41 (October). Paper accessed November 2006 http://www.yorku.ca/yciss/whatsnew/documents/WP41-Barnes.pdf.

Barnett, Michael and Martha Finnemore. 2004. *Rules for the World.* Ithaca: Cornell University Press.

Barnett, Michael N. 1995. "The New United Nations Politics of Peace: From Juridical Sovereignty to Empirical Sovereignty," *Global Governance* 1(1): 79–97.

Becker, Jo. 2003. "Child Soldiers and Armed Groups," *Conference on Curbing Human Rights Abuses by Armed Conflict,* Centre of International Relations, University of British Columbia, Vancouver (14–15 November). Paper accessed February 2007, http://www.armedgroups.org/images/stories/pdfs/becker_paper.pdf.

Berg, Robert J. 2006. "The UN Intellectual History Project: A Review of the Literature," *Global Governance* 12(3): 325–341.

Berman, Jacqueline. 2004. "'This Season's Hottest Accessory': Human Security, Biopolitics, and the 'Securitization' of Everyday Life," Paper presented at the Annual Convention of the International Studies Association, March 17–20, Montreal, CA.

Berman, Jacqueline. 2007. "The 'Vital Core:' From Bare Life to the Biopolitics of Human Security and Human Trafficking" in *Protecting Human Security in a Post-9/11 World: Critical and Global Insights,* edited by Giorgio Shani, Makoto Sato, and Mustapha Kamal Pasha. Palgrave Press, pp. 30–49.

Bhatia, Michael V. 2003. *War and Intervention: Issues for Contemporary Peace Operations.* Bloomfield: Kumarian Press, Inc.

Black, Maggie. 1996. *Children First: The Story of UNICEF, Past and Present.* New York: Oxford University Press.

166   *References*

Blanchard, Eric M. 2003. "Gender, International Relations, and the Development of Feminist Security Theory," *Signs: Journal of Women in Culture and Society* 28(4): 1289–312.

Bobrow, Davis B. 1996. "Complex Insecurity: Implications of a Sobering Metaphor." *International Studies Quarterly*, 40: 435–50.

Bob, Clifford. 2005. *The Marketing of Rebellion: Insurgents, Media, and International Activism.* Cambridge: Cambridge University Press.

Bob, Clifford (ed). 2008. *The International Struggle for New Human Rights.* Philadelphia, Pennsylvania: University of Pennsylvania Press.

Boli, Jon and George M. Thomas. 1999. "INGOs and the Organization of World Culture," in *Constructing World Culture International Non-governmental Organizations since 1875,* edited by J. Boli and G. Thomas. Stanford: Stanford University Press, pp. 13–49.

Booth, Ken. 1991. "Security and Emancipation," *Review of International Studies* 17: 313–27.

Booth, Ken. 1995. "Human Wrongs and International Relations," *International Affairs* 71: 103–22.

Booth, Ken. 1997. "Security and Self: Reflections of a Fallen Realist," in *Critical Security Studies,* edited by Keith Krause and Michael C. Williams. Minneapolis: University of Minnesota Press.

Booth, Ken, ed. 2005. *Critical Security Studies and World Politics.* Boulder, CO: Lynne Rienner Publishers.

Bourloyannis, Christine. 1993. "The Security Council of the United Nations and the Implementation of International Humanitarian Law," *Denver Journal of International Law and Policy* 20(3): 43.

Boutros-Ghali, Boutros. 1992. *An Agenda for Peace: Preventative Diplomacy, Peacemaking and Peacekeeping.* A/47/277 – S/24111 (17 June).

Boyer, Mark A., Brain Urlacher, Natalie Florea Hudson, Anat Niv-Solomon, Laura Janik, Michael J. Butler, Scott W. Brown, Andre Ioannou. 2009. "Gender and Negotiation: Some Experimental Findings from an International Negotiation Simulation," *International Studies Quarterly* 53(1): 23–47.

Breen, Claire. 2003. "The Role of NGOs in the Formulation of and Compliance with the Operational Protocol to the Convention on the Rights of the Child on Involvement of Children in Armed Conflict," *Human Rights Quarterly* 25: 453–81.

Brown, Michael E., ed. 2003. *Grave New World: Security Challenges in the twenty-first Century.* Washington D.C., Georgetown University Press.

Browning, Christopher and Matt McDonald. 2007. "Securitization and Emancipation," paper presented at the Annual International Studies Association Conference, Chicago, IL.

Bunch, Charlotte. 1990. "Women's Rights as Human Rights," *Human Rights Quarterly* 12: 486–98.

Bunch, Charlotte. 2002. "Feminism, Peace, Human Rights, and Human Security," *Canadian Women's Studies* 22(2): 6–15.

Bunch, Charlotte. 2004. "A Feminist Human Rights Lens on Human Security," *Peace Review* 16(1): 29–34.

Burke, Anthony. 2002. "Aporias of Security," *Alternatives* 27(1): 1–27.

Butler, Judith. 1997. *Excitable Speech: A Politics of the Performative.* NY: Routledge.

Butler, Michael J. and Mark A. Boyer. 2003. "Bosnian Peacekeeping and EU Tax Harmony: Evolving policy frames and changing policy processes," *International Journal* 58: 389–416.

Buzan, Barry. 1983. *People, States and Fear.* Brighton: Harvester Wheatsheaf.

Buzan, Barry. 1991. *People, States and Fear, 2nd Edn.* Boulder, CO: Lynne Rienner.

References 167

Buzan, Barry. 2004. "A Reductionist, Idealistic Notion that Adds Little Analytical Value," *Security Dialogue*. 35(3): 369–70.

Buzan, Barry and Ole Wæver. 1997. "Slippery? Contradictory? Sociologically untenable? The Copenhagen School Replies," *Review of Internationally Studies* 23: 241–50.

Buzan, Barry, Ole Wæver, and Jaap de Wilde. 1998. *Security: A new framework for analysis*. Boulder, CO: Lynne Rienner Publishers.

Campbell, John L. 1998. "Institutional Analysis and the Role of Ideas in Political Economy," *Theory and Society* 27: 377–409.

Cantwell, N. 1992. "Non-governmental Organizations and the United Nations Convention on the Rights of the Child," *91 Bulletin on Human Rights* 19: 16–24.

Caprioli, Mary. 2004. "Democracy and Human Rights Versus Women's Security: A Contradiction?" *Security Dialogue* (35): 411–28.

Carpenter, Charli R. 2003. "'Women and Children First': Gender, Norms and Humanitarian Evacuation in the Balkans 1991-1995," *International Organization* 57: 661–94.

Carpenter, Charli R. 2005. "'Women, Children, and Other Vulnerable Groups': Gender, Strategic Frames and the Protection of Civilians As a Transnational Issue," *International Studies Quarterly* 49(2): 295–334.

Carpenter, Charli R. 2007. "Setting the Advocacy Agenda: Theorizing Issue Emergence and Nonemergence in Transnational Advocacy Networks," *International Studies Quarterly* 51: 99–120.

Carrillo, Roxanna. 1992. *Battered Dreams: Violence Against Women as an Obstacle to Development*. NY: UNIFEM.

Cavalcanti, Henrique B. 2005. "Food Security," in *Human and Environmental Security: An Agenda for Change*, edited by Felix Dodds and Tim Pippard. London: Earthscan.

Carver, Terrell. 1996. *Gender is not a Synonym for Women*. Boulder, CO: Lynne Rienner Publishers.

Center for Conflict Resolution (CCR). 2005. "Women and Peacebuilding in Africa: Seminar Report," Policy advisery group meeting supported by CCR and UNIFEM, Cape Town, South Africa (27–28 October). Accessed May 2007 http://ccrweb. ccr.uct.ac.za/fileadmin/template/ccr/pdf/Vol_9-WPA_Report_Final_Web-small.pdf.

Chen, Lincoln, et al., eds. 2003. *Global Health Challenges for Human Security*. Cambridge: Harvard University Press.

Childs, Sarah and Krook, Mona Lena. 2006. "Gender and Politics: The State of the Art," *Politics* 26(1): 18–28.

Chinkin, Christine. 2004. "Gender, International Legal Framework and Peacebuilding," in *Gender and Peacebuilding*, edited by Kari Karamé. Oslo: NUPI, pp. 27–45.

Claude Jr., Inis L. 2004. "Forward to the Second Edition," *The United Nations and Changing World Politics, Fourth Edition*. By Thomas G. Weiss, David P. Forsythe, and Roger A. Coate. Boulder, CO: Westview Press.

Coalition to Stop the Use of Child Soldiers. 2006. "Next Steps for the UN Security Council on Children and Armed Conflict." International Secretariat, London: www.child-soldiers.org (accessed 1 April 2007).

Coalition to Stop the Use of Child Soldiers. 2008. *Child Soldiers Global Report*. International Secretariat, London: http://www.childsoldiersglobalreport.org/ (accessed 30 December 2008).

Cohen, Cynthia Price. 1997. "The United Nations Convention on the Rights of the Child: A Feminist Landmark," *William and Mary Journal of Women and Law* 3: 29–78.

168   References

Cohen, Cynthia Price and Per Miljeteig-Olssen. 1991. *Status Report: United Nations Convention on the Rights of the Child* 8 N.Y.L. Sch. J. Human Rights.

Cohn, Carol. 1987. "Sex and Death in the Rational World of Defense Intellectuals," *Signs* 12(4): 687–98.

Cohn, Carol. 1993. "Wars, Wimps, and Women: Talking Gender and Thinking War," in *Gendering War Talk,* edited by Miriam Cooke and Angela Woollacott. Princeton, NJ: Princeton University Press, pp. 227–46.

Cohn, Carol. 2003–2004. "Mainstreaming Gender in UN Security Policy: A Path to Political Transformation," *Boston Consortium on Gender, Security and Human Rights, Working Paper No. 204.* Paper accessed December 2006, http://www.genderandsecurity.org/working.htm.

Cohn, Carol. 2004. "Feminist Peacemaking," *The Women's Review of Books* XXI(5): 8–9.

Cohn, Carol. 2006. "Motives and Methods: Using multi-cited ethnography to study US national security discourses," in *Feminist Methodologies for International Relations,* edited by Brooke A. Ackerly, Maria Stern, and Jacqui True. Cambridge: Cambridge University Press, pp. 91–107.

Cohn, Carol, Helen Kinsella, and Sheri Gibbings. 2004. "Women, Peace and Security: Resolution 1325," *International Feminist Journal of Politics* 6(1): 130–40.

Collier, Paul, V.L. Elliot, Håvard Hegre, Anke Hoeffler, Marta Reynal-Querol and Nicholas Sambanis. 2003. *Breaking the Conflict Trap: Civil War and Development Policy.* Washington: World Bank and Oxford University Press.

Commission on Human Security. 2003. *Human Security Now.* New York, NY: United Nations Publications. Accessed October 2005 at http://www.humansecurity-chs.org/finalreport/English/FinalReport.pdf.

Conaway, Camille Pampell and Salome Martinez. 2004. *Adding Value: Women's Contribution to Reintegration and Reconstruction in El Salvador.* Washington, D.C.: Hunt Alternatives Fund.

Connell, Robert W. 2005. "Change Among the Gatekeepers: Men, Masculinities and Gender Equality in the Global Arena," *Signs: Journal of Women in Culture and Society* 30(3:) 1801–25.

Connelly, Patricia M., Tania Murray Li, Martha MacDonald and Jane L. Parpart. 2000. "Feminism and Development: Theoretical Perspectives," in *Theoretical Perspectives on Gender and Development,* edited by Jane L. Parpart, Patricia M. Connelly, and V Eudine Barriteau. Ottawa, ON, Canada: International Development Research Centre, pp. 51–160.

Cooley, Alexander and James Ron. 2002. "The NGO Scramble: Organizational Insecurity and the Political Economy of Transnational Action," *International Security* 27: 5–39.

Coomaraswamy, Radhika. 2006. *Report of the Special Representative of the Secretary-General for Children in Armed Conflict.* A/61/275.

Corner, Lorraine. 2004. "Women Transforming the Mainstream—a think piece," *Development Bulletin* 64: 11–15.

Cox, Robert. 1986. "Social Forces, States and World Orders: Beyond International Relations Theory," in *Neorealism and Its Critics,* edited by Robert O. Keohane. NY: Columbia University Press.

Crawford, Neta. 1991. "Once and Future Security Studies," *Security Studies* 1: 283–313.

Cutillo, Alberto. 2006. "International Assistance to Countries Emerging from Conflict: A Review of Fifteen Years of Interventions and the Future of Peacebuilding," Policy Paper, The Security-Development Nexus Program, International Peace Academy (February). Paper accessed April 2007 at www.ipacademy.org/Programs/Research/ProgReseSecDev_Pub.htm.

References 169

Cynthia, Enloe. 1990. "Womenandchildren: Making Feminist Sense of the Persian Gulf War," *The Village Voice* (25 September).

D'Amico, Francine. 1999. "Women Workers in the United Nations: From Margin to Mainstream?" in *Gender Politics in Global Governance,* edited by Mary K. Meyer and Elisabeth Prügl. Boulder, CO: Rowman & Littlefield Publishers, Inc., pp. 19–40.

de la Rey, Cheryl and Susan McKay. 2006. "Peacebuilding as a Gendered Process," *Journal of Social Issues* 62(1): 141–53.

DeGroot, Gerard J. 2001. "A Few Good Women: Gender Stereotypes, the Military and Peacekeeping," in *Women and International Peacekeeping,* edited by Louise Olsson and Torunn L. Tryggestad. London: Frank Cass Publishers, pp. 23–38.

Der Derian, James. 1995. "The Value of Security: Hobbes, Marx, Nietzsche, and Baudrillard." In *On Security,* edited by Ronnie D. Lipschutz. NY: Columbia University Press, pp 24–45.

Deudney, Daniel. 1990. "The Case Against Linking Environmental Degradation and National Security," *Millennium* 19(3): 461–76.

Dirasse, Laketch. 1999. "Conflict, Development, and Peace in Africa: Gender Perspectives," *Conflict Trends,* (April), pp. 12–15.

Dombrowski, Peter, ed. 2005. *Guns and Butter: The Political Economy of International Security.* Boulder, CO: Lynne Rienner Publishers.

Doyle, Michael W. 2001. "War Making and Peace Making: The United Nations' Post-Cold War Record," in *Turbulent Peace: The Challenges of Managing International Conflict,* edited by Chester A. Crocker, Fen Osler Hampson, and Pamela Aall. Washington, D.C.: United States Institute for Peace Press, pp. 529–560.

Ekiyor, Thelma. 2006. "Engendering Peace: How the Peacebuilding Commission Can Live up to UN Security Council Resolution 1325." *Dialogue on Globalization, Briefing Papers Friedrich Ebert Stiftung.* New York (June). Paper accessed May 2007 at http://www.fes-globalization.org/publicationsNY/BriefingPaper%20NYThelma June2006.pdf.

Elbe, Stefan. 2006. "Should HIV/AIDS Be Securitized?" *International Studies Quarterly* 50(1): 119–44.

Elshtain, Jean Bethke. [1987] 1995. *Women and War.* Chicago: University of Chicago Press.

Enloe, Cynthia. 1989. *Bananas, Beaches, and Bases: Making Feminist Sense of International Politics.* Berkeley: University of California Press.

Enloe, Cynthia. 2000. *Maneuvers: The International Politics of Militarizing Women's Lives.* Berkeley: University of California Press.

Enloe, Cynthia. 2005. "What if Patriarchy *Is* 'the Big Picture'? An Afterward," in *Gender, Conflict, and Peacekeeping,* edited by Dyan Mazurana, Angela Raven-Roberts and Jane Parpart. Oxford: Rowman & Littlefield: 280–283.

Ensalaco, Mark. 2005. "The Right of the Child to Development," in *Children's Human Rights: Progress and Challenges for Children Worldwide,* edited by Mark Ensalaco and Linda C. Majka. New York, New York: Rowman & Littlefield Publishers, Inc., pp. 9–29.

Finnbogadóttir, Vigdís. 1995. "Statement by the President of Iceland for the Fourth World Conference on Women," as cited in the *Report of the Fourth World Conference on Women* A/CONF.177/20/Rev.1, Beijing, China (4–15 September): 197–199. Accessed May 2007 http://daccessdds.un.org/doc/UNDOC/GEN/N96/273/01/PDF/N9627301. pdf?OpenElement.

Finnemore, Martha and Kathryn Sikkink. 1998. "International Norm Dynamics and Political Change," *International Organization* 52(4): 887–917.

170   References

Fitzsimmons, Tracy. 1998. "Engendering a New Police Identity?" *Peace Review* 10(2): 269–74.

Fitzsimmons, Tracy. 2005. "The Postconflict Postscript: Gender and Policing in Peace Operations," in *Gender, Conflict, and Peacekeeping*, edited by Dyan Mazurana, Angela Raven-Roberts, and Jane Parpart. Boulder, CO: Rowman & Littlefield Publishers, Inc, pp. 185–201.

Fleshman, Michael. 2003. "African Women Struggle for a Seat at the Peace Table," *African Recovery*, United Nations Department of Public Information 16(3): 16.

Florea, Natalie, Mark Boyer, Scott Brown, Michael Butler, Magnolia Hernandez, Kimberly Weir, Paula Johnson, and Clarisse Lima. 2003. "Negotiating from Mars to Venus: Some Findings on Gender's Impact in Simulated International Negotiations," *Simulation and Games* 34(2): 226–48.

Florini, Ann, ed. 1999. *The Third Force: The Rise of Transnational Civil Society*. Tokyo: Japan Center for International Change and Carnegie Endowment for International Peace.

Friedman, Elisabeth. 1995. "Women's Human Rights: The Emergence of a Movement," in *Women's Rights, Human Rights: International Feminist Perspective*, edited by Julie Peters and Andrea Wolper. NY: Routledge, pp. 18–35.

Fukuyama, Francis. 1992. *The End of History*. New York: Free Press.

Gallie, W.B. 1962. "Essentially Contested Concepts," *The Importance of Language*, edited by Max Black. Englewood Cliffs, NJ: Prentice-Hall, pp. 121–146.

Galtung, Johan. 1976. "Three Approaches to Peace: Peacekeeping, peacemaking, and peacebuilding," in *Peace, War and Defense: Essays on Peace Research, Vol.1* edited by Johan Galtung. Copenhagen: Ejlers, pp. 282–304.

Geneva Centre for the Democratic Control of Armed Forces (DCAF). 2006. "United Nations Approaches to Security Sector Reform," Background paper for workshop on "Developing a SSR Concept for the United Nations" 7 July 2006. Accessed May 2007 at http://www.dcaf.ch/publications/kms/details.cfm?lng=en&id=25482&nav1=4.

Gerschutz, Jill Marie and Margaret P. Karns. 2005. "Transforming Visions into Reality: The Convention on the Rights of the Child," in *Children's Human Rights: Progress and Challenges for Children Worldwide*, edited by Mark Ensalaco and Linda C. Majka. New York, New York: Rowman & Littlefield Publishers, Inc. (31–51).

Geske, Mary B. and Mark Ensalaco. 2005. "Three Prints in the Dirt: Child Soldiers and Human Rights," in *Children's Human Rights: Progress and Challenges for Children Worldwide*, edited by Mark Ensalaco and Linda C. Majka. New York, New York: Rowman & Littlefield Publishers, Inc., pp. 111–26.

George, Jim. 1994. *Discourses of Global Politics: A Critical (Re) Introduction to International Relations*. Boulder, CO: Lynne Rienner Publishers.

Glennon, Michael J. 2003. "Why the Security Council Failed," *Foreign Affairs* 82(3): 16–35.

Goldstein, Joshua. 2001. *War and Gender*. London: Cambridge University Press.

Haftendorn, Helga. 1991. "The Security Puzzle: Theory-Building and Discipline-Building in International Security," *International Studies Quarterly* 35: 3–17.

Hamber, Brandon, Paddy Hillyard, Amy Maguire, Monica McWilliams, Gillian Robinson, David Russell, and Margaret Ward. 2006. "Discourses in Transition: Re-Imaging Women's Security," *International Relations* 20(4): 487–502.

Hamill, James. 1998. "From Realism to Complex Interdependence? South Africa, Southern Africa, and the Question of Security," *International Relations*. 14(3): 1–30.

References   171

Hamilton, Heather B. 2000. "Rwanda's Women: The Key to Reconstruction," *Journal of Humanitarian Assistance*. Posted 10 May 2000 at www.jha.ac/greatlakes/b001.htm.

Hampson, Fen Olser. 2004. "A Concept in Need of a Global Policy Response," *Security Dialogue*. 35(3): 349–50.

Hampson, Fen Osler with Jean Daudelin, John B. Hay, Holly Reid, and Todd Martin. 2001. *Madness in the Multitude: Human Security and World Disorder*. Oxford: Oxford University Press.

Hansen, Lene. 2000. "The Little Mermaid's Silent Security Agenda and the Absence of Gender in the Copenhagen School," *Millennium: Journal of International Studies*, 29(2): 285–306.

Hansen, Lene. 2006. *Security As Practice: Discourse Analysis and the Bosnian War*. London: Routledge.

Harding, Sandra. 1991. *Whose Science? Whose Knowledge? Thinking from Women's Lives*. Ithaca, NY: Cornell University Press.

Hedley, Bull. 1977. *The Anarchical Society*. New York, NY: Columbia University Press.

Held, David and Anthony McGrew. 2001. *The Global Transformations Reader*. Cambridge: Polity Press.

Helms, E. 2003. "Women as Agents of Ethnic Reconciliation? Women's NGOs and International Intervention in Postwar Bosnia-Herzegovina," *Women's Studies International Forum* 26(1): 15–33.

Hendrickson, Dylan and Andrzej Karkoszka. 2005. "Security Sector Reform and Donor Policies," in *Security Sector Reform and Post-Conflict Peacebuilding*, edited by Albrecht Schnabel and Hans-Georg Ehrhart. Oxford: United Nations University Press, pp. 19–44.

Hertel, Shareen. 2006. *Unexpected Power: Conflict and Change among Transnational Activists*. Ithaca, NY: Cornell University Press.

Heyzer, Noeleen. 2004. "UNIFEM Multi-Year Funding Framework 2004–2007," Speech made to the Executive Board of UNDP/UNFPA, First Regular Session, United Nations, New York (29 Janurary).

Heyzer, Noeleen. 2006a. "A Message from Noeleen Heyzer," in *Voice, Influence, Justice, and Security: The Keys to Inclusion and Sustainable Peace Building*, NY: UNIFEM.

Heyzer, Noeleen. 2006b. "Women's Roles in Peace Consolidation," Statement made to the Security Council Open Debate on Women, Peace, and Security (26 October). Accessed speech text at http://www.peacewomen.org/un/6thAnniversary/Open_Debate/UNIFEM.pdf.

Hill, Felicity, Mikele Aboitiz and Sara Poehlman-Doumbouya. 2003. "Non-governmental Organizations' Role in the Buildup and Implementation of Security Council Resolution68.

Hill, Felicity. 2004–2005. "How and When Has Security Council Resolution 1325 (2000) on Women, Peace, and Security Impacted Negotiations Outside the Security Council?" *Uppsala University Master's Thesis*. Paper accessed online August 2006 at http://www.hdcentre.org/datastore/Felicity%20Hill%20-%201325%20thesis.pdf.

Holsti, Kal J. 1999. "The Coming of Chaos: Armed Conflict in the World's Periphery," in *International Order and the Future of World Politics*, edited by T.V. Paul and John A. Hall. Cambridge: Cambridge University Press, pp. 283–310.

Hubert, Don. 2004. "An Idea that Works in Practice," *Security Dialogue*. 35(3): 351–2.

Hudson, Heidi. 2005. "Doing Security as Though Humans Matter: A Feminist Perspective on Gender and the Politics of Human Security," *Security Dialogue* 36(2): 155–74.

172   References

Hudson, Natalie Florea. 2005. "En-gendering UN Peace Operations," *International Journal,* 60(3): 785–806.

Human Security Now. 2003. NY: Commission on Human Security. Accessed May 2007 at http://www.humansecurity-chs.org/finalreport/index.html.

Huysmans, Jef. 1998a. "Security! What Do You Mean? From Concept to Thick Signifier," *European Journal of International Relations* 4: 226–55.

Huysmans, Jef. 1998b. "Revisiting Copenhagen: Or, On the Creative Development of a Security Studies Agenda in Europe," *European Journal of International Relations* 4(4): 479–505.

Hyndman, Jennifer and Malathi de Alwis. 2003. "Beyond Gender: Toward a Feminist Analysis of Humanitarianism and Development in Sri Lanka." *Women's Studies Quarterly* 31: 212–22.

Jahan, Rounaq. 1995. *The Elusive Agenda: Mainstreaming Women in Development.* London: Zed Books.

Jain, Devaki. 2005. *Women, Development, and the UN: A Sixty-Year Quest for Equality and Justice.* Bloomington, IN: Indiana University Press.

Joachim, Jutta. 2007. *Agenda Setting, the UN and NGOs: Gender Violence and Reproductive Rights.* Washington, D.C.: Georgetown University Press.

Jolly, Richard. 2001. "Implementing Global Goals for Children: Lessons from UNICEF Experience," in *United Nations-Sponsored World Conferences: Focus on Impact and Follow-up,* edited by Michael G. Schechter. Tokyo, Japan: United Nations University, pp. 10–28.

Jones, B. and C. Cater. 2001. "From Chaos to Coherence? Toward a Regime for Protecting Civilians in War," in *Civilians in War,* edited by S. Chesterman. Boulder, CO: Lynne Reinner, pp. 237–62.

Kakonen, Jyrki, ed. 1994. *Green Security or Militarized Environment.* Aldershot: Darmouth Publishing Company.

Karamé, Kari, ed. 2004. *Gender and Peacebuilding in Africa.* Oslo, Norway: Norsk Utenrikspolitisk Institutt (NUPI).

Katzenstein, Peter J. 1996. *The Culture of National Security: Norms and Identity in World Politics.* NY: Columbia University Press.

Karns, Margaret P. and Karen Mingst. 2004. *International Organizations: The Politics and Processes of Global Governance.* Boulder, CO: Lynne Rienner Publishers.

Keck, Margaret and Kathryn Sikkink. 1998a. *Activists Beyond Borders: Advocacy Networks in International Politics.* New York: Cornell University Press.

Keck, Margaret and Kathryn Sikkink. 1998b. "Transnational Advocacy Networks in Movement Society," in *The Social Movement Society: Contentious Politics for a New Century,* edited by David S. Meyer, and Sidney Tarrow. Lanham, MD: Rowman & Littlefield, pp. 217–262.

Kennedy, Paul. 2006. *The Parliament of Man: The Past, Present, and Future of the United Nations.* NY: Random House.

King, Angela E.V. 2001. "Forward," in *Gender, Peace, and Conflict,* edited by Inger Skjelsbæk and Dan Smith. London: Sage.

King, Gary and Christopher J.L. Murray. 2001. "Rethinking Human Security," *Political Science Quarterly.* 116(4): 585–612.

Klare, Michael T. 1998. "The Era of Multiplying Schisms: World Security in the Twenty-First Century," in *World Security: Challenges for a New Century, 3ʳᵈ Edition,* edited by Michael T. Klare and Yogesh Chandrani. New York, NY: St. Martin's Press, pp. 59–77.

References   173

Klot, Jennifer. 2002. "Women and Peace Processes—An Impossible Match?" in *Gender Processes—an Impossible Match?* Edited by Louise Olsson. Uppsala, Collegium for Development Studies: 17–25.

Kolodziej, Edward. 1992. "Renaissance in Security Studies? Caveat Lector!" *International Studies Quarterly* 36: 421–38.

Krause, Keith and Michael Williams. 1996. "Broadening the Agenda of Security Studies: Politics and Methods," *Mershon International Studies Review* 40: 229–254.

Laurenti, Jeffrey. 2006. "Grand Goals, Modest Results: The UN in Search of Reform," *Current History* 104: 431–37.

Lehrer, Jim. 2005. "UN Looks to Move from Peacekeeping to Peacebuilding," *PBS Online Newshour: Background Report* (9 September 2005). Article accessed October 2006 at http://www.pbs.org/newshour/bb/international/un_reform/peace_building.html.

Leonard, Stephen. 1990. *Critical Theory in Political Practice*. Princeton: Princeton University Press.

Linklater, Andrew. 2005. "Political Community and Human Security," in *Critical Security Studies and World Politics,* edited by Ken Booth. Boulder, CO: Lynne Rienner Publishers, pp. 113–31.

Liotta, P.H. 2002. "Boomerang Effect: The Convergence of National and Human Security," *Security Dialogue* 33(4): 473–88.

Lipschutz, Ronnie D., ed. 1995. *On Security*. New York: Columbia University Press.

Litfin, Karen. 1999. "Constructing Environmental Security and Ecological Interdependence," *Global Governance* 5(3): 359–78.

Lloyd, Jane. 2006. "Women Peacekeepers Making a Difference," *UN Chronicle,* XLIII(1): online edition. Article accessed January 2009 at http://www.un.org/Pubs/chronicle/2006/issue1/0106p06.htm.

Longford, Michael. 1996. "NGOs and the Rights of the Child," in *The Conscience of the World: The Influence of Non-governmental Organizations in the UN System,* edited by Peter Willetts. Washington, D.C.: Brookings Institute, pp. 214–30.

Luck, Edward C. 2006. *UN Security Council: Practice and Promise*. London: Routledge.

Lyytikäinen, Minna. 2007. "Gender Training for Peacekeepers: Preliminary overview of United Nations peace support operations," *Gender, Peace, and Security—Working Paper #4* INSTRAW. Paper accessed December 2008 at www.un-instraw.org.

McDonald, Matt. 2002. "Human Security and the Construction of Security," *Global Society* 16(3): 277–95.

MacFarlane, S. Neil and Yuen Foong Khong. 2006. *Human Security and the UN: A Critical History*. Bloomington, IN: Indiana University Press.

Mackay, Angela. 2003. "Training the Uniforms: gender and peacekeeping operations," *Development in Practice* 13(2&3): 217–23.

McKay, Susan. 2004. "Women, Human Security, and Peace-building: A Feminist Analysis," in *Conflict and Human Security: A Search for New Approaches to Peace-building,* edited by Hideaki Shinoda and Ho-Won Jeong. IPSHU English Research Report Series NO. 19. Paper accessed February 2007 at http://home.hiroshima-u.ac.jp/heiwa/Pub/E19/Chap7.pdf.

McSweeney, Bill. 1996. "Identity and Security: Buzan and the Copenhagen School," *Review of International Studies* 22: 81–93.

Martin, J.P. and Mary Lesley Carson, Eds. 1996. *Women and Human Rights: The Basic Documents*. New York: Columbia University Press.

Mathews, Jessica Tuchman. 1989. "Redefining Security," *Foreign Affairs.* 68(2): 162–77.

174   References

Mayanja, Rachel. 2008. "Statement to the Security Council Open Debate on Women, Peace and Security," New York, NY: United Nations. Online. Accessed December 2008 at www.peacewomen.org/un/8thAnniversary/Open Debate/Mayanja.pdf.

Mazurana, Dyan and Susan McKay. 1999. *Women and Peacebuilding*. Montreal, Canada: International Centre for Human Rights and Democratic Development.

Mazurana, Dyan, Angela Raven-Roberts, and Jane Parpart, Eds. 2005. *Gender, Conflict, and Peacekeeping*. Lanham, MD: Rowman & Littlefield Publishers, Inc.

Mearsheimer, John J. 1994. "The False Promise of International Institutions," *International Security* 19: 5–49.

Meintjes, Sheila, Anu Pillay, and Meredeth Turshen, eds. 2002. *The Aftermath: Women in Post-Conflict Transformation*. London: Zed Books.

Milliken, Jennifer, ed. 2003. *State Failure, Collapse and Reconstruction*. Oxford: Blackwell Publishing.

Mingst, Karen, and Margaret P. Karns. 2007. *The United Nations in the twenty-first Century, 3rd Edition*. Boulder, CO: Westview Press.

Mohanty, Chandra, Ann Russo, and Lourdes Torres, eds. 1991. *Third World Women and the Politics of Feminism*. Bloomington: Indiana University Press.

Morphet, Sally. 2007. "Review Essay: Future Prospects for the United Nations," *Global Governance* 13: 139–150.

Mueller, John. 1989. *Retreat from Doomsday: The Obsolescence of Major War*. Rochester, New York: University of Rochester Press.

Murphy, Criag. 2006. *The United Nations Development Programme: A better way?* Cambridge, MA: Cambridge University Press.

Nakaya, Sumie. 2003. "Women and Gender Equality in Peace Processes: From Women at the Negotiating Table to Postwar Structural Reforms in Guatemala and Somalia," *Global Governance* 9: 459–76.

Ndacayisaba, Goretti. 2007. "Interview with the PeaceWomen Project," (February): 1–5. Available at http://www.peacewomen.org/resources/Burundi/GorettiDushirehamwe.html.

Neack, Laura. 2007. *Elusive Security: States First, People Last*. Lanham, MD: Rowman & Littlefield.

Newman, Edward. 2001. "Human Security and Constructivism," *International Studies Perspectives* 2 (3): 239–251.

NGO Working Group on Women, Peace, and Security. 2006. *SCR 1325 and the Peacebuilding Commission*. New York, NY: NGO Working Group on Women, Peace and Security. Available at www.womenpeacesecurity.org.

O'Neill, William G. 2006. "Kosovo Field Notes, Police Reform," NY: UNIFEM (21 November), pp. 1–17.

O'Neill, William G. 2007a. "Report on Gender and Police Reform in Post-Conflicts For UNDP/BCPR, UNIFEM, DPKO/UN Police/Best Practices," NY: UNIFEM (4 January), pp. 1–34.

O'Neill, William G. 2007b. "Liberia Field Notes, Police Reform," NY: UNIFEM (4 January), pp. 1–11.

Oberleitner, Gerd. 2005. "Human Security: A Challenge to International Law?" *Global Governance* 11: 185–203.

Oestreich, Joel E. 1998. "UNICEF and the Implementation of the Convention on the Rights of the Child," GlobalGovernance 4(2): 183–98.

Oestreich, Joel E. 2007. *Power and Principle: Human Rights Programming in International Organizations*. Washington, D.C.: Georgetown University Press.

References   175

Ogata, Sadako. 2003. "Human Security and State Security," *Human Security Now*. Final Report from the UN Commission on Human Security: p. 5. Available at http://www.humansecurity-chs.org/finalreport/index.html.

Ogata, Sadako and Johan Cels. 2003. "Human Security—Protecting and Empowering the People," *Global Governance* 9: 273–82.

Olsson, Louise. 2000. "Mainstreaming Gender in Multidimensional Peacekeeping: A Field Perspective," *International Peacekeeping*, 7(3): 1–16.

Olsson, Louise. 2001. "Mainstreaming Gender in Multidimensional Peacekeeping: A Field Perspective," *International Peacekeeping*, 7(3): 1–16.

Olsson, Louise and Torunn L. Tryggestad, eds. 2001. *Women and International Peacekeeping*. London: Frank Cass Publishing.

Otto, Dianne. 2004. "Securing the 'Gender Legitimacy' of the UN Security Council: Prising gender from its historical moorings," in *Faultlines of International Legitimacy*, edited by Hilary Charlesworth and Jean-Marc Coicaud. Tokyo: United Nations University Press. Accessed May 2007 at http://papers.ssrn.com/sol3/papers.cfm?abstract_id=585923.

Owen, Taylor and P. H. Liotta. 2007. "In All But Name: The Uncertain Future of Human Security in the UN," paper presented at the Annual International Studies Association Conference, Chicago, IL.

Paris, Roland. 2001a. "Human Security: Paradigm Shift or Hot Air?" *International Security* 26(2): 87–102.

Paris, Roland. 2001b. "Broadening the Study of Peace Operations," *International Studies Review* 2(3): 27–44.

Paris, Roland. 2003. "Human Security: Paradigm Shift or Hot Air?" in *Global Politics in a Changing World*, edited by Richard W. Mansbach and Edward Rhodes. Boston, MA: Houghton Mifflin Company, pp. 255.

Paris, Roland. 2004. "Still an Inscrutable Concept," *Security Dialogue*. 35(3): 370–1.

Passy, Florence. 1999. "Supranational Political Opportunities as a Channel of Globalization of Political Conflicts," in *The Case of the Rights of Indigenous Peoples. In Social Movements in a Globalizing World*, edited by D. della Porta, H. Kriesi and D. Rucht. London: Macmillan Press, pp. 148–69.

Peacebuilding Support Office (PBSO). 2007. *Draft Concept Note on the Design of Integrated Peacebuilding Strategies.* (February). Paper accessed April 2007 at http://www.reformtheun.org/index.php?module=uploads&func=download&fileId=2124.

Pearson, Michael. 2001. "Humanizing the Security Council," in *Canada Among Nations 2001: The Axworthy Legacy*, edited by Fen Osler Hampson et al. Oxford: Oxford University Press, (pp. 127–51).

Pearson, Ruth and Cecile Jackson. 1998. "Introduction: Interrogating development: feminism, gender and policy," in *Feminists Visions of Development: Gender Analysis and Policy*, edited by Cecile Jackson and Ruth Pearson. London: Routledge, pp. 1–16.

Peou, Sorpong. 2002. "The UN, Peacekeeping and Collective Human Security: From *An Agenda for Peace* to the Brahimi Report," *International Peacekeeping* 9(2): 52–4.

Petchesky, Rosalind. 2002. "Violence, Terror, and Accountability: Reports from the Field," Paper presented at the National Council for Research on Women Annual Conference 2002, "Facing the Global and National Crises: Women Define Human Security," New York, 2002. http://www.ncrw.org/interest/2002annconf.htm.

Peters, Julie and Andrea Wolper. 1995. *Women's Rights Human Rights: International Feminists Perspectives*. NY: Routledge.

Peterson, V. Spike and Anne Sisson Runyan. 1998. *Global Gender Issues, second edition*. Boulder, CO: Westview.

176   *References*

Podder, Sukanya. 2006. "The Children and Armed Conflict Agenda and the United Nations: Assessing a Decade of Engagement," *Institute for Defense Studies and Analyis,* (http://www.idsa.in/publications/stratcomments/SukanyaPodder280706.htm, accessed 4 March 2007).

Porter, Elisabeth. 2003. "Women, Political Decision-Making, and Peace-Building," *Global Change, Peace & Security* 15(3): 245–62.

Price-Smith, Andrew. 2001. *The Health of Nations: Infectious Disease, Environmental Change, and Their Effects on National Security and Development.* Cambridge: MIT Press.

Prins, Gwyn. 2004. "AIDS and Global Security," *International Affairs* 80(5): 931–952.

Reardon, Betty A. (1993). *Women and Peace: Feminists Visions of Global Security.* Albany, NY: State University of New York.

Rees, Stuart and Lynda-ann Blanchard. 1999. "Human Security through International Citizenship," in *Worlds Apart: Human Security and Global Governance,* edited by Majid Tehranian. London: I.B. Tauris Publishers.

Rehn, Elisabeth and Ellen Johnson Sirleaf. 2002. *Women, War and Peace: The Independent Experts' Assessment on the Impact of Armed Conflict on Women and Women's Role in Peace-building.* New York: United Nations Development Fund for Women.

Reimann, Kim D. 2006. "A View from the Top: International Politics, Norms and the Worldwide Growth of NGOs," *International Studies Quarterly* 50(1): 45–67.

Roberts-Davis, Tanya. 2006. "Peacebuilding Commission Opens: UN Reform Process Rolls on—Will Women's Voice Be Heard?" *International Women's Tribune Centre (IWTC) Women's Globalnet* 304 (10 July 2006): 1–3. Article accessed September 2006 at www.iwtc.org.

Rosenau, James N. 1994. "New Dimensions of Security: The interaction of globalizing and localizing dynamics," *Security Dialogue.* 25(3): 255–81.

Rothschild, Emma. 1995. "What is Security?" *Daedalus, Journal of the American Association for the Advancement of Science,* 124(3): 53–98.

Roughneen, Simon. 2006. "Challenges Ahead for UN Peace Commission," *International Relations and Security Network* (24 January 2006). Article accessed October 2006 at http://www.isn.ethz.ch/news/sw/details.cfm?ID=14509.

Schalkwyk, J. 1998. *Building Capacity for Gender Mainstreaming: UNDP's Experience.* New York: GIDP/UNDP.

Schechter, Michael G. 2005. *United Nations Global Conferences.* New York: Routledge, Taylor and Francis Group.

Schnabel, Albrecht and Hans-Georg Ehrhart. 2005. *Security Sector Reform and Post-Conflict Peacebuilding.* Oxford: United Nations University Press.

Searle, John. 1969. *Speech Acts: An Essay in the Philosophy of Language.* Cambridge: Cambridge University Press.

Searle, John. 1977. "A Classification of Illocutionary Acts," in *Syntax and Semantics,* edited by P. Cole and J. Morgan. New York: Academic Press, pp. 59–82.

Searle, John. 1991. "What is a Speech Act," in *Pragmatics: A Reader,* edited by Steven Davis. Oxford: Oxford University Press, pp. 254–64.

Sheehan, Michael. 2005. *International Security: An Analytical Survey.* Boulder, CO: Lynne Rienner Publishers.

Shinoda, Hideaki. 2007. "Toward a Sustainable Strategy of Peacebuilding: An Examination of Negative and Positive Justifications of Security Sector Reform," Paper Presented at the Annual Convention of the International Studies Association, Chicago, IL (March).

References   177

Shultz, Richard, Roy Godson and Ted Greenwood, eds. 1993. *Security Studies for the 1990s*. New York: Brassey's.

Sjoberg, Laura and Caron Gentry. 2007. *Mothers, Monsters, and Whores: Women's Violence in Global Politics*. Zed Books.

Sjoberg, Laura. 2006. *Gender, Justice, and the Wars in Iraq*. Lanham, MD: Rowman and Littlefield Publishers.

Smith, Dan. 2001. "The Problem of Essentialism," in *Gender, Peace, and Conflict*, edited by Inger Skjelsbæk and Dan Smith. London: Sage, pp. 32–46.

Smith, Jackie. 2000. "Social Movements, International Institutions and Local Empowerment," in *Global Institutions and Local Empowerment. Competing Theoretical Perspectives*, edited by K. Stiles. London: MacMillan and St. Martin's Press.

Snyder, Anna. 2000. "Peace Profile: Federation of African Women's Peace Networks," *Peace Review* 12(1): 147–53.

Snyder, Margaret. 1995. *Transforming Development: Women, poverty and politics*. London: Intermediate Technology Publications.

Spees, Pam. 2003. "Women's Advocacy in the Creation of the International Criminal Court: Changing the Landscapes of Justice and Power," *Signs: Journal of Women in Culture and Society* 28: 1233–54.

Sterling-Folker, Jennifer, ed. 2006. *Making Sense of International Relations Theory*. Boulder, CO: Lynne Rienner Publishers.

Stockholm International Peace Research Institute (SIPRI). 2006. Annual Yearbook 2006: Armaments, Disarmaments and International Security. Oxford: Oxford University Press. Accessed January 2007 at http://yearbook2006.sipri.org.

Suhrke, Astri. 1999. "Human Security and the Interests of States," *Security Dialogue* 30(3): 265–76.

Sylvester, Christine. 1994. *Feminist Theory and International Relations in a Postmodern Era*. Cambridge: Cambridge University Press.

Teriff, Terry, Stuart Croft, Lucy James, and Patrick M. Morgan. 1999. *Security Studies Today*. Cambridge, MA: Polity Press.

Thomas, Caroline. 2004. "A Bridge Between Interconnected Challenges Confronting the World," *Security Dialogue*. 35(3): 343–54.

Thomas, Caroline. 2001. "Global Governance, Development and Human Security: Exploring the Links," *Third World Quarterly* 22(2): 159–75.

Thomas, Nicholas and William T. Tow. 2002. "The Utility of Human Security: Sovereignty and Humanitarian Intervention," *Security Dialogue*. 33(2): 177–92.

Tickner, J Ann. 1992. *Gender in International Relations: Feminists perspectives on achieving global security*. New York, NY: Columbia University Press.

Tickner, J. Ann. 1995. "Revisioning Security," in *International Relations Theory Today*, edited by Ken Booth and Steve Smith. Cambridge: Polity Press: 175–97.

Tickner, J. Ann. 1998. "Continuing the Conversation," *International Studies Quarterly* 42(1): 205–10.

Tickner, J. Ann. 1999. "Why Women Can't Run the World: International Politics according to Francis Fukuyama," *International Studies Review* 1(3): 3–11.

Tilly, Charles. 1999. *Durable Inequality*. CA: University of California Press.

True, Jacqui. 2003. "Mainstreaming Gender in Global Public Policy," *International Feminist Journal of Politics* 5(3): 368–96.

True, Jacqui. 1996. "Feminism," in *Theories of International Relations*, edited by Scott Burchill and Andrew Linklater. London: Macmillan, pp. 210–51.

178   References

True-Frost, C. Cora. 2007. "The Security Council and Norm Consumption," *International Law and Politics* 40: 115–217.

Ullman, Richard. 1983. "Redefining Security," *International Security*. 8(1): 129–53.

United Nations. 1994. *An Agenda for Development: Report of the Secretary-General* A/48/935, New York: United Nations.United Nations. 1992. *An Agenda for Peace, Preventative Diplomacy, Peacemaking and Peace-keeping*, Report of the Secretary-General pursuant to A/47/277—S/24111, New York: United Nations.

United Nations. 1995. *Supplement to An Agenda for Peace: Position Paper of the Secretary-General on the Occasion of the Fiftieth Anniversary of the United Nations* A/50/60-S/1995/1, New York: United Nations.

United Nations. 1997. *Renewing the United Nations: A Programme for Reform* A/51/950, New York: United Nations.

United Nations. 2000. *Report of the Panel on United Nations Peacekeeping Operations.* A/55/305-S/2000/809. New York: United Nations.

United Nations Brandt Report. 1980. *Report of the Independent Commission on International Development Issues, North-South: A Programme for Survival.* London: Pan Books.

United Nations Development Fund for Women (UNIFEM). 2004. *Getting It Right, Doing It Right: Gender and Disarmament, Demobilization, and Reintegration*, NY: UNIFEM.

United Nations Development Fund for Women (UNIFEM). 2005. *Programme Framework—Peace and Security, Phase II 2006–2009*, NY: UNIFEM

United Nations Development Fund for Women (UNIFEM). 2005. *Securing the Peace: Guiding the International Community towards Women's Effective Participation throughout Peace Processes.* (October) NY: UNIFEM.

United Nations Development Fund for Women (UNIFEM). 2006a. *Voice, Influence, Justice, and Security: The Keys to Inclusion and Sustainable Peace Building*, NY: UNIFEM.

United Nations Development Fund for Women (UNIFEM). 2006b. "Briefing Notes at the Request of the Deputy Secretary General: On Women, Peace,and Security," (16 November)

United Nations Development Fund for Women (UNIFEM). 2006c. "CEDAW and Security Council Resolution 1325: A Quick Guide," Accessed November 2008 at http://www.unifem.org/attachments/products/CEDAWandUNSCR1325_eng.pdf.

United Nations Development Programme (UNDP). 1994. *UN Human Development Report.* New York, NY: Oxford University Press.

United Nations Economic Commission for Africa (UNECA). 1998. *Post-Conflict Reconstruction in Africa: A Gender Perspective.* African Women's Report, Addis Ababa: UNECA.

United Nations Fund for Women (UNIFEM). 2001–02. *Annual Report: Working for Women's Empowerment and Gender Equality.*

United Nations Fund for Women (UNIFEM). 2007. *GBV Offices—A Sign of Progress in UNIFEM Partnership with Rwandan Police.* NY: UNIFEM.

United Nations International Research and Training Institute for the Advancement of Women. 2006. "Building Peace Through Gender Equality," Santo Domingo, Dominican Republic (www.un-instraw.org).

United Nations International Research and Training Institute for the Advancement of Women (INSTRAW). *Gender and Security Sector Reform Working Group: Background Information.* http://www.un-instraw.org/en/docs/SSR/Website_Background.pdf (accessed 27 April 2007).

References 179

United Nations Secretary-General. 2002. *Report of the Secretary-General on Women, Peace, and Security* S/2002/1154. Available at http://www.un.org/womenwatch/daw/public/eWPS.pdf.

United Nations Secretary-General. 2004. Report of the Secretary-General's High-Level Panel on Threats, Challenges, and Change. *A More Secure World: Our Shared Responsibility.* A/59/565. NY: United Nations. Available at www.un.org/secureworld/report.pdf.

Uvin, Peter. 2004. "A Field of Overlaps and Interactions," *Security Dialogue* 35(3): 352–353.

Van Evera, Stephen. 1997. *Guide to Methods for Students of Political Science.* Ithaca, NY: Cornell University Press.

Wæver, Ole. 1995. "Securitization and Desecuritization," in *On Security,* edited by Ronnie Lipschutz. New York: Columbia University Press, pp. 46–86.

Wallensteen, Peter and Patrik Johansson. 2004. "Security Council Decisions in Perspective," in *The UN Security Council: From the Cold War to the twenty-first Century,* edited by David M. Malone. Boulder, CO: Lynne Rienner Publishers, pp. 17–33.

Walt, Stephan. 1991. "The Renaissance of Security Studies," *International Studies Quarterley* 35: 211–239.

Weiss, Thomas G. 2004. "The Humanitarian Impulse," in *The UN Security Council: From the Cold War to the twenty-first Century,* edited by David M. Malone. Boulder, CO: Lynne Rienner Publishers, pp. 37–54.

Weiss, Thomas G., Tatiana Carayannis, Louis Emmerij, and Richard Jolly. 2005. *UN Voices: The Struggle for Development and Social Justice.* Bloomington, IN: Indiana University Press.

Weldon, Laurel. 2006. "Inclusion, Solidarity, and Social Movements: The Global Movement Against Gender Violence," *Perspectives.* 4: 55–74.

Weschler, Joanna. 2004. "Human Rights," in *The UN Security Council: From the Cold War to the twenty-first Century,* edited by David M. Malone. Boulder, CO: Lynne Rienner Publishers, pp. 55–68.

West, Lois A. 1999. "The United Nations Women's Conferences and Feminist Politics," in *Gender Politics in Global Governance,* edited by Mary K. Meyer and Elisabeth Prügl. Boulder, CO: Rowman & Littlefield Publishers, Inc., pp. 177–93.

Whitworth, Sandra. 2004. *Men, Militarism, and UN Peacekeeping: A Gendered Analysis.* Boulder, CO: Lynne Rienner Publishers.

Williams, Michael C. 1997. "The Institutions of Security: Elements of a Theory of Security Organizations," *Cooperation and Conflict* 32(3): 287–307.

Williams, Michael. 2003. "Words, Images, Enemies: Securitization and International Politics," *International Studies Quarterly* 47(4): 511–31.

Wilton Park Conference Presentations. 2008. "Women Targeted or Affected by Armed Conflict: What role for military peacekeepers?" (27–9 May): 1–11. Accessed November 2008 at http://www.unifem.org/news_events/event_detail.php?EventID=175.

Wilton Park Summary Report. 2008. "Women Targeted or Affected by Armed Conflict: What role for military peacekeepers?" (27-29 May): 1–11. Accessed November 2008 at http://www.unifem.org/news_events/event_detail.php?EventID=175.

Wolfers, Arnold. 1952. "'National Security' as an Ambiguous Symbol." *Political Science Quarterly,* 67(3): 481–502.

Wolfers, Arnold. 1962. *Discord and Collaboration: Essays on International Politics.* Baltimore: John Hopkins Press.

180 *References*

Wyeth, Vanessa Hawkins. 2006. "Getting the Peacebuilding Commission off the Ground: Including Civil Society," *Dialogue on Globalization, Briefing Papers Friedrich Ebert Stiftung*. New York. Paper accessed May 2007 at http://www.globalpolicy.org/reform/topics/pbc/2006/09pbcngos.pdf.

Wyn Jones, Richard. 1999. *Security, Strategy and Critical Theory*. London: Lynne Rienner Publishers.

Zald, Mayer. 1996. "Culture, Ideology, and Strategic Framing," in *Comparative Perspectives on Social Movements,* edited by Doug McAdam, John D. McCarthy, and Mayer Zald. Cambridge: Cambridge University Press.

Zalewski, Marysia. 1996. "'All These Theories Yet the Bodies Keep Piling Up': Theory, Theorists, and Theorizing," in *International Theory: Positivism and Beyond,* edited by Steve Smith, Ken Booth and Marysia Zalewski. Cambridge: Cambridge University Press, pp. 340–53.

Zalewski, Marysia and Jane Parpart, eds. 1998. *The 'Man' Question in International Relations*. Boulder, CO: Westview.

Zwingel, Susanne. 2005. "From intergovernmental negotiations to (sub)national change: A transnational perspective on the impact of CEDAW," *International Feminist Journal of Politics*. 7(3): 400–24.

Index

A More Secure World 124, 128, 141n21
Afghanistan 51,83, 103
African Women in Crisis (AFWIC) 99–102
Agenda for Development 123
Agenda for Peace 69–70, 90n10, 122–3; references to women and gender 126
agenda-setting 1, 39, 146; and GAD 39; 'backdoor moves' 112, 146, 151; norm diffusion and the significance of the UN 148–9; role of NGOs 152–3
Alvarez, Enrique 133–4
Amajan, Safia 103
Anderlini, Sanam 9, 18n6, 47, 100, 119, 127, 141n18, 146
Angola 123
Annan Kofi A. 6, 7, 70, 123–4, 126–7, 129
Antrobus, Peggy 97
Arria Formula meeting 10, 13, 20n33, 46
Axworthy, Lloyd 4, 26

Barnes, Karen 122–3, 135, 137, 139
Barnett, Michael 125
Beijing Conference *see* Fourth World Conference on Women (1995)
Beijing Platform for Action 8, 11, 20n42, 101, 117n33
Berman, Jacqueline 28, 40, 113, 118n48, 154n6
Blanchard, Eric 4, 34–7
Booth, Ken 23, 25, 33, 34; gender and security 37;
Boserup, Ester 97, 115n4
Boston Consortium on Gender, Security and Human Rights 9
Boznia-Herzegovina 53, 110
Brahimi Report 124, 126, 140n15, 141n21; references to women and gender 126

Brandt Commission 6
Bunch, Charlotte 38, 99, 116n12
Burundi 48, 55, 56–7 *Table*, 58–9, 84, 100, 152; PBC 119, 122, 131–2, 134–6
Buzan, Barry 3, 10, 18n1, 22–3, 25, 30, 32, 41n26, 148–9

campaign 23, 38–9, 42n44; adoption of SCR 1325 11–12, 14, 17, 96, 116n19, 120; to end the use of child soldiers 88, 93n51; 'women's rights as human rights' 99, 116n12
Campbell, John 111
Canada: human security 21n48, 70, 90n13; SCR 1325 2, 8, 13, 19n23, 28, 59, 70
Caprioli, Mary 21n49
Carillo, Roxanna 99
Carpenter, R. Charli 1, 39, 72, 153
Central African Republic 55, 56–7 *Table*, 83
Chad 55, 56–7 *Table*
child protection advisors 80 *Table*,
children in armed conflict 16; child soldiers 71, 80 *Table*, 83–4, 87–8; Democratic Republic of the Congo 83–4; Graça Machel report 72, 75–6, 91n26; human rights violations against 93n52; monitoring and reporting procedure 83; 'name and shame' initiative 82, 93n50; NGO involvement 75–6, 91n30; protection-based approach 72, 80 *Table*, 81 *Figure*, 85 *Figure*, 82–3, 85 *Figure*, 86–8; SCR 1612 81 *Figure*, 83–4, 85 *Figure*, 87; Security Council resolutions on 67–8, 79–89; Security Council Working Group 67, 83–7, 93–4n59; security framework 76, 79; Special Rapporteur 67; Special Representative of the

182 *Index*

Secretary-General (SRSG) 68, 75–6, 79, 84, 87–8, 91n29; success of thematic issue in the Security Council 73–6
Chinkin, Christine 123
Chowdhury, Anwarul 12
Claude Jr., Inis L. 7
Côte d'Ivoire 55, 56–7 *Table*, 84, 100
Coalition to Stop the Use of Child Soldiers 83–4, 87
Cohn, Carol 1–2, 4–5, 9–15, 19n21, 19n28, 20n39, 35, 48, 63n4, 63n40, 70–2, 90n13, 96, 152
Commission on the Status of Women 11–12, 43n46; drafting of CEDAW 77
content analysis for Security Council resolutions 80 *Table*, 80–7
Convention on the Elimination of All Forms of Discrimination Against Women (CEDAW) 51–4, 64n20, 76–8, 92n40, 117n33, 120, 147; lack of institutional role for NGOs 77;
Convention on the Rights of the Child (CRC) 73–80, 90n19, 91n27–28 92n39, 88; children's agency 94n60; Optional Protocol on the CRC 82, 92n33, 93n51; UNICEF's role 73–4, 76, 77; reporting process 74; World Summit for Children 77, 91n28;
Coomaraswamy, Radhika 67, 84, 87
Copenhagen School (CS) 23, 29–30, 34, 42n34, 149–50, 153
critical security studies 4, 33–4, 37–8, 121, 146
Cutillo, Alberto 124, 129, 137

Darfur 55, 56–7 *Table*, 59, 67
Decade for Women (1975–1985) 20n43, 77, 121
Democratic Republic of the Congo 56–7 *Table*, 71, 83–4
Dirasse, Laketch 100, 116n15
disarmament, demobilization and reintegration (DDR) 48, 81, 105–7, 118n37, 133
domestic violence 102–3, 107–110, 135
Doyle, Michael 125

East Timor 51, 55, 56–7 *Table*, 123
Ekiyor, Thelma 120, 132, 134
Elshtain, Jean Bethke 35
Enloe, Cynthia 18n17, 35, 50, 64n8–9, 64n14, 71, 117n28, 138
Ensalaco, Mark 73, 90n19

feminism: activism 4, 16–17, 19n21, 60, 72, 153; Global South 7–8; International Relations (IR) theory 4–5, 20n35, 23, 32, 35, 42n36, 48, 138; perspective on WID 39; United Nations 6, 60, 97, 144
feminist security theory (FST) 4–5, 34–7; addressing andocentric biases 42n37; on institutionalization 114
Fitzsimmons, Tracy 103, 107, 118n39
Fourth World Conference on Women (1995) 102, 120; importance to SCR 1325 11, 100, 116n21–3; preparatory meeting 100–1
framing processes 1, 42n45, 47, 114, 145; how movements frame 3–4; impact of 3, 46, 110–1; issue-alignment 72

Galtung, Johan 140n9
gender: as a problem-solving tool 61–2, 114, 137; conceptual confusion 150–1; definition of 7; essentializing notions of 17, 36, 42n38–40, 49, 50, 58, 63; gender architecture within the UN system 54, 65n29–30,76, 78, 92n44, 92n46, 150
gender balance 126–7, 131–3, 141n20, 141n32; tokenism 137
Gender Development Index 18n16
gender mainstreaming 8, 43n47; additive, integrative, transformative 8, 39, 58, 61–2, 114, 127–8, 137–9, 148, 152–4; critique of 42n42, 114; evolution of 38; existing research on 4; focus on women only 43n46; ghettoizing effect 133, 148; need to focus on men and masculinity 7, 36–7, 42n41, 61, 114, 127–8, 137, 150; myth of gender neutrality 37, 48, 117n29, 127, 139, 144; within the UN 39, 126–7
gender training: UN peacekeeping operations 55
gender-based violence 42n32, 102–103, 107, 114, 118n39, 151; indicator for political stability 87; police reform in post-conflict societies 108–111, 112; rape as war crime 71, 90n15; sexual exploitation and violence 60, 71, 86–7, 111–12; Special Rapporteur on Violence Against Women 93n48
Geneva Centre for the Democratic Control of the Armed Forces (DCAF) 104, 105 *Table*

Geneva Declaration of the Rights of the
    Child 73
Ghana 55, 100
Gibbings, Sheri 70
Goetz, Anne Marie 38–9, 66n39, 111
Goldstein, Joshua 15, 19n27

Haiti 55, 56–7 *Table*
Hansen, Lene 1, 10, 32–3, 154n5
Harding, Sandra 37
Hertel, Shareen 112, 114, 151, 153
Heyzer, Noeleen 12, 102, 105, 114,
    118n40
High Commission for Human Rights 70–1
Hill, Felicity 11–14, 18n4, 148, 154n9
Hudson, Heidi 28, 37, 113
Human Development Report 26, 29;
    components of human security 41n13
human security 3, 5, 25–9, 145; and
    feminism 37; Canada and the Security
    Council 70; compared to critical
    security studies 42n35, 113–14;
    creating political space 14, 25, 102,
    146; criticisms of 28, 146, 150–1;
    discourse 14, 31; framework for action
    29, 106–7, 144–6; human development
    27, 102; human rights 27–28, 62–3,
    102, 147; link to humanitarian and
    human rights law 70–2;
    operationalizing 41n19, 112–14,
    115n16, 145; relationship to national
    security 27, 41n15–16; role of the state
    146–7; UN Commission on 6, 27; UN
    context 6, 26–9
Human Security Network 14, 20n47,
    90n13, 146

*In Larger Freedom: Towards Security,
    Development, and Human Rights for
    All* (2005) 121, 129
International Alert 8, 11, 20n40, 135,
    142n42
International Monetary Fund 124, 130
International Security 25

Jain, Devaki 5, 97, 115n4, 115n10, 133
Jebb, Eglantyne 73
Joachim, Jutta 1, 152–3

Karamé, Kari 127
Kihunah, Milkah 135
Klot, Jennifer 63n3, 72
Kosovo 56–7 *Table*, 61, 109, 123

Kosovo Women's Network 109
Kvinna till Kvinna 61

Liberia 48, 55, 56–7 *Table*, 100, 109–110,
    127, 152
Liotta, P.H. 147
Luck, Edward 69, 71

MacFarlane and Khong 23–4, 26, 29,
    40n11, 41n20
Mano River Union Women Peace Network
    (MARWOPNET) 127
Mathews, Jessica Tuchman 25
Mazurana, Dyan 126–7
McAskie, Carolyn 132
McDonald, Matt 145–6
McKay, 126–7, 140n8
militarism 20n45, 22, 25, 36, 48, 62–3,
    154
Miller, Alice 49
Mozambique 100
Muddell, Kelli 135
Murphy, Craig 112, 115n1

Nadjibulla, Vina 132, 136
national action plans on SCR 1325 51,
    64n17, 148
Neack, Laura 41n12
NGO Working Group on Women, Peace
    and Security (NGOWG) 2; advocating
    for 1325 11, 13–14; original members
    8, 20n38, 132; report on the PBC
    124–6, 128; WPS network 8, 137;
norm-building process 1, 33, 38, 63, 71,
    85, 91n23, 152; norm diffusion 5, 39,
    148–9, 153; UN and norm creation 3,
    5–6, 15, 18n15, 87–88

O'Neill, William 108–110
Oestreich, Joel 74; UNICEF/CRC model
    74–7
Ogata, Sadako 6
Organization for Economic Cooperation
    and Development (OECD) 104

Paris, Roland 28, 41n13, 123, 125, 139
participant-observer 10
peacebuilding: definition of 122–3;
    women's role 127, 136
police 31,146; all-female contingent 55;
    community policing projects 110, 113;
    contributions by UN Member States
    58, 86; gender training by UN of

184   Index

national troops 109, 112, 114; Kosovo
Police Gender Unit 109; Liberian
National Police and the Task Force on
Gender Violence 109–110; security
sector reform 60, 95, 103–115, 105
Table; Rwanda Police Gender-Based
Violence Desk Office 108–9
protection of civilians 14, 70, 89n5, 90n11

Reardon, Betty A. 36
Reimann, Kim 76, 79, 92m34
Report of the Panel on United Nations
Peace Operations *see* Brahimi Report
Robinson, Mary 70–1
Rome Statute for the International
Criminal Court 71, 80
Rothschild, Emma 23, 40n9
Rwanda 64n20, 70, 100, 108–9

Secretary-General's High Level Panel on
System-Wide Coherence (2006) 54,
141n21–2
Secretary-General's High Level Panel on
Threats, Challenges, and Change
(2004) 6, 126
securitization (theory) 5, 29–33, 153;
applied to HIV/AIDS 32, 64n11, 70; as
a strategy 2, 31–2, 150–1;
desecuritization 32; feminist critique of
32–3; process of 3, 31, 40; SCR 1325
45–6, 62; speech acts 12–13, 30, 31,
42n33; studying discourse 10, 46, 95;
women's activism 38, 151
security framework 1–4, 9, 80 *Table*, 81
Figure, 85 *Figure*, 144, 149; accuracy
of 18n7; advantages of 16, 59, 151;
connection to UN mission 47, 120; for
nonmilitary issues 23; humanitarian
and human rights law 72, 76, 147;
implications of 3, 48–9, 131;
instrumental argument 45–6, 61–2, 88,
116n19, 127; limitations of 17, 150–1;
link to Former Ambassador Chowdhury
12–13; opening political space 59–60,
62, 151; political framework 22, 31,
37; repacking 'old' issues 112–14, 151;
*Report on the Fourth World Conference
on Women* 100–1; SCR 1325 44–6;
tension present for WPS activist 143–4;
women's movement 5, 22, 50, 63, 100
security sector reform (SSR) 10, 16, 60,
95–6, 102–7, 109–113
security studies 4–5, 40n5, 145; critical
approaches 24–5, 33–7, 42n35,

113–14, 121
security: traditional conceptions of 3, 5,
16, 21n49, 23–6, 69, 95, 144
security-development nexus 121, 123, 125,
137, 146
sexual and gender-based violence see
gender-based violence
sexual harassment 60, 103
Sierra Leone 48, 56–7 *Table*; PBC 119,
122, 127, 131, 134–6
Smith, Jackie 153
Snyder, Margaret 18n11, 97–100, 115n3
Somalia 57, 84, 91, 100
Steinberg, Donald 117n29
Sudan 51–2, 55, 56–7 *Table*, 59, 79, 84,
100, 152
Suhrke, Astri 147
Sylvester, Christine 36

Thomas, Caroline 41n22
Tickner, J. Ann 22, 35, 36, 37, 48
transnational advocacy networks 4–5, 13,
152–3; women's organizations 13
True, Jacqui 8, 17, 35, 36

Ullman, Richard 22, 25
United Kingdom 51, 65n22
United Nations Charter Chapter VII 81–2
United Nations Children's Fund
(UNICEF) 73, 83, 88, 91n24; annual
report 73, 78; Children in Especially
Difficult Circumstances (CEDC) 74;
drafting of the CRC 74; institutional
relationship with the CRC 74;
United Nations Department of
Peacekeeping Operations (DPKO) 13,
107; DPKO Gender Advisor/Unit 55,
66n38; gender affairs offices/gender
advisors 55, 58–9, 66n32, 148; gender
training 55, 86; *Policy Directive:
Gender Equality in UN Peacekeeping
Operations* 55; sex-disaggregated data
58; UNIFEM Partnership 111–12,
118n37
United Nations Development Program
(UNDP) 27–8, 77, 98, 107–8, 112,
114, 115n1
United Nations Economic and Social
Council (ECOSOC) 8, 77, 130
United Nations Fund for Women
(UNIFEM) 2; advocating for 1325
11–14; annual reports 102, 116n17;
catalyst for change 98, 103, 108, 110,
114, 115n10; Consultative Committee

95, 97–8; DPKO partnership 111–12; development focus 97–8, 115n2, 115n8–9; 'door-opening function' 99–101, 151; engaging in the security framework 101–3, 110–1; gender justice 117n34; *Governance, Peace and Security* division 96, 102–3, 106, 111, 116n25, 132, 154n8; human security approach 106–7, 112–13, 118n47; implementing SCR 1325 within the PBC 132, 135; policing projects 107–10, 118n39–40; role in CEDAW process 77–8; security sector reform 16, 95–6, 102–7, 145–6, 148; VFDW 77, 97–8; weak institutional and financial status 77–9, 92n41; web portal 19n22

United Nations General Assembly (GA): children's rights 73, 75; gender architecture 54; human rights 45; PBC 119–120, 129, 132, 142n33; resolutions 10; VFDW/UNIFEM 78, 97–8, 102, 116n17, 116n24

United Nations Intellectual History Project (UNIHP) 5

United Nations Methodist Women's Division 126,

United Nations Office of the Special Advisor on Gender Issues (OSAGI) 66n38, 92n44

United Nations Peacebuilding Commission (PBC) 17, 119–22, 124–6, 146, 148; civil society access 133–7; country-specific strategic planning 134–7; *Draft Concept Note on the Design of Integrated Peacebuilding Strategies* 129–130; gender balancing 131–133; Peacebuilding Fund 130, 139; Peacebuilding Support Office (PBSO) 119, 130–2, 135–6, 141n32; purpose, mandate and structure 120–2, 128–130, 140n3; reference to SCR 1325 131, 134, 138–9

United Nations Security Council 3, 89; gendered war system 15, 48; historical inactivity on gender issues 44–5; human security agenda 71, 146; humanitarian concerns 69–70; impact of SCR 1325 on the SC 144–5; language on women and gender 48; legal nature of resolutions 64n16; legitimacy issues 67, 83, 148; on non-traditional security issues 64n6, 69–72, 88; relevancy of human rights 72;

resolutions and accountability mechanisms 80 *Table*, 81 *Figure*, 85 *Figure*, 82–7; role within UN system 5, 143; targeting of for a resolution on WPS 9

United Nations Security Council Resolution 1325 2, 44, 85 *Figure*; accountability and enforcement 54, 63, 65n25, 67, 82, 85–6, 105; assumptions about pacifism 50; dual strategy of protection and participation 15, 99, 116n13; European Union 18n10; feminist understanding of 138–9; future of 16, 152, 154; goals of 41n14, 44–5; implementation challenges 59–60, 65n24, 66n31, 66n35, 78, 85–7, 89n1; implementation within DPKO 55–60, 56–57 *Table*; implementation within PBC 125–8, 131–7; impact on the role of the state 48–9, 113–14, 138, 144; importance of language 48–50; independent expert's assessment 78–9, 93n47; limitations of 60–2, 63n3; mandating UNIFEM's work in post-conflict SSR 105–7, 117n33; national action plans 51, 64n17, 148; origins of idea to advocate for 11, 72; PBC 17, 120–2; progress of 16, 46–60, 62–3, 148; relevancy to CEDAW 51–4, 64n20–2; role of NGOs 11–15, 149, 152; successes in Burundi 58–9; successes in Sudan 59; women involved in peace processes 48; women's contributions to peace and security processes 47, 88, 100, 120, 138, 139n1; *Women's Participation and Gender Perspectives in Security Council Resolutions Checklist* 62; women's representation in decision-making 58, 89, 106, 111

United Nations Security Council Resolution 1820 16, 69, 85 *Figure*, 86–8, 105; PBC 140n4; progress of 86; criticisms of 86–7, 93n57

United Nations Training Institute for the Advancement of Women (INSTRAW) 10, 115n5

United Nations Universal Declaration of Human Rights (UDHR) 73, 76

United States 52, 91n27, 93n57

Wæver, Ole 23, 29–32, 42n31, 49, 63, 149, 150

Weiss, Thomas 69, 90n8

186   *Index*

Welsh School 33–4
Weschler, Joanna 72
Whitworth, Sandra 3, 36, 42n42, 61, 66n33, 114, 137
Wilton Park Conference (2008) 111–12
Windhoek Declaration and the Namibian Plan of Action 13, 20n44
women: conflation with gender 50, 109, 137, 151; definition of 7–8; their agency 13, 16, 44, 50, 89, 94n60; violence against 67, 99, 108; 'women and children' as a vulnerable group 44, 68, 71–2
'Women, Peace and Security' network 8, 11, 35, 95, 119, 153–4; approach to security 37–9, 88, 137, 145, 151, 154; bandwagoning mechanism 14, 63; Canada and human security 70;
connection to children and armed conflict advocacy 72; involvement in development of PBC 126–7, 130; norm diffusion 16, 19n19, 148–9; relationship with UNIFEM 96, 100, 114; role in shaping UN security agenda 120–1, 138–9, 143–5, 148
Women's League for International Peace and Freedom (WILPF) 8, 19n21, 48, 135
women's movement 3, 5, 37, 121; emancipatory goals 3, 34, 50, 144, 153; GAD 39, 153; opening political space 58–60, 62; WID 38–9, 61, 62, 97, 112, 153; women's rights as human rights 38, 99, 116n12
World Bank 124, 130

eBooks – at www.eBookstore.tandf.co.uk

A library at your fingertips!

eBooks are electronic versions of printed books. You can store them on your PC/laptop or browse them online.

They have advantages for anyone needing rapid access to a wide variety of published, copyright information.

eBooks can help your research by enabling you to bookmark chapters, annotate text and use instant searches to find specific words or phrases. Several eBook files would fit on even a small laptop or PDA.

NEW: Save money by eSubscribing: cheap, online access to any eBook for as long as you need it.

Annual subscription packages

We now offer special low-cost bulk subscriptions to packages of eBooks in certain subject areas. These are available to libraries or to individuals.

For more information please contact webmaster.ebooks@tandf.co.uk

We're continually developing the eBook concept, so keep up to date by visiting the website.

www.eBookstore.tandf.co.uk